Post-9/11 Horror in American Cinema

Post-9/11 Horror in American Cinema

KEVIN J. WETMORE, JR.

continuum

The Continuum International Publishing Group
80 Maiden Lane, New York, NY 10038
The Tower Building, 11 York Road, London SE1 7NX

www.continuumbooks.com

© Kevin J. Wetmore, Jr, 2012

All rights reserved. No part of this book may be reproduced, stored in a retrieval system, or transmitted, in any form or by any means, electronic, mechanical, photocopying, recording, or otherwise, without the written permission of the publishers.

Library of Congress Cataloging-in-Publication Data

Wetmore, Kevin J., 1969-
 Post-9/11 horror in American cinema / by Kevin J. Wetmore.
   p. cm.
 Includes bibliographical references and index.
 ISBN-13: 978-1-4411-3295-6 (hardcover : alk. paper)
 ISBN-10: 1-4411-3295-3 (hardcover : alk. paper)
 ISBN-13: 978-1-4411-9797-9 (pbk. : alk. paper)
 ISBN-10: 1-4411-9797-4 (pbk. : alk. paper) 1. Horror films–United States–History and criticism. 2. Motion pictures–United States–History–21st century. 3. Terrorism in motion pictures. 4. September 11 Terrorist Attacks, 2001–Influence. I. Title.
 PN1995.9.H6W435 2012
 791.43'6164--dc23
                        2011045916

ISBN: HB: 978-1-4411-3295-6
      PB: 978-1-4411-9797-9

Typeset by Fakenham Prepress Solutions, Fakenham, Norfolk NR21 8NN

Contents

Acknowledgements vi
List of Illustrations viii
Introduction: Terror and Horror 1

1 9/11 as Horror 23
2 Documenting the Horror 57
3 'Because you were home': Anonymous and Random Death 81
4 'Torture Porn' and What It Means to Be American 95
5 Hopeless Bleak Despair, or How I Learned to Stop Worrying and Love *The Mist* 116
6 Fear of/from Religion 137
7 They Won't Stay Dead: The Ghosts, Zombies and Vampires of 9/11 153
8 Manufacturing Fear 168
9 Horrific Nostalgia: Remaking the Slasher Film 192

Conclusion 201
Notes 204
Filmography 209
Bibliography 218
Index 227

Acknowledgements

Thanks are due to many individuals for the development of this study. Thanks to Katie Gallof and David Barker of Continuum, for guiding this volume from initial proposal to final realization, and to the anonymous readers whose insights and suggestions made the volume infinitely stronger and more focused.

Thanks to the film-makers who in the wake of one of the most terrible days in American history were not afraid to keep looking into the abyss. As Clive Barker has said, there is no delight the equal of dread, even in dark times.

Thanks to the William H. Hannon Library at Loyola Marymount University, which was invaluable in locating sources. Thanks as well to Vidiots in Santa Monica for its phenomenal library of rare, classic and current horror films on VHS and DVD. Thanks to Matt Frank of LMU's IT department for help with the images.

Thanks to Anthony Miller for ideas, sources, support and encouragement. David Sanchez's guidance on apocalypticism and American fundamentalism was invaluable. Numerous friends and colleagues were subjected to my taste in cinema and offered their support, ideas and feedback: Tom Quinn, and the Quinn family (Mary Ann, Shea and Kaleigh), Josh 'Worm' Miller, Meg Bodi, Sarah Broyles, Jo Ann 'Badger' Mendelson, Grant Garinger, SJ, Cody Kopp, Jim and Beth Holmes, Nenad 'Neno' Pervan, Katharine Noon and Mark Seldis, and Andy and Jennifer Allen.

Thanks to my family, Kevin Sr., Eleanor, Lisa, John, Sean, Tom, Eileen and Toni. Thanks especially to Lacy Hornick, who watched them all (willingly), talks horror and culture with me, and has shared the delight of dread. This one is for her.

Writing about 9/11 is to engage a very sensitive subject that is still a living wound for many Americans. My apologies to anyone disturbed by the images and ideas in this book. My purpose has been to understand how we understand 9/11 through horror cinema and how horror films have reproduced 9/11. No offence has been

ACKNOWLEDGEMENTS

intended, and I certainly do not take the events of that day or its consequences lightly. This book should not be seen as in any way making light of or downplaying the tragedy of September 11. It is my hope that by looking into the abyss, we understand ourselves, our culture and what we may have become in the ten years since.

Any mistakes, errors or inaccuracies are, alas, my own.

List of Illustrations

Figure 1.1 Although set in Los Angeles, *Skyline* features a shot of New York City's skyline burning with the Statue of Liberty in the foreground. After 9/11, New York is the central site of horror. 25

Figure 1.2 In *Vanishing on 7th Street*, as Luke emerges from his apartment to a deserted street, a plane crashes to the ground behind him. 26

Figure 1.3 A plane in flames flies low over the heads of the protagonists before crashing into city buildings in *Pulse*, an American remake of the pre-9/11 Japanese film *Kairo*. 27

Figures 1.4 & 1.5 9/11 literalized: the crashed plane in your living room in *War of the Worlds*. 28

Figure 1.6 From *Inside 9/11*, a cameraman flees along with a crowd, looking back at the smoke cloud behind them. The moving camera offers a very different fleeing crowd image than before. 30

Figure 1.7 From *Cloverfield*, the crowd flees as does the camera, held by Hud. 30

Figure 1.8 From *War of the Worlds*, the crowd flees the initial attack, the camera moving with them. 30

Figures 1.9 and 1.10 From National Geographic's *Inside 9/11*, the collapse of the South Tower, the iconic cloud of dust and debris as the building sheds material as it falls. 31

Figure 1.11 From *Diary of the Dead*, a fireball over a neighbourhood as a building burns and collapses. 32

Figure 1.12 From *Cloverfield*, in the distance, the monster is not particularly visible, but the building it destroys is. The debris falls in patterns suggestive of the collapse of the Twin

Towers. The lights in the building go out and then the entire structure collapses straight down. 32

Figure 1.13 The plane crash from *Vanishing on 7th Street* results in burning buildings, collapsed infrastructure and a debris cloud full of flames rushing down the street toward Luke. 33

Figure 1.14 Flying objects propel things into buildings in *Skyline*, sending clouds of smoke, dust and debris everywhere and pulling the human bodies out of those clouds and up into the ships. 33

Figure 1.15 An empty, deserted, smoke-filled street in Manhattan (from *Inside 9/11*). 34

Figure 1.16 An empty, deserted, smoke-filled street in *Vanishing on 7th Street*. 35

Figure 1.17 A slow-moving crowd of refugees approaches a burning and debris-filled Boston in *War of the Worlds*. 35

Figure 1.18 Wall of the missing and lost in *War of the Worlds*. 36

Figure 1.19 Amid the other student notices, missing person fliers are found in *Pulse*. 37

Figure 1.20 *The Happening*'s horror begins with bodies falling from the roof of a construction site, echoing The Falling Man. 40

Figure 1.21 *Skyline* reverses The Falling Man with hundreds of bodies tumbling upward to their deaths. 41

Figure 1.22 The decapitated head of the Statue of Liberty, showing scars in *Cloverfield*. 51

Figures 1.23a–c Marlena as monster suicide bomber. Inside the military post, she explodes. 53

Figure 2.1 From National Geographic's 'Witness 9/11', amateur photographers and videographers record the burning and collapsing World Trade Center from the roof of their apartment building. 58

Figures 2.2 and 2.3 From *Diary of the Dead*: Jason films Debra who films Jason; an echo chamber of self-documenting and recording horror. 64

Figure 2.4 Jigsaw as terrorist: jihadist-style videos present the *Saw* killer's victims with their fate. 75

Figure 2.5 *Saw* as terrorist video as seen on the internet: The disguised 'terrorist' in close-up, making his demands. 76

Figure 2.6 Videos of hostages taken by terrorists: *Saw*. 77

Figure 2.7 The screen within the screen: the camera makes the alien attack both more and less real, both safer and less safe in *War of the Worlds*. 79

Figure 8.1 *Cry Wolf* (2005): The email text forms the background of the conversation between Dodger (Lindy Booth) and Owen (Julian Morris). 182

Figures 8.2, 8.3, 8.4, 8.5 Literalization of a metaphor: The transformation of the transmission of the email about the Wolf into the physical body of the Wolf in *Cry Wolf*. 184–5

Introduction

Terror and Horror

Every day, particularly after September 11th, every day was September 12th. You got up and you thought it might happen again.

CONDOLEEZZA RICE
FORMER NATIONAL SECURITY ADVISOR
ON *THE DAILY SHOW*, 13 OCTOBER 2010

There have been a few films made about the terror attacks of September 11 and many more about the war on terror and the wars in Afghanistan and Iraq that came afterwards. Of the former, *United 93*, about the passengers' attempt to retake the fourth plane, *World Trade Center*, Oliver Stone's least political film, which concerned the rescue of first responders trapped under the rubble of the twin towers, and *Fahrenheit 9/11*, Michael Moore's scathing documentary on the Bush administration's immediate responses to the attacks, remain the widest seen and best known. Of the latter, there are far more, including *Lions for Lambs*, *Rendition*, *Grace is Gone*, *The Messenger*, *In the Valley of Elah*, *Rendition*, *Home of the Brave*, the Academy Award winning *The Hurt Locker*, and the odd satire *American Dreamz*. Although of varying quality (although many are quite good), what most of these films have in common is that audiences initially did not go to see these films in theatres. The box office numbers for most of the above are quite low. It is almost as if American filmgoers did not want to see 9/11 and its military and political aftermath on the screen. The poor box office also reflects the failure of realistic representation to capture the experience of the events of 9/11 and afterwards. Kristiaan Versluys argues that the 'synecdochic imagination' is unable to make Oliver Stone's *World Trade Center* stand for the entirety of the events of 9/11, and instead reduces it down to a disaster movie of the week for television. The films about 9/11 in the immediate wake of 9/11 are, in the words of Matthew J. Morgan, 'triumphant narratives', celebrating American victories during and after the terror attack (2009: 2). But 9/11 did not feel like a victorious experience. Again, Versluy's 'synechodic imagination' reminds us not of victory but of fear and horror. The heroic, dramatic and action genres fail to present 9/11 in a manner that captures the experience and the understanding of that experience.[1]

Instead, the terror attacks and wars that followed have been co-opted into other genres, most notably horror. Where *World Trade Center* fails, *War of the Worlds* (2005) and *Cloverfield* (2008) step in and embrace the fear and horror of the events, not the heroism. In a study of how culture plays a role in emotionally processing the attacks, Reed Johnson sees popular culture as representing 9/11 'indirectly and elliptically' (2011: E7). This book concerns how 9/11 has been reproduced as horror movie, how the war on terror has been framed through and by horror cinema and how the genre itself has been influenced and transformed in the decade since the fall of the twin towers. Joseph Natoli asks how one can prove the world is different after September 11. His response is, 'I can't. I don't … I go to movies and I am aware of the difference' (2007: 9). I agree: the same holds true for me as well. For the past decade I, a life long horror fan, have gone to the cinema, rented DVDs and had them sent to me through Netfilx, and seen them on television and I am aware that horror has changed. One key difference between pre-9/11 and post-9/11 horror is that the former frequently allows for hope and the latter just as frequently does not. In pre-9/11 horror, there is almost always a way to stop the evil. Jason, Michael and Freddy, though they will return in the next sequel, can be defeated by the 'final girl'. Regan MacNeil can be exorcized, Pazuzu driven from her by a priest's sacrifice. A hydrophobic Roy Scheider can blow up a shark by shooting the son of a bitch when he smiles. Though half your group dies and the bikers have invaded the mall, the pregnant woman and the S.W.A.T. officer can climb to the mall's roof and take the helicopter somewhere else. Buffy can and will slay vampires, even if she dies a couple of times while doing it. Heroic human qualities such as love, bravery, resourcefulness and intelligence will eventually defeat the monster. The horror film ends in hope up to September 10.

After 9/11, nihilism, despair, random violence and death, combined with tropes and images generated by the terrorist attacks began to assume far greater prominence in horror cinema. There is a line in John Carpenter's *Prince of Darkness* (1987) (a film that actually does allow for hope), typed out by a possessed linguist: 'You will not be saved by the holy spirit. You will not be saved by the god Plutonium. In fact, YOU WILL NOT BE SAVED' (emphasis in original). This prediction proves faulty, as at least four members of the scientific team and a priest played by Donald Pleasance are, in fact, saved from the titular Prince of Darkness, not to mention the entire world being (temporarily) spared Armageddon, at least until 'the year 1999'. Whereas that film merely plays at hopelessness (as most pre-9/11 films do), now we get true hopelessness and nihilism that shows that evil can and will conquer all. There is not even a temporary sparing in the post-9/11 film. Heroic human qualities cannot and will not save the day or defeat the evil.[2]

Stephen King offers an analysis of political horror as epitomized in *Earth vs. the Flying Saucers* in *Danse Macabre* that ends in what he terms 'reintegration': 'that same feeling that comes when the roller coaster stops at the end of its run and you get off with your best girl, both of you whole and unhurt' (1982: 14). After 9/11, that reintegration seemed less realistic and more difficult to achieve. In films like *Cloverfield*, *The Mist*, *Strangers* and *Paranormal Activity* there is no stepping off whole and unhurt. These films kill most if not all of their main characters and leave the audience with no sense of reintegration. In fact, in the last one, the best girl is possessed by a demon, kills her boyfriend and then vanishes, only to show up in a sequel where she then kills her sister and her sister's entire family in order to gain possession of their infant son. This volume offers a survey of the various ways horror films capture and respond to the 9/11 experience, frequently indirectly, through heightened senses of insecurity, vulnerability, meaninglessness, hopelessness, bleak despair and uncertainty, not to mention specific film-making techniques that echo the experience of 9/11.

The title as problem

Although accurate in terms of the content, every single word of the title of this volume is problematic. 'Post-9/11' relates to specific moment in time and a specific event, but has also come to refer to a mindset. Politicians, pundits and media figures use 'pre-9/11' and post-9/11' to categorize ways of viewing the world and the subsequent necessary actions we must individually and collectively take. The words refer to the terrorist attacks on the United States on 11 September 2001, but also all that has come after: the wars in Afghanistan and Iraq; the creation of the Transportation Safety Administration (TSA) and Department of Homeland Security; the passing of the USA PATRIOT Act; not to mention numerous other terrorist attacks carried out by Islamic extremists in other nations since September 2001. The phrase thus refers to a day, an event, a period, a mindset and a cultural shift.

'Horror' is a specific genre, but one that finds its boundaries blurred, and with numerous subgenres. Hybrid films, such as *Skyline* are science fiction, but contain many horror elements: invasion, body horror, terror within one's own home, a small group of survivors attempt to defeat something monstrous and are slowly killed off one by one. In much the same way, *The Thing*, *Alien*, *Invasion of the Body Snatchers* and *Event Horizon* are all films that blend science fiction and horror. Conversely, some films contain elements of horror cinema, but do not function in the way that more standard horror films do. For example, both *30 Days of Night* and *Twilight* reimagine the vampire motif, but only the former is horror. The latter shares more in common with alienated teen dramas than it does with scary movies. *Nightmare on Elm Street 5* is not really horror, not in the way the original is, not in the way *The Exorcist* is, primarily because of its use of humour and the simple fact that by that point in the series, audiences identified more with Freddy than with his victims and attended the films to laugh and be grossed out, not filled with dread.

Different scholars have defined the genre in different ways, none of which is particularly satisfactory or all-encompassing. Noël Carroll specifies the genre as 'art horror' (as opposed to 'natural horror') in which an 'emotional effect', specifically fear, is generated through an encounter with the monstrous (1990: 12, 8, 42). The monstrous in this case refers not only to 'categorically impossible beings' but also monstrous humans: Hannibal Lecter, Norman Bates and John Kramer (Jigsaw, from the *Saw* films) are all monstrous (and monsters) as well (1990: 206). His definition is useful, but not comprehensive, as Carroll focuses primarily on the monster as that which is outside. He observes, 'the horror film is essentially xenophobic', and monsters represent 'a predatory Other' which 'reinforces negative imagery of those political/social entities which threaten the established social order' (1990: 196). This definition, however, allows one to ignore fears generated from within: the *Hostel* films and the *Saw* films, for example, are rooted in American ambivalence and concern that we have become a nation that tortures. In those films, the fear is of being tortured by monsters, in Carroll's sense, but also it is of becoming a torturer. The fear is not just of Other but what Self becomes in response of other. In many post-9/11 horror films, the film does not end with the defeat of the monster and the return of the status quo in the social order. The paradigm shift in horror reflects the paradigm shift after 9/11. We cannot return to the status quo.

In this case, I am relying on the simple definition that the primary purpose of a horror film is to cause fear in the audience. As a result, some films are discussed in this survey that use horror conventions but are not considered 'horror'. *Buried*, for example, is not considered a genre film, although it contains almost nothing but horror elements and its overarching narrative is derived almost entirely from Edgar Allen Poe's stories. More fear and dread are created in *Buried* than in all of the *Twilight* films. In short, if it creates fear, a film is fair game for this study.

'American' as a term fails to represent the complexity and transnational nature of contemporary cinema production and reception, as well as the global nature of 9/11. In the case of the former, the United States' two most lucrative exports are weapons and films. As a result, both are emblematic of American culture and have far-reaching influences and implications on the world stage. There is an international visual language and influence of film that has developed over the last few decades. Asian cinema has profoundly influenced Quentin Tarantino, who then has a reciprocal influence on Asian cinema. Some of the films discussed here are American remakes of foreign films: *[Rec]* becomes *Quarantine*, *Ringu* becomes *The Ring*, and, in the most identity-bending film discussed here, the Austrian film *Funny Games* (1997) is remade by the same director as *Funny Games* (2007) in the United States with expatriate British actors in the lead. Furthermore, the economics of film production has reduced Hollywood's geographic importance. Films are made with American money and some American actors, but filmed in Toronto or Vancouver, or in Eastern Europe in order to become more profitable. I am not suggesting that American popular culture does not continue to dominate, merely that cultural flow is not unidirectional and that 'American' is not an uncomplicated term.

In the case of the latter, as Versluys observes, 'In a time of globalized witnessing and shared vicarious experience, an event like 9/11 is a rupture for everybody. As a consequence, there is a globalized need to comprehend, to explain and to restore' (2009: 4). Moreover, as will be outlined below, terrorism was and is not just an American concern. Before and after 9/11 there have been significant terror attacks throughout the world, and the tension between the experience of terror as a global phenomenon and a local phenomenon is reflected in a global cinema that reflects 'glocal' terror, and therefore similar horror. There is a reason why Japanese horror films concerning angry spirits that employ technology to kill (frequently referred to as 'J-horror') rose to prominence after the 1995 Aum Shinrikyō sarin gas attacks in the Tokyo subway, just as there is a reason why American remakes of those films began appearing after 9/11.[3]

Lastly, 'cinema' does not exist in a vacuum. Art does not mean, it generates meaning, and cinema is influenced and influences other media as well as popular perception. Part of the challenge of analysing film texts in the present era is the existence of 'fluid texts', in John Bryant's terminology (2002: 1). Not only are multiple viewings of a single film possible, but the new technology of DVDs and Blu-Ray allows for multiple versions of the same film to be placed on the same source and viewed sequentially or interactively.

Alternate endings, deleted scenes, variant versions ('the version not seen in theatres!'), director's cuts and extended versions mean that there is no single 'text' of a film, but a fluid text that contains all the multiple variants. The DVD of *Land of the Dead* contains scenes not seen in the theatrical release, for example. There are different versions and endings possible on the DVD of *Paranormal Activity*. As a result, like all films, post-9/11 horror cinema consists of fluid texts that change and transform upon subsequent viewings.

Films' meanings also change with time, as does our perception of those films. We must also note the ideological assumptions about the films, which are often seen as reactionary, but which just as often are simultaneously reactionary and revolutionary. Some films are obviously reactionary, some films engage the ambiguity of America's role in the world (either intentionally or inadvertently), and many films studied here contain both regressive and progressive elements. In this study, I as writer and you as reader must remember there is no blanket response, horror is not monolithic, audience experiences are not monolithic and even a single individual's reactions may change with time and subsequent viewing. I was distinctly underwhelmed the first time I saw the remake of *Dawn of the Dead* (2004). Since then, however, repeated viewings have led me to discover multiple layers in that film that have raised my respect for it. It is my hope that this book will allow the reader to view the films discussed herein through new lenses and discover elements not before seen.

Terror

The terror attacks of September 11 were the largest terror events and terror spectacles seen to date. Chapter 1 will go into more details, but on September 11, 2001, a group of 19 hijackers, trained and financed by a group called al Qaeda whose de facto leader was Osama bin Laden, a wealthy Saudi-born Islamic extremist, using box cutters and the claims of possessing a bomb, commandeered four passenger airplanes, resulting in those planes being used as missiles to attack and destroy the Twin Towers of the World Trade Center in New York City, as well as hit the Pentagon. The fourth plane, United 93, was intended to hit the White House or the Capitol building, but an attempt to retake the plane by the passengers resulted in the terrorists crashing it into the ground in a field in Pennsylvania. The official death total was 2,973 killed during the attacks, including the people in the buildings and the people on the planes.[4] The attacks shocked the United States and directly resulted in wars in Afghanistan (whose government under the Taliban sheltered al Qaeda), and Iraq (which actually had nothing to do with the terror attacks), as well as greater restrictions and security legislation within the United States such as the USA PATRIOT Act.[5] The post-9/11 period also includes a decade's worth of catastrophes, terrorist attacks and natural disasters which have only heightened our collective sense of vulnerability, paranoia and pessimism. Contributing to this period of seemingly increasing despair are the experiences of Hurricane Katrina in 2005, two lingering wars, the economic meltdown of 2008, the Gulf oil spill of 2010, and significant terror attacks around the globe since.

Immediately in the wake of 9/11 came the Anthrax attacks, which initially were perceived as another Islamic extremist attack. In October of 2001, five envelopes were mailed in Princeton, New Jersey. The envelopes each contained a photocopied letter with differing texts including the phrases '09-11-01', 'Death to America', 'Death to Israel', and 'Allah is Great', along with weaponized, powdered anthrax. The addressees and presumed targets of the letters were American Media, Inc., the Boca Raton-based publisher of the *National Enquirer*, the *New York Post*, NBC News anchor Tom Brokaw, then-Senate majority leader Tom Daschle, and Senator Patrick Leahy. Five people died from inhaled anthrax: two postal workers, the photo editor of American Media, and two women in New York and Connecticut whose mail became contaminated from contact with the anthrax-filled envelopes. Although in the immediate post-9/11 climate the envelopes were seen as the next terror attack by al Qaeda, suspicion rapidly shifted to individuals closer to home. The first suspect was former Army scientist Steven Hatfill. The inquiry, however, eventually shifted to Bruce Ivins, a scientist with the army's bio-defense labs, who committed suicide when he learned he was going to be charged with the attacks.[6]

The Anthrax attacks evoked a powerful fear of bio-warfare and weapons of mass destruction (biological and chemical, not to mention 'dirty bombs' – standard explosives mixed with radioactive material in order to contaminate large areas and irradiate the victims) in the media and citizenry. We have had plague movies and fears of bioterrorism before (*The Andromeda Strain, The Crazies, The Hot Zone*, etc.) but post-9/11 the shift indicated a greater possibility of reality: *28 Days Later, The Crazies, Resident Evil*, as well as such neo-medievalist fare as *Black Death* and *Season of the Witch* (both of which feature the bubonic plague as backdrop and inciting incident), all depict societies at the mercy of plagues. What all these films have in common is the development of the virus by the government as a bio-weapon and its inadvertent release through accident or act of terror. Thomas Fahy, for example, sees *Cabin Fever* as a use of horror cinema 'to explore modern-day fears about biological terrorism in post-9/11 America', employing slasher movie clichés in order to engage a larger context of fear (2010: 3).

Terror has remained the fundamental concern of American society since, and post-9/11 terror attacks on passenger planes bound for the United States as well as terror attacks in other nations by Islamic militants have only added to that concern. On 20 December 2001, Richard 'The Shoe Bomber' Reid attempted to detonate plastic explosives hidden in his sneakers on American Airlines Flight 63 from Paris to Miami. In October 2002, a Bali Nightclub was bombed, leaving 202 dead, including a few vacationing Americans. On 11 March 2004 the Madrid train bombings occurred, killing 191. In September of that year, a school in Beslan, Russia, was taken over by Muslim separatists and over 300 were killed. July of 2005 saw the London Underground bombings, which killed 53. In November of that year three hotels were bombed in Amman, Jordan, killing 67. Coordinated shooting attacks by Islamic militants in Mumbai, India in November 2008 killed 174. Echoing Richard Reid, on 25 December 2009, Umar Farouk Abdumutallab, better known as 'The Underwear Bomber' attempted to blow up Northwest Flight 253 from Amsterdam to Detroit with plastic explosives sewn into his underwear. Five suicide bombings in Pakistan in January, March, May, July and September of 2010 left a total of 441 dead. A second attack in Mumbai, India in July 2011, this time with bombs, left 21 dead: not to mention the Times Square bomber, a failed attempt to carry out a terror attack within the United States in New York City on New Year's Eve, which was stopped, and the more successful shootings at Fort Hood. In every case, these deaths were a means to an end. All of these attacks were spectacles designed to demonstrate to the West and its allies in the Middle East and Asia that it is vulnerable and can be hurt.

As noted above, the role of the horror film is to cause fear. The role of the terrorist attack is also to cause fear. Both the horror film and terrorism are rooted in the visual experience of horrifying images that cause dread and terror. Terrorism, as Orr and Klaić observe, is a 'paratheatrical' activity, 'a performance with an involuntary audience' and 'a form of social drama' (1990: 8). In describing international acts of terrorism, pre-9/11 volumes such as Edward S. Herman and Gerry O'Sullivan's *The Terrorism Industry* frequently use the words 'drama' and 'theatre' to describe what terrorism is, at heart (1989: 42). Gabriel Weimann, in an article entitled 'Mass Mediated Theatre of Terror – Must the Show Go On?' describes contemporary terrorism as 'programmed, preplanned and well-choreographed theatre' (1988: 2). Indeed, Brian Michael Jenkins concludes his survey of terrorism by noting, 'Terrorism is aimed at the people watching, not at the actual victims. Terrorism is theatre' (1975: 158). Terrorism is a public performance aimed at an international audience, with active performers in the form of the perpetrators and unwilling, involuntary performers in the form of the victims and, by extension, their families.

The terror attacks on September 11, 2001 were not aimed at those who died in them. They were not aimed at the people on the planes or in the buildings. Those individuals, tragic though their deaths were, were simply a means to an end for the terrorists. The actual targets, the greater victims, so to speak, are those forced to watch, unable to help, hope or change anything. The terror attacks were a spectacle designed to show that the United States was vulnerable, that it could be attacked and badly hurt, that it could not protect its own people. As Tom Engelhardt reminds us, only a relative handful of people experienced the terror attacks of September 11 directly. For most of the nation, it was a mediated 'on screen spectacle', resulting in numerous commentators seeing the experience as being like a film or something from Hollywood (2006: 15). Numerous commentators on the day and since have observed it was 'like a movie'.

In short, 9/11 was terrorism at its most spectacular designed to cause the greatest amount of fear. The whole point was for the people of the United States to witness Americans dying horribly and to react out of fear and panic. 9/11 was terror, but therefore it was also horror. 'The perpetrators fully assumed the horror of their acts; this horror is part of the fatal attraction which draws them towards committing them', writes Slavoj Žižek (2002: 136). Whereas the Nazis, for example, tried to keep their atrocities secret and hidden, even if it was an open secret, the perpetrators of the terror attacks of 9/11 counted on the events being played out in front of the world. 9/11 was a *show*. That show demonstrated not just the attacks themselves, but also that the US was left in a state of vulnerability.

The pre-9/11 film moment which might summarize a significant post-9/11 realization occurs in Brian DePalma's *The Untouchables* (1987). Agent Oscar Wallace (Charles Martin Smith), an accountant who has joined Eliot Ness's team of crusading federal agents in their war against organized crime is charged with the everyday task of escorting an informant from the courtroom in an elevator to the garage from which the prisoner will be taken to a federal penitentiary. During the performance of this simple task, he, the prisoner, and other policemen are killed off-screen by Frank Nitti (Billy Drago). When the elevator doors open, the bodies are revealed and written on the elevator wall in their blood is the word 'Touchable'. Ness's team is called 'the untouchables' because they will not take bribes, but Nitti's message written in the blood of one of the members of the team interprets that nickname in a different way and reminds Ness and his men that they can be killed in horrible ways and their bodies violated as well. After 9/11, the United States, which saw itself as 'untouchable' in terms of moral conduct, realized it was 'touchable' in terms of violence done against it. The oceans and the military and economic might which had protected the United States in the past proved to be illusory barriers to those who wished to do us harm. Mohamad Atta and his colleagues proved that the United States was 'touchable' in all senses of the word. Al Qaeda claimed that the attacks were 'retaliation in kind' for American military and economic policies throughout the Muslim world (quoted in *The 9/11 Commission Report* 2004: 47).

The media, politicians and the culture at large developed a new concept of terrorism as a direct result of September 11. Whereas previously, terrorism was perceived as violent criminal acts for political or ideological purposes that deliberately targeted non-combatants, after

9/11, terrorism was conceptualized as an existential threat. It was not the actions of a few individuals attempting to use violence for political or social gain, it was a threat to all life and human existence itself. Frank Furedi terms this 'catastrophic terrorism', and 9/11 is the paradigmatic example (2007: 51).

This vulnerability (whether perceived or real) has shaped not only American domestic and foreign policy for the last decade, it has also profoundly shaped our culture. Our 'heightened sense of vulnerability,' writes Frank Furedi, 'has encouraged an attitude of fatalism, pessimism and a dread of terrorism' out of proportion to its actual possibility and repercussions (2007: 13) This attitude is reflected in our popular culture and filtered through horror cinema. As the purpose of horror is to generate fear in the audience, it becomes perhaps one of the best vehicles for allowing our culture to process the experience of terror.

The elements, tropes, themes and memes of post-9/11 horror are not necessarily new. New York City has often been a site of horror: *King Kong* (both original and 1976 remake), *Q*, *Rosemary's Baby* and *C.H.U.D.*, to name but some. Even Jason Vorhees could not stay away from the city that never sleeps. Everybody dies in *Night of the Living Dead*, in *Children Shouldn't Play with Dead Things* and in *Cannibal Holocaust*.

John Carpenter's *The Thing* is an exercise in unremitting nihilism, paranoia and hopelessness in which the best one can hope for is that one dies frozen in the snow so that the thing does not reach civilization. Evil wins, perhaps more often in horror films regardless of period, than in any other genre. *Rosemary's Baby*, *Burnt Offerings*, *Lifeforce*, *Invasion of the Body Snatchers*, *The Blair Witch Project* and *Children Shouldn't Play with Dead Things*, to name but an immediate few, all end with the forces of evil victorious and/or the deaths of most of the significant characters. David Cronenberg's films frequently end in a kind of bleak nihilism (James Marriott states that Cronenberg 'is one of the few directors in North America allowed the luxury of an unhappy ending' (2007: 255)). Not to put too fine a point on it, post-9/11 horror did not invent the bleak ending, nihilism, the deaths of all the protagonists or the triumph of evil. However, just as a paradigm shift occurred in the United States politically, culturally and socially on 9/11, so too a paradigm shift has also occurred in American cinema.

What David Edelstein calls 'viciously nihilistic' (2006), referring specifically to *The Devil's Rejects*, can be applied to many post-9/11 horror films, such as *The Strangers*, *Cloverfield* and *30 Days of Night*. Stephen King's *The Mist* features one of the bleakest endings of the last ten years and is painfully nihilistic in its outlook on our prospects for survival, let alone happiness.

Numerous critics have also indicated the strong link between humour and horror. Yet despite the presence of such films as *Shaun of the Dead* or *Zombie Strippers* the violence of post-9/11 horror is not jokey or playful. The remakes of *Friday the 13th* and *Nightmare on Elm Street* lack the playful squeamishness the originals and their sequels came to embody. Their villains are again true monsters, evil beings that can only be resisted but not defeated. We cannot laugh as we do at the comic grotesqueries of the deaths in *Nightmare on Elm Street 4, The Dream Child* or *Jason X*, which are hardly frightening and serve as gross-outs at best, causing screams of laughter more than fright. The remakes feature violent, horrible, painful deaths, meant to display our vulnerability to evil, just as the terror attacks of 9/11 did.

Horror after 9/11: methodology and contexts

The conventional wisdom in Hollywood after the attacks was that audiences would want 'comfort films' and films that displayed American pride and heroics. A few days after September 11, President of the Motion Picture Association of America Jack Valenti wrote in *Variety* that terrorists 'try to make us afraid' and that Hollywood had a moral obligation to 'tell visual stories which offers our fellow citizens an interlude so sorely needed at this time' (2001: 1). Yet by 2005, Lions Gate was devoting 20 per cent of its cinematic output to horror (Lee, 'Horror' E8). Between September 2005 and April 2006, seven horror films opened at the top of the box office, including *Saw II* (Gordon, 2006: 60). This same period saw the emergence of the Afterdark Horrorfest, the *Masters of Horror* series on Showtime (and its subsequent decline and de-fanging as *Fear*

Itself on network television), not to mention the huge popularity of American adaptations of J-horror, the advent of so-called 'torture porn', the development of entire new horror series such as the *Saw* franchise, the return to horror films for director Sam Raimi (who traded in his *Evil Dead* director's hat for a *Spiderman* suit), and the remake of almost three dozen horror films from the past three decades. Although we live in a generation of the 'reboot' (*Star Trek*, for example) and the delayed sequel (*Tron*, for example), horror remakes are the massive dark heart of the phenomenon.

As noted above, horror becomes a means of indirectly dealing with the experiences of 9/11 and the decade of despair which followed. Continuous coverage as the events unfolded on that day represented an attempt to understand them but also an attempt to contain the experience. Horror cinema after 9/11 sought to and seeks to understand, contain and explicate the experience as well. Horror films do not exist in a vacuum as autonomous texts but rather contain deliberate engagement with contemporaneous culture. Horror films do not simply mean; they generate meaning based on audience experience. We must also remember, as Andrew Tudor astutely perceives, 'horror movies are neither direct cause nor an unmediated reflection of their audiences' attitudes and activities' (1989: 212). Furthermore, to focus on specific fears in specific contexts is of limited use, as it ignores larger emergent patterns (Tudor 1989: 213). Lastly, there is no one totalizing perspective on either September 11 (and its attendant meanings and resonances within our culture) or horror cinema. As such, I will not rely on a single methodology.

Thus, an approach to post-9/11 horror requires a methodology that engages multiple films with multiple points of view, engaging multiple ideologies, functioning in multiple ways, while aimed at multiple constituencies. Traditionally, much horror film criticism has been rooted in psychology and gender politics. Hollywood does not always uniformly express or reinforce dominant ideological concerns, especially as related to gender. Carol Clover (1992) and Tony Williams (1996) have already convincingly argued this fact over a decade and a half ago. Horror criticism has seen a shift away from gender in the wake of September 11. There are two primary ways to understand gender and politics after 9/11. On the one hand, 9/11 transforms horror, rendering gender no longer a central issue. A collapsing building or crashing plane does not care about one's gender, orientation or relationship with one's father: everybody dies. Random and anonymous death is not concerned with oppression or gendered identity. Although Islamic fundamentalists have regressive attitudes towards women, the deaths on 9/11 had less to do with gender and maintaining the patriarchy or sexual purity than with nationality and attacking the entirety of the socio-cultural-political reality of the United States of America. The result is that horror cinema ignores the rules of gender established by the genre as well. For example, Clover's famous 'final girl' becomes the 'final couple' in the remake of *Friday the 13th* or *Hatchet*. The 'final girls' of *Wolf Creek*, *The Devil's Rejects*, and *Martyrs* all die horrible, painful deaths, despite their resourcefulness. The terror attacks of 9/11, having no gender bias, render such analysis moot.

Conversely, however, as Susan Faludi convincingly argues in *The Terror Dream*, whereas the events of 9/11 do not display gender bias, the manner in which those events are interpreted, presented publicly and reconstructed for meaning do, in fact, display a great deal of gender bias. The immediate media consensus was that feminism was no longer relevant or even useful in the wake of 9/11, and in extreme cases may even be to blame for the attacks, because of its ostensible contribution to the 'feminizing' of the American male, its commitment to multiculturalism and its devotion to opposing 'traditional values' (2007: 20–2). When the stories of 9/11 are told, men are the active heroes and women are the passive victims or the grieving widows left behind. The heroic contributions of women to the downing of United 93 and the rescue efforts at Ground Zero, as well as the pain and loss of the widowers left behind are ignored or at least downplayed by the media (2007: 57–8). In short, 9/11 was not gender biased, but our culture's understanding and reconstruction of it is. Faludi has already convincingly made this argument, so I will not pursue it here. I do, however, want to recognize and demonstrate the shifting and protean challenges of analysing horror cinema either through traditional methodologies and the challenges presented by ignoring such methodologies altogether.

These conflicting impulses manifest in the cinema of post-9/11 horror, sometimes overtly and sometimes covertly; but they do render psychoanalysis and gender studies problematic for understanding the fears at the root of contemporary horror cinema. In his seminal text *Dreadful Pleasures*, now a quarter of a century old, James Twitchell argues that the attraction of horror for the audience is psychosexual: 'Horror has little to do with fright; it has more to do with laying down the rules of socialization and extrapolating a hidden code of sexual behavior' (1985: 66). Twitchell relies upon a Freudian model for viewing horror and its appeal which was already limited and not entirely encompassing when it was published (Douglas Cowan, for example, convincingly argues that the fear generated from watching *The Exorcist* is not necessarily rooted in childbirth, adolescence or sexual behaviour but in a genuine fear of the reality of demons). After September 11, Twitchell's suppositions become much more tentative. At the very least, horror has everything to do with fright and with coping not with social codes but the very real threat of death.

Sexual anxiety has been overridden (although not entirely banished by) other anxieties: the ephemeral and ghostly fear associated with terrorism; new body horror rooted in torture, and the fear associated with the power of religion, to name but three. The explosion of pseudo-documentaries, zombie films and 'torture porn' has less to do with maintaining the patriarchy and controlling female sexuality and more to do with domesticating the experience of terrorism. To say so is not to suggest that the same retrogressive sexual politics are not present in these films, nor to suggest that gender constructions have been radically transformed in horror since September 11.

Trauma studies represent a new methodology that has begun to offer genuine insights into both horror cinema and the experience of 9/11. Linnie Blake reads horror films through trauma studies, analysing 'the mode in which traumatic historical events are representationally transmitted in space and time' (2008: 1). Stephen Prince argues that films allow viewers 'to bear witness to trauma' without actually visiting trauma upon them (2009: 12–13). Lastly, Schopp and Hill observe, 'If the products of a nation's popular culture can both reflect cultural dreams – or nightmares – and cultivate a dark national fantasy made real by trauma, then we need to consider how that same popular culture reflects our efforts to negotiate the complex cultural reverberations of that trauma' (2009: 14). In other words, horror cinema allows us to represent and to witness horrific events without being genuinely traumatized by them. In doing so, it allows us to process and cope with the genuine traumas we have experienced. Many of these ideas are rooted in Aristotelian notions of catharsis.[7] In *The Poetics*, Aristotle argues that audiences go to the theatre in order to experience catastrophe so that they might feel pity and terror. By experiencing these emotions in a controlled, artificial environment, we are able to encounter tragedy, but then purge the negative emotions from us in a catharsis. We leave the theatre in a better emotional condition than we entered. This phenomenon, however, is tricky. When Phrynicus, an ancient Athenian playwright, wrote *The Fall of Miletus*, a play about the true story of the conquest of the city, an Athenian colony in Asian Minor, by the Persian army and the slaughter of every last man, woman and child afterwards, the audience was indeed moved to pity and terror. Unfortunately for Phrynicus, the emotions were too real and the tragic event too recent to be sufficiently represented on stage. The poet was fined for using a literary tragedy to remind the city of a genuine tragedy and the city also banned the presentation of contemporary events on stage. Greek tragedy predominantly used myth as its source material after this event.[8]

From its origins, drama recognized that tragic distance was needed in order for catharsis to work and for the audience to enjoy the spectacle of violence and catastrophe. Bearing in mind all of these suppositions, cautions and theories, in this volume I propose to use a blend of methodologies in which we focus on the various elements of horror films that engage the images, spectacles and motifs of September 11 and the horrific decade which followed. I will consider narrative elements such as plot and characters, as well as filmic and cinematic elements (editing, including use of montage, point of view shots, scores and sound effects, lighting), as well as what is not present.

In particular, I am interested in sociophobics, 'the study of human fears as they occur and are experienced in the context of the sociocultural systems humans have created' (Scruton 1986: 9). David L. Scruton makes a case that 'fear is a social act that occurs within a cultural matrix. 'To fear' and 'to be afraid' are social events which have social consequences' (1986: 10). The events of 9/11 generated fear: the United States continues to this day to function in a state of fear and paranoia. Horror films, at least those viewed in a cinema, are also social experiences. We go to the theatre to fear together. Even when viewed on DVD at home, horror cinema can be a social experience when viewed with friends or family, or can become a social experience when later discussed with others.

The purpose of this volume then is to tease out the theoretical implications not just of these different films but also the larger themes and patterns than begin to emerge in the wake of September 11. What do these films teach us about 9/11? What do they teach us about horror and fear? When viewed as an entire genre, how has the horror film changed in the last decade? I will be surveying themes, motifs, tropes that have risen to prominence in the decade since the terror attacks. In order to do so, I am less interested in close readings of entire films but looking at trends manifested and reflected across different types of films and subgenres. This also indicates one of the shifts in cinema: the permeability of genre, hybrid genres and the advent of specific subgenres: 'torture porn', 'post-millennial horror road movie', 'military horror movie' and 'post-torture porn retro-slasher'.[9]

Horror is both emotional and intellectual. I also therefore will be looking at the intellectual processes behind the experience of the films alongside their intended emotional effect. I am, however, wary of universalizing audience experiences, or perceiving my experience as normative. Likewise, I am cautious of explorations of horror cinema that are overly theory laden and apt to confirm either first impressions or one's own preconceptions. Lastly, I am also cautious not to read too deep into the films here and to recognize that no one walks out of a horror film saying, 'I was terrified by that reaffirmation of patriarchy and the reinscription of codes of sexual behaviour,' or 'That use of the zombie as a metaphor for the American *lumpenproletariat* scared the hell out of me'. In the end, the fear is what matters. It is what we seek when we go to such films and it is what brings us back to genuine horrifying experiences. Horror films are 'sociophobic windows' to use Douglas Cowan's term, into the things that frighten us, individually and collectively, and should not be reduced down to simple psychoanalysis (2008: 10).

Let me also state from the outset that I am not proposing a simple teleology from monolithic pre-9/11 horror to monolithic post-9/11 horror, as if a switch had been flipped on that day. Instead, I am proposing a shift in emphasis, tropes and elements, many if not all of which existed before 9/11, but which became foregrounded in the period afterwards. I am proposing the elements and images of 9/11 began to present themselves in horror cinema for the purpose of coping with the fears generated not only by the terror attacks but by the events and culture afterwards. These include the wars in Afghanistan and Iraq, the anthrax attacks of 2001, the subsequent terror attacks, detailed above, Hurricane Katrina, the economic collapse of 2008 and catastrophic earthquakes in Chile, New Zealand, Japan, Haiti and other natural disasters. We must remember that not everything in new horror can be traced to 9/11: other factors come into play as well. The rise of realistic video games and their adaptation into films, the influence of J-horror and other international echoes, the rise of social media and the omnipresence of technology are all sources for horror in the new millennium.

The book breaks down various elements and tropes of post-9/11 horror into specific chapters. Chapter 1, entitled '9/11 as Horror' is in two parts. The first part considers the imagery of 9/11 and how horror films have appropriated it. The second part offers close readings of films that have reproduced the experience of 9/11 as a horror film in different ways and considers different understandings of the meaning of that event.

The second chapter considers the rise of the pseudo-documentary. Films such as *Cloverfield, Diary of the Dead, [REC]* (and its American remake, *Quarantine*), *Paranormal Activity* and *Apollo 18* all rise out of two other mediated phenomena: the experience of 9/11 and its subsequent representation through television documentaries, news reports and other media and the increased presence and awareness of terrorist-made videos. In the case of the former, the actual experience of 9/11 was, for the majority of people all over the world, a fragmented, highly mediated one in which a variety of camera shots, shaky footage from mobile, hand-held cameras and footage from a variety of sources are combined together to frame a single narrative. In the case of the latter, internet videos made by terrorists, frequently depicting the brutal, violent and bloody death of a westerner began to circulate soon after 9/11. The experience of viewing these also shaped the 'found footage' horror film, as well as the use of video in such films as *Saw*.

The third chapter focuses primarily on *The Strangers* and *Funny Games* (both original and remake) as manifestations of a change in the approach to and understanding of death in horror films. Whereas many slasher films of the eighties and nineties posit a moral universe, in which death comes for those fornicate, drink, do drugs or otherwise violate a moral code, post-9/11 horror posits a world in which death is random and anonymous. You are tortured and killed for no other reason than you were home at that time. The chapter concludes with a brief analysis of the *Final Destination* films.

The fourth chapter seeks to locate 'torture porn' films in the conflicted national discourse on 'enhanced interrogation'. The sociophobic reflects not only the fear of being tortured by evil foreigners, but also the fear that we ourselves may be torturers. Rooted in these films is also a conflicted exploration of what it means to be an American in the world today. Chapter 5 focuses on hopeless, bleak despair and the trope of nihilistic endings. In many films after September 11, it is not enough for characters to die, they must be hopeless, helpless and despairing. They must witness loved ones die horribly. The chapter focuses on such films as *The Mist*, *Drag Me to Hell* and *Paranormal Activity* which do not allow for catharsis. The bleak endings result in a denied catharsis that leaves one in a state of despair.

Although fear of religion is a major theme in horror cinema since its origins, after-9/11 horror cinema has focused on religion in particular. Driving the terrorist attacks was a radical Islamic fundamentalism. Interestingly, no mainstream horror film has used Islamic fundamentalists as a source for horror. Instead, the fear of religion has been diverted into three streams. The first is a fear of American fundamentalism. Films such as *The End of the Line*, *The Reaping* and *The Mist*. In these films, fundamentalist characters are shown to be of great danger to society, causing a great deal of damage and death. The second stream is a variation of the first, comprised of films in which religious people are revealed to be devil worshippers. Films such as *The Reaping*, *House of the Devil* and *The Last Exorcism* feature Christian characters revealed to be secret devil worshippers. The last stream is one that acknowledges the reality of evil as posited in religion. As Cynthia Freeland observed in 2000 in *The Naked and the Undead*, horror films 'provide one very large, popular, ongoing and accessible body for symbolizing evil' (2000: 2). Post-9/11 horror shows that evil is real, and that exorcism does not always work. The devil, demons and evil spirits become symbols for terrorists, but the tools for fighting them (prayer, ritual exorcism, and the presence of holy people) do not always have efficacy.

Chapter 7 also visits a mainstay of horror cinema: the traditional monsters of ghosts, zombies and vampires, all of which (as well as werewolves) return with a vengeance (literally) after 9/11. The chapter considers how these traditional creatures of horror movies change from the nineties to the post-9/11 period and what they tell us about our changing fears. Similarly, in Chapter 8, 'Manufacturing Fears', the creation of fear is a major theme. In this case, however, the fear is real, the threat is not. In the films *The Village*, *Cry Wolf* and *Four Boxes*, individuals seeking to advance their own agendas create imaginary monsters in order to achieve an effect, The fear they generate, however, has unintended consequences that results in death and destruction. It is no coincidence that these films were all made after the start of the war in Iraq.

The final chapter considers what I term 'horrific nostalgia'. In the wake of the terror attacks, over three dozen horror films from the sixties, seventies, and eighties have been remade, especially numerous slasher films: *Halloween, Friday the 13th, Black Christmas, A Nightmare on Elm Street, My Bloody Valentine, Sorority Row* and *Prom Night*, to name but some of the more well-known ones. All of these remakes evince sociocultural shifts from the original to the post-9/11 version, but, perhaps more significantly, there is something more happening here than producers cashing in on recognizable properties. In remaking eighties slasher films, Hollywood, in its own way, is remaking the eighties. The George W. Bush administration is re-imagined as a second Reagan era, in which American strength is projected and in which the threats were more manageable and less horrifying. A conclusion rounds out the volume.

This volume was written not only to identify the patterns and motifs of post-9/11 horror, but also because I am a fan of horror cinema. It is a strange thing to critique that which you love. Yet, as with families and friends, it is the things we love the most that we know the best. As do most horror fans, I seek out my favoured genre at all levels. To be a horror fan is to know the triumph of hope over experience. Each film I see I hope will be another *Exorcist*, another *Night of the Living Dead*, another *Ringu*. Experience has taught me that most of the films I see will be another *Leprechaun in the Hood*, another *Blood Monkey*, another *Freddy's Dead: The Final Nightmare*.

Regardless of quality or popularity, I take all the films in this study at face value and ask that the reader does so as well. I reserve judgement on the quality of the films, instead focusing on the images, elements and motifs recurring throughout the genre. These films all reflect the culture that produced them. The fact that some do so better or more intelligently than others, or that some do so poorly, or in a manner designed cravenly and crassly to make a profit rather than a quality film, does not change the fact that they still offer a vision of our world. My focus has been on more mainstream films, but I have reviewed many movies from every level of the genre and have found these themes reflected at all levels.

Finally, a spoiler alert is due. In this volume, I reveal endings, identities, plot twists and other information that can and will ruin the viewing experience if the reader is not familiar with the cinematic texts. See the films first, then read this book, for your own satisfaction.

1

9/11 as Horror

In his article for *The Nation*, '9/11 in a Movie-Made World', Tom Engelhardt argues that the United States has cinematically imagined '9/11' long before it happened (2006: 15). Our cinema has presented the destruction of New York, of the United States and of the world many, many times. When such a visual catastrophe did occur, multiple commentators observed that it was 'like a movie'. Cinema taught us how to perceive, receive and understand the events unfolding that day (on a screen, for most observers). Conversely, the images of that day were immediately iconic, many (but not all) repeated endlessly in the days and weeks that follow, and continue to be presented publicly each anniversary of the attacks.

As noted in the Introduction, however, Hollywood has by and large eschewed presenting images of 9/11 itself directly. Instead, the images and experiences have been distanced and displaced into genre narratives. Just as the ancient Athenians no longer allowed historical representation in the theatre of Dionysus, but filtered their fears, hopes and social dramas through mythic subject matter, so, too, does the United States explore 9/11 through the fantastic, the monstrous and the horrific. This chapter is in two parts. The first part considers the tropes and images of 9/11 and how horror films have appropriated them. The second part offers brief readings of three films that have reproduced 9/11 as a horror film in different ways and offering different understandings of the meaning of that event: *War of the Worlds* (2005) and *Cloverfield* (2008), which write 9/11 as large horror, and *Mulberry Street* (2006) which reproduces it as smaller, personal horror. All three films present New York as a site of horror.

Part 1

Iconic elements, images and tropes

Several elements, tropes and images dominate post-9/11 horror. No one film has all of the elements and images and no image or trope appears in every film. But together these elements represent ways in which horror cinema has appropriated 9/11 and its imagery, not least of which in order to contain it, understand it and re-experience it under safer conditions or with a different ending.

First is the idea of New York City as 'ground zero', a term usually associated with nuclear destruction. The city itself was not destroyed, but the imagery of destruction and the specific images from that day of deserted streets, and conversely larger crowds fleeing, combined with gray ash, dust and debris covering everything and everyone and the overall picture of New York was of a city in ruins. 'Ground zero' also indicates the heart of an attack. New York had always been a site of horror in cinema, as noted in the Introduction, but 9/11 made it *the* site of horror.

Until 9/11, Los Angeles was the preferred city to destroy in American culture. Mike Davis reports that between 1952 and 1999, Los Angeles was destroyed in novels and films an average of three times every year, far more than New York or London, the next two most destroyed cities (1999: 276). Since Hollywood is solipsistic, Hollywood is also one of Hollywood's favorite targets. Los Angeles is prominently featured in films of global destruction, even if not the primary setting of the film.[1] Yet, after 9/11 it is New York that becomes the site of primary destruction, death, mayhem and attacks. New York is 9/11, in a way the other sites are not. I have heard anecdotally from New Yorkers of tourists asking 'where 9/11 is', referring to the footprints of the Twin Towers. Linguistically, this question indicates not only that 9/11 is now perceived as a place, not an event, but that the place it is located is solely the province of Manhattan. Nor is the Pentagon or the field in Shanksville, Pennsylvania referred to as 'ground zero'. 9/11 has a hierarchy: New York is where 9/11 happened; the Pentagon and United 93 are secondary sites in the public imagination. As a result, New York is the centre of post-9/11 horror.

Figure 1.1 Although set in Los Angeles, *Skyline* features a shot of New York City's skyline burning with the Statue of Liberty in the foreground. After 9/11, New York is the central site of horror.

I do not suggest that New York was not a primary setting for horror before 9/11 (it most certainly was) nor do I suggest that all post-9/11 horror is set in New York (it is not: it takes place all over the United States and the world, in both urban and rural settings). I do argue, however, that New York has gained primacy as a site of horror in a way that it was not before the terror attacks. Even films whose original narrative is set elsewhere find a home in post-9/11 New York City. The novel *The War of the Worlds* is set primarily in London; the 1953 film is set primarily in Los Angeles; but the 2005 film is set in New Jersey, New York and the road to Boston. The 1954 novel *I Am Legend* is set in Los Angeles, the film *The Omega Man* is set in Los Angeles, the 2007 *I Am Legend* is set in New York. Even films such as *Skyline*, all but a few minutes of which are set in Los Angeles and specifically in Marina del Rey on L.A.'s Westside, cannot resist a shot of the Statue of Liberty and the skyline of New York City under attack by the same aliens (see figure 1.1). While the film-makers ostensibly do so to show that the entire nation, if not the world, is undergoing the same attack, it is interesting that no other city is represented. M. Night Shyamalan's film *The Happening* is set primarily in Philadelphia and rural Pennsylvania, but it opens with mysterious suicides in Central Park and at a construction site in New York City. When the United States is attacked, New York is attacked, even if the film's focus is on a different locale. New York also serves as a locale for every type of horror. Although 'hillbilly horror' is better suited to the South or the West, films such as *Stag Night* (2008) relocates it to the New York City subway system.

The image of New York burning, or attacked or on fire is therefore one of the first and most iconic images to emerge out of 9/11. The attacks were experienced as images long before they were understood as information. Writing in the *New York Times*, C. James confessed, 'the images were terrifying to watch, yet the coverage was strangely reassuring because it existed with such immediacy, even when detailed information was scarce'.² On the day itself, we were overwhelmed with lots of images and underwhelmed with little information, only mostly speculation. The images themselves, however, were frightening, evocative and have since been employed to reconnect to the terror of the day itself. Iconic images include

Figure 1.2 In *Vanishing on 7th Street*, as Luke emerges from his apartment to a deserted street, a plane crashes to the ground behind him.

planes crashing, crowds fleeing, buildings being destroyed, walls covered in photos and fliers of the missing and the dead, empty streets and falling bodies, evocative of 'The Falling Man'.

Planes crash in films in which the crash of the plane is not integral to the plot. *Knowing* (2009) shows a plane on approach to Boston's Logan Airport (where two of the 9/11 flights, American Airlines 11 and United 175 originated) crashing into a field next to a gridlocked highway. *Vanishing on 7th Street* shows a plane crashing into a deserted and windswept city street (see figure 1.2). *Pulse* (2006), the American remake of the Japanese film *Kairo* (2001), recreates an image from the original, a plane in flames passing low over the protagonists before crashing behind city buildings, an image made all the more stunning and relevant in the American version (see figure 1.3).

Steven Spielberg's controversial *War of the Worlds*, which will be explored in greater detail below, literalizes a metaphor for the experience of 9/11. Working class everyman Ray Ferrier (Tom Cruise) hides with his children in the basement of a upper middle

Figure 1.3 A plane in flames flies low over the heads of the protagonists before crashing into city buildings in *Pulse*, an American remake of the pre-9/11 Japanese film *Kairo*.

class suburban home for safety while journeying from New Jersey (another 9/11 flight origin point) to Boston. During the night there is a huge crash and destruction above their heads, which the film implies may be the aliens attacking in their tripods. In the morning, Ray emerges from the basement to literally find a crashed jet in the

Figures 1.4 and 1.5 9/11 literalized: the crashed plane in your living room in *War of the Worlds*.

living room. He slowly enters the destroyed space to see a jet engine on fire in the living room (see figure 1.4). Just as the constant stream of images on September 11 literally brought the image of the second plane crashing into the South Tower into American's living rooms (and offices, and bedrooms, and kitchens, etc.), Spielberg has crashed a plane into a suburban living room. As Ray emerges through the hole in the house to see the rest of the crashed fuselage outside, we see that the entire neighbourhood is unrecognizable from the images of the previous night (see figure 1.5). The only thing visible is smoke and wreckage, nothing else, nothing 'normal' can be seen. The crashed plane is in the living room, and it has changed the world forever. We might read this single image as THE visual metaphor of Spielberg's film.

Spielberg has said that for him the unforgettable visual of 9/11 was 'the image of everybody in Manhattan fleeing across the Brooklyn Bridge' (quoted in Gordon 2008: 253). Although we have seen images of crowds fleeing before, from *War of the Worlds* (1953), *Independence Day* (1996), *Gojira* (Godzilla, 1954), and numerous disaster films, the image changed in two ways on 9/11. First is the transformation in the nature of the image itself. The crowds fleeing in the above-mentioned films run past a static camera. Crowds move past a camera that is capturing the image, but is separate from the events itself. As a result of much footage from 9/11 coming from cameramen and women who were running themselves, a very different crowd-fleeing scene has risen to prominence: flashes of a fleeing crowd combined with unrecognizable images as the person holding the camera runs (see figures 1.6, 1.7 and 1.8). As one can see from the images from *Cloverfield* and *War if the Worlds*, crowds now flee not past the camera, but with it, creating a jarring, shaky series of images echoing the camera work of 9/11.

Also echoing the images of that day is the slow-moving crowd. Both *War of the Worlds* and *Cloverfield* feature this second changed image – the slow migration of large numbers of people away from city centres on foot. They are not running, but they are moving en masse. *The Happening* also shows this image, albeit writ small, as Elliot Moore (Mark Wahlberg) leads a small group from Philadelphia out to the suburbs and then rural Pennsylvania on foot. In all three of these films, the slow-moving, walking mass of humanity treads

Figure 1.6 From *Inside 9/11*, a cameraman flees along with a crowd, looking back at the smoke cloud behind them. The moving camera offers a very different fleeing crowd image than before.

Figure 1.7 From *Cloverfield*, the crowd flees as does the camera, held by Hud.

Figure 1.8 From *War of the Worlds*, the crowd flees the initial attack, the camera moving with them.

through or across familiar landmarks, and then begin to run when confronted with new threats. In *Cloverfield*, the crossing of the Brooklyn Bridge is recreated in the film, just before the creature then attacks the bridge, causing the crowd to panic and begin running.

Figures 1.9 and 1.10 From National Geographic's *Inside 9/11*, the collapse of the South Tower, the iconic cloud of dust and debris as the building sheds material as it falls.

Figure 1.11 From *Diary of the Dead*, a fireball over a neighborhood as a building burns and collapses.

Figure 1.12 From *Cloverfield*, in the distance, the monster is not particularly visible, but the building it destroys is. The debris falls in patterns suggestive of the collapse of the Twin Towers. The lights in the building go out and then the entire structure collapses straight down.

9/11 AS HORROR

Figure 1.13 The plane crash from *Vanishing on 7th Street* results in burning buildings, collapsed infrastructure and a debris cloud full of flames rushing down the street toward Luke.

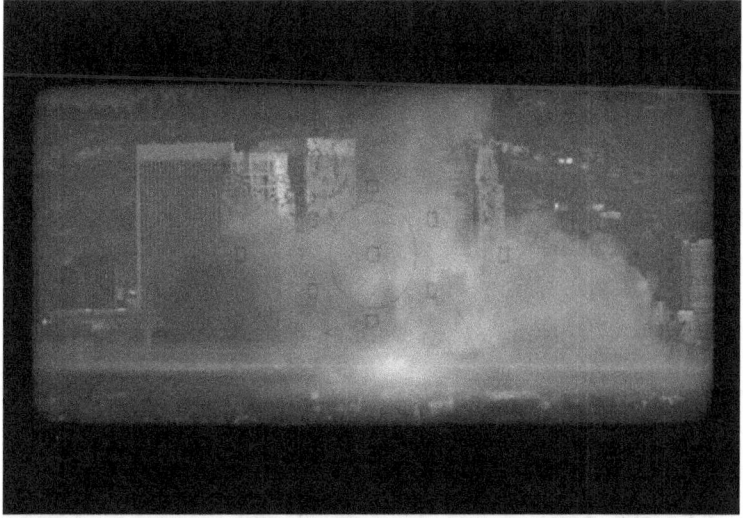

Figure 1.14 Flying objects propel things into buildings in *Skyline*, sending clouds of smoke, dust and debris everywhere and pulling the human bodies out of those clouds and up into the ships.

Other iconic images recur in film after film. Perhaps one of the most central images of 9/11 is the collapse of the Twin Towers: buildings falling leaving behind tell-tale smoke and dust (see figure 1.9 and 1.10). As the wreckage burns and falls, a huge cloud of dust and ash is created. This image is repeated in *Diary of the Dead* (2007) (see figure 1.11), *Cloverfield* (see figure 1.12), *War of the Worlds*, *Vanishing on 7th Street* (see figure 1.13), *Pulse*, and *Skyline* (see figure 1.14). Just as on 9/11, cameras showed us images of empty streets with papers blowing in them, New York as a deserted ghost town with smoke obscuring its emptiness (see figure 1.15), so, too, do horror films use this image. *Vanishing on 7th Street* features a deserted city with a debris cloud moving down an empty street (see figure 1.16). Empty streets in huge urban areas indicate horror in *I Am Legend* (2007), *Last of the Living* (2009, New Zealand), *Pulse*, and the disturbingly empty and abandoned London of *28 Days Later* (2002) and *28 Weeks Later* (2007). Dust and ash cover everything, and once thriving urban centres are deserted in these films, echoing the images of lower Manhattan on the afternoon of September 11. Sometimes the films will combine the images, as in *War of the Worlds*, in which a slow-moving mass of people walk towards a burning Boston, wreckage and debris everywhere (see figure 1.17).

Figure 1.15 An empty, deserted, smoke-filled street in Manhattan (from *Inside 9/11*).

Figure 1.16 An empty, deserted, smoke-filled street in *Vanishing on 7th Street*.

Figure 1.17 A slow-moving crowd of refugees approaches a burning and debris-filled Boston in *War of the Worlds*.

Another iconic image from 9/11 is the wall of fliers and photographs.[3] Immediately after 9/11, numerous photos, fliers and posters began appearing in the streets of New York, depicting missing individuals, friends and family members. The first few days after the attacks made travel in New York difficult, and communication also challenging, so hopeful loved ones put up fliers and photos in hopes that someone might know where a missing individual was, or if someone had been knocked unconscious, they might be tracked to a hospital. Within days, these fliers became memorials, simply hoping in the identification of bodies. The wall of photos and fliers springs up in *War of the Worlds* the day after the aliens begin attacking (see figure 1.18). Indeed, this image was one of the most controversial in the film, as it seems to exist in the film only to call to memory 9/11. *Pulse* uses a university campus kiosk as a more subtle echo, in which a student hangs a flier to let others know how to fight the evil spirits coming through the web (see figure 1.19). Mixed within the advertisements, calls for rides and other fliers are also missing person and 'have you seen' posters, subtly echoing the 9/11 missing-cum-memorial photos.

Figure 1.18 Wall of the missing and lost in *War of the Worlds*.

Figure 1.19 Amid the other student notices, missing person fliers are found in *Pulse*.

In addition to the collapse of the buildings, one of the most iconic and horrific, not to mention written about images is The Falling Man. The horror of the burning and collapsing towers was matched only by the horror of seeing individuals jump or fall from the buildings. The exact numbers are unknown, but some researchers believe more than 200 people fell or jumped to their deaths from the towers, the vast majority of whom were from the North Tower (Flynn and Dwyer 2004: A1). The *New York Times* reported, 'Those who came through the windows of the towers provided the starkest, most harrowing evidence of the desperate conditions inside' (Flynn and Dwyer 2004: A1). Dwyer and Flynn refer to the floors above the plane strikes as 'an unforgiving place', stating that not everyone was jumping, many were also inadvertently falling in the attempt to get air in a crowd of people at an open window (2005: 137). The end result, however, regardless of the reason, was falling bodies.

The bodies, as they fell, were virtually unidentifiable. The anonymity of the jumpers was preserved despite the presence of recording technology. Photos of those falling from the towers were 'typically too far away to capture faces' (Flynn and Dwyer 2004: A1). Instead, those who fell became image and sound. The documentary

9/11 contains something far more chilling than any fictional movie: as the firefighters move through the connecting mezzanine below the towers, the microphone picks up the sounds of multiple impacts, spaced out every few seconds. The firefighters realize (as does the viewer) that we are hearing the sound of bodies hitting the roof.

The most famous image of falling is Richard Drew's photograph of a man, almost perfectly straight and vertical, not flailing, directly between the two towers, although he has fallen from the North Tower. The image is known as 'The Falling Man', and it is both one of the most iconic and also obscured. The photo was run in many major papers once and then vanished from the public sphere. Two years later, in *Esquire* magazine, Tom Junod attempted to ascertain the identity of the man in the photo, as well as analyse why the photograph was so powerful. Junod points out that of all the images of 9/11: planes hitting buildings, the collapse of the towers, the smouldering wreckage in a field in Pennsylvania, etc., only the falling bodies have become taboo. The jumpers horrified onlookers more than the smoke pouring from the buildings (Junod 2003: 179), and in almost every set of images in both actual footage and recreations, the falling bodies are not included.

Although falling to one's death has been a trope in horror cinema since its origins, jumpers and falling bodies have risen to prominence in post-9/11 films. The film *1408* (2007), based on a Stephen King story and set in a hotel in New York City, features ghosts recreating their own leaps out the fourteenth floor window of the titular room. Mike Enslin (John Cusack) climbs out onto the window ledge to escape the haunted room and nearly slips and falls to his death, echoing an image seen frequently on September 11: the individual seeking to escape the hell inside inadvertently losing their grip and then falling horrifically. Falling bodies mimicking the Falling Man are seen in *Pulse* (2006), *Quarantine* (2008), *The Descent* (2005) and *The Ruins* (2008). The threat of falling is present in such films as *Cloverfield*, in which characters must climb through one leaning skyscraper in order to rescue a friend trapped near open windows several hundred feet up in another skyscraper.

M. Night Shyamalan's *The Happening* (2008) employs the imagery of Falling Man in its opening sequence. The film opens in a park in an urban setting, in which individuals begin to act strangely, distant screams are heard, and finally, a young woman reading on a bench (Alison Folland) stabs herself in the neck with a hair pin. The film then cuts to a construction site, a familiar enough image in urban areas, where a group of construction workers stand around telling each other jokes. A subtitle informs the viewer that the location is 'Three Blocks from Central Park, New York City, 8:59 AM'. This text does three things. First, it establishes the previous scene as taking place in Central Park in New York, even though the majority of the rest of the film will take place in Philadelphia and rural Pennsylvania. Second, it has the effect of calling to mind the experience of 9/11, in which, unexpectedly, at a few minutes before nine in the morning, a catastrophe struck a famous New York landmark and its environs. Shyamalan not only establishes the location and time, the specific location and time are meant to call the beginning moments of the terror attacks and the public awareness of them (those on the planes were obviously aware earlier). Third, by giving a locale that is both specific yet imprecise, and focusing on New York, he frames the following events as a form of attack, which, in fact they are, this time improbably, with plants as terrorists, driving human beings to kill themselves and each other.

Suddenly, a body hits the ground behind them. The men rush over, check the man, and call for an ambulance, when a second body falls behind them, then a third, then a stream of eight more bodies in rapid succession hit the ground. Shyamalan has now either shown bodies hitting the ground or allowed the sound of a body hitting the ground to echo, or both, when he then has a POV (point-of-view) shot of the foreman's view, looking up from the ground. We are shown the top of the building as individuals almost seem to be jumping off the building in lines. Shyamalan employs slow motion here, so the audience may see the bodies tumble off the roof, not resisting, and then tumble through space, the wind blowing clothing as they fall and pick up speed. In the North Tower on 9/11, Flynn and Dwyer report individuals 'piled four and five deep into the windows' (2004: B8). Junod writes, 'For more than an hour and a half, they streamed from the building, one after another, consecutively rather than en masse, as if each individual required the sight of another individual jumping before mustering the courage to jump himself or herself' (2003: 178). According to one witness, the people who fell or jumped 'didn't struggle', they simply dropped (quoted in Faludi 2007: 289). And that is precisely the image Shyamalan places on screen: individuals throwing themselves consecutively off the building, not struggling or resisting, but simply dropping to their deaths. In a horror film, Shyamalan does what the media stopped doing after September 12, which is to show the two taboo images of 9/11: people jumping and bodies hitting.

Figure 1.20 *The Happening*'s horror begins with bodies falling from the roof of a construction site, echoing The Falling Man.

Narratively, in *The Happening*, it makes sense to show the body hitting first (effect) and then the jumping (cause). The overall effect, however, is to reverse the Falling Man. First we see impact, then we see bodies in flight. The second to last shot of the scene is of numerous bodies jumping or falling from the roof and descending through space (figure 1.20). But we never see or hear them hit after the initial bodies strike the ground. Thus, Shyamalan gives the audience impact, then the fall. Visually, this is a reversal of the Falling Man. Other films have also reversed the Falling Man trope. In *Skyline* (2010) the aliens attack Los Angeles early in the morning. As Jarrod (Eric Balfour) and Terry (Donald Faison) watch, buildings come apart and bodies fly upward into the air in a bizarre inversion of Falling

Man. They fall upwards to their deaths, which serve the needs of the invaders, but reverses Falling Man. In *Skyline* there is neither the sight nor the sound of impact. Bodies 'fall' upwards to their deaths in a bizarre inversion of gravity. The image is one of a thousand 'Falling Mans', suspended between buildings, ground and the ships above them (figure 1.21). This reversal, of falling upwards to one's death, preserves the horror of The Falling Man without reproducing it directly.

Figure 1.21 *Skyline* reverses The Falling Man with hundreds of bodies tumbling upward to their deaths.

Most horror films, however, maintain the fear of falling to one's death in more straightforward images. In *Frozen* (2010), three friends are trapped atop a ski lift at a resort that closes down for a few days. Mechanical problems, weather, wolves and human incompetence conspire to place the characters in a very difficult situation. The film focuses on their choice: stay put and possibly freeze to death or jump and possibly get badly injured, die or be attacked by wolves. Dan (Kevin Zegers) jumps, breaking his legs and is devoured by a pack of wolves. Joe (Shawn Ashmore) climbs down and is attacked by the same wolves and killed. Parker (Emma Bell) falls while climbing and is rescued by a man in a passing car who stops;

his face is never seen. The choice of fall/jump versus die from the conditions of your environment very much echoes the experience within the Towers on 9/11.

Devil (2010) begins with a body falling off a building and landing on a truck, which subsequently rolls down the street. The police must trace the journey back to the point where broken glass litters the ground. They believe the person must have jumped and is a suicide, because the body is holding a rosary. Religious security guard Ramirez (Jacob Vargas) informs the others that a suicide always precedes an attack by the devil, who will gather to him a group of people, killing them slowly until only one is left, who will then die in front of the person he or she loves the most. The film begins with a falling body hitting the ground and then narrates an assault on a skyscraper in Philadelphia. We might also note, tangentially, that M. Night Shyamalan, who gave us the falling bodies of *The Happening*, produced and wrote the story of *Devil*.

Christine Muller reads the images of bodies falling from the towers as a recognition of 'powerlessness', and also 'hopelessness': there is nothing to be done either by the falling person or by those witnessing the fall, only to wait for the inevitable end (2009: 59). The Falling Man and his cinematic echoes tap into very deep fears from 9/11, while also promoting a sense of vulnerability and despair. Conversely, however, in films in which falling images are employed, they are employed fairly early in the film (also echoing 9/11: as noted above, most of those who fell, did so early from the North Tower, for a variety of reasons). Once the falling is over, the film begins to contain the threat and reintegrate the damaged community. *War of the Worlds* shows the family reunited. *The Happening* ends with a new nuclear family created out of the experience. Even *Skyline* ends with the hero's brain taking over an alien body and becoming the defender of his girlfriend and presumably Los Angeles.

Another trope of the post-9/11 horror film is the lack of a 'big picture'. In sci fi/horror films of the fifties and sixties (and for that matter, the seventies, eighties and nineties), the audience is shown both the everyman protagonist and the President coping with the horror. In *Independence Day*, for example, the threat is not only encountered by New York cable company manager David Levinson (Jeff Goldblum) and a fighter pilot (Will Smith), the audience is privy to the White House crisis room and the thoughts of the President (Bill Pullman) and his staff. 'The top' of the social and political pyramid is shown coping with horror. As a result, the audience is privy to the latest intelligence, all the information available and the thoughts of the top minds working to fight it, just as the president is.

The actual experience of 9/11 for most Americans lacked the information and the 'big picture' of such films. Government officials were never seen, but only reported on –fleeting words conveyed quickly as individuals moved to 'unnamed locations' in order to secure their safety. After President Bush left the classroom in Florida that morning, he boarded Air Force One and was flown to an 'undisclosed location', pausing to make a brief speech on television. Only national media figures were giving information, and mostly that was conjecture and expert hearsay: what the government was doing in response to the attacks, whether additional attacks were coming or already underway, and if there was another, different kind of event also planned for that day, were all unknowns for the people watching.

This experience is captured in films such as *Cloverfield*, where the characters only briefly catch news announcements in an electronics store after the immediate attack. Otherwise, they remain in the dark as to what is happening, where the creature is and how the counter attack is going. They occasionally encounter soldiers, who are as confused as they are. In *War of the Worlds*, no one knows what is going on. Spielberg captures this effectively during the mass refugee walking scene in which a rapid montage of strangers passing along contradictory information demonstrates that rumours are flying, but no one knows anything for certain. There is no president in *Skyline*, *Vanishing on 7th Street* or *Battle: Los Angeles*. There is no mayor or governor in *Mulberry Street* or *Quarantine*. Post-9/11, the only source of information in a horror film is the television and the rumours that other people share. The leadership is not seen or heard from. We suffer horror in a vacuum of information and nothing from the top of the social pyramid.

As a result, another trope is the initial belief that anything horrific happening is the work of 'terrorists', even when it obviously is not. In *War of the Worlds*, as the tripods are burning people all around them with heat rays, Robbie asks Ray, 'Is it terrorists?' Ray, who has seen a tripod emerge from underground but has no idea what is actually happening, responds, 'They came from somewhere else!' Robbie asks, 'You mean like Europe?'; he is incapable of grasping the magnitude of the situation. Yet the first thought being that terrorists are the ones behind any horror, achieves several effects. First, it is a natural impulse in the wake of 9/11. When anything happens in the United States in which people die by violence, the first thing the media asks is, 'is it terrorists?' Second, by establishing that the threat is not terrorists, it takes terrorists down a level of scary: there are worse things out there than terrorists. The implication being, of course, we can deal with terrorists, and we have a chance of dealing with this new threat. By replacing terrorists as the scariest thing we can think of, the threat of terrorism is reduced somewhat in the audience's minds. Lastly, it also equates the horror of the film with terrorism. Though terrorists are less frightening, they are no less monsters for it. Terrorists and monstrous aliens and evil shadow creatures are conflated and equated into an equivalent threat.

Something similar occurs in *The Happening*. The mysterious rash of suicides is initially blamed on terrorists employing some sort of nerve agent. When the patrons of a diner watch an uploaded video of man's arm ripped off by a lion when he walked into its cage at a zoo, a woman responds, 'Mother of God! What kind of terrorists are these?' Even after a news report announces that the phenomenon has spread to small, rural towns from the big cities, and that 'They're not sure it's terrorists now', many viewers in the film continue to believe they are under a terrorist attack. Terror is equated to and is presented as horror. Terrorists horrify and horrific monsters terrify.

Although to my knowledge we have yet to see a mainstream horror film featuring Islamic or Muslim 'monsters', the monsters themselves, being equal, as noted above, to terrorists, serve as a synecdoche for that which frightens us. The villains in horror cinema are 'primitive' and evil, especially if human, suggesting the cave-dwelling Taliban that oversaw the planning of the 9/11 attacks. *Mulberry Street*'s monsters are humans that have been bitten by rats and transformed into plague-carrying rat zombies. Their ears sharpen, their eyes grow more rat-like, they grow rat teeth and their entire appearance becomes more rat-like. They are human vermin, out to destroy New York City. They might have looked like 'us' once, but now they are an evil pestilence, to be fought against by citizen and military alike.

Another popular primitive, evil substitute for terrorists comprises American rednecks and hillbillies. We have had rural 'monsters' before: *Deliverance* (1972), *Southern Comfort* (1981) and the original *Texas Chainsaw Massacre* (1974). But, as Linnie Blake astutely perceives 'the backwoods South ... becomes a symbolic analogue for the faceless and savage threat of Islamic anti-Americanism' in the post-9/11 rural horror films (2008: 143). These new films are what Finn Ballard calls 'Post-millennium road horror': a group of young protagonists journey 'into an unknown and hostile location' and meet a killer or group or family of killers (2008). The killers are frequently inbred, rural, almost cave-dwelling primitive cannibals, setting up a conflict between poor rural whites and the multi-cultural, multi-ethnic, highly educated urban dwellers who have 'invaded' their territory. Though Ballard considers these 'post Millennium' horror, I would argue they are predominantly post-Iraq War horror. The educated elites from the developed cities 'invade' the hostile territory of primitive savages with their own cultures, values and faith and it results in a 'conflict of civilizations' in which the savage rednecks abuse and kill the urbanites until the urbanites are forced to react with overwhelming violence in return.

The redneck monsters can stand for many things: the 'Red Staters' feared by the filmmakers; the desert-dwelling, 'primitive', rural middle easterners; and the irrational and savage terrorist, as viewed and constructed by the popular media. In the *The Hills Have Eyes* remake (2006), for example, the hero literally uses an American flag to kill one of the mutants attacking him and his family. The symbolism is rather heavy-handed and blatant. *The Hills Have Eyes II* (2007) repeats and enhances the idea by making the victims of the desert-dwelling monster cannibals a platoon of soldiers training for desert warfare in the Middle East. To save their lives, they must fight back and kill every last primitive desert-dweller.

Homogenous groups of primitive killers allow the American audience to relax and not think. 'Anti-Americanism' means that these backwards, savage degenerates simply hate Americans with no need for Americans to examine themselves or their own behaviour to see if there is cause for the 'bad guys' to believe what they believe.

'Evil' becomes a useful title to hang upon these individuals, because then it explains away why they are attacking and justifies anything done to them in response. As Linnie Blake concludes:

> In a post-9/11 climate of paranoia, economic self-interest and cultural essentialism, hillbilly horror can thus be seen to explore the traumatic cultural aftermath of terrorist atrocity illustrating how the bombing of the World Trade Center has been re-narrativised, re-visioned and re-remembered in the service of nationally specific military industrial ends.
>
> (2008: 12–13)

In other words, primitive human monsters expropriate the horror of 9/11 for the purposes of patriotism, advancing a national narrative that keeps us as 'the good guys' and allows for extreme violence in response to those who would hurt us. *Stag Night* literalizes this by placing primitive rural cannibals in the New York City subway system and having the New Yorkers taking the last train home from a bachelor party, fight back and kill them. Joe (Karl Geary), recognizing he will die, commits suicide by grabbing the third rail rather than letting the cannibals stab him to death. As they reach for his body, they too are electrocuted. Even in films seemingly completely unrelated to 9/11, like the remake of *The Hills Have Eyes*, the elements, images and tropes of the terror attacks (and the wars carried out in response afterwards) recreate 9/11 as a horror film, just one that justifies our response to 9/11.

When the monsters are not primitive rural killers they are just as often as not utterly alien. There is a direct link between 9/11, the wars that followed and the predominance of 'war' movies against extraterrestrials. *Alien* may have been a 'haunted house in space' film (which is how it was pitched), but alien films after September 11 are first and foremost war movies. *Battle: Los Angeles*, *Skyline*, *War of the Worlds* and *Monsters* all present humanity at war with alien invaders, the last as a *Behind Enemy Lines* with monstrous killer squids in Mexico. We are not just being pursued in the woods outside Camp Crystal Lake or down Elm Street in these films. This assault is a global one and one that is a war for our very survival. As clumsy as *War of the Worlds* may be in terms of its use of 9/11 iconography, it set the stage for several films that imagine terrorists as aliens. W. J. T. Marshall posits that 9/11 'was an attack by *aliens*, by 'foreign bodies' that had taken advantage of American hospitality to infiltrate our borders' (emphasis in original) (2011: 46). The direct result is the trope of the monstrous alien Other that seeks to not only kill us but to leave our nation and country in ruin. While *Independence Day* followed this model in 1996, it did so in a manner that included broad comedy and feel-good cuteness. The current group of films are bleak and unremittingly realistic in their depiction of combat as not heroic, but a simple matter of survival.

Part 2

War of the Worlds as 9/11

Saving Private Ryan (1998) uses handheld camera and POV shots running through a landscape to emphasize the graphic realism and the horrors of experiencing the D-Day landing. This technique functions in much the same way it does in a horror film, as we see, sometimes fleetingly, bodies blown apart, limbs shot off, individuals killed in mid-sentence, in short, true body horror. The opening sequence is a cinematic confirmation that war is indeed hell. Steven Spielberg emulates these shots and this experience in *War of the Worlds*, his next war film.

Spielberg's *War of the Worlds* is a film that aggressively recreates the experiences of 9/11 as a horror film. The question that critics and scholars have continually asked is, why? To what purpose does Spielberg blatantly employ (exploit?) the images of 9/11 in order to tell the story and evoke emotion in the audience. *War of the Worlds* has been perceived as a science fiction narrative in America, but it may help to remember that the term 'science fiction' had not even been coined when H. G. Wells published the novel in 1898 (Edwards, 2005: 35). Les Edwards believes 'the SF trappings of the story ... the glittering machines and ultratechnology' obscure the 'dark heart of the tale' (2005: 36). It is, after all, a novel in which London is utterly destroyed by invading monsters. Often forgotten in the novel is the fact that Wells's Martians literally consume humans, eating their bodies and drinking their blood. They are space vampires, of a sort. They consume us, destroy our lands and offer nothing in return. For Wells, the novel was also a political critique of colonialism, imagining what would happen if a technologically advanced race did to England what England was doing to the peoples of Africa, Asia and the Caribbean.

War of the Worlds as socio-political metaphor has been demonstrated by its protean transformations into other media. Orson Welles's 1938 Hallowe'en adaptation, which provoked a genuine panic, reflects the concerns of a nation seeing Europe on the brink of war and concerned for its own future. The 1953 George Pal film, directed by Byron Haskin, and produced as the Korean War was entering its third year, is an extended Cold War metaphor, with Martians as godless communists, attempting to invade the United States to use it for their own nefarious purposes. Small town American family values, Christianity and the rock-jawed bravery of American men (and one woman) stop the invasion. Spielberg's 2005 film, therefore, enters a long line of adaptations which reinterprets the Martians in terms of the threat of the day, in this case, terrorists.

Spielberg's film also changes the nature of the alien threat. Although clearly different from us, they are already here. The weapons are already here, buried under our cities. They ride the lighting down into them. Just like 9/11, those who would attack us are already present within society. Not a purely external attack, instead employing what was already here, what Thompson calls 'anxiety of proximity' (2007: 148). Unlike, say, *Invasion of the Body Snatchers*, the aliens in *War* will never pass for one of us. The fear is not that anyone could be one, but that they are among us, are not like us, and we cannot do anything about it.

Spielberg's film has proven controversial because of its obvious use of 9/11 imagery and themes, splitting critics into two camps. One group sees the film as attempting to contain the trauma of 9/11 by appropriating its imagery in order to provide an ending in which the family survives and the enemy eventually defeated. The other sees *War of the Worlds* as exploiting the pain of 9/11, employing its imagery for no reason other than its power to shock. Stephanie Zacharek was appalled by the film, writing in *Salon* that it was 'all visuals and no vision', and that it is a 'cheap', 'shallow' and 'sadistic [and] mean-spirited' film that 'mines real-life tragedy' as fodder for a blockbuster (2008). Timothy Noah, in a *Slate* review entitled '9/11 Was No Summer Movie' judged *War of the World* 'offensive' for its 'explicit and quite obviously deliberate' visual references to 9/11: 'The annihilation of people and buildings is signaled by white ash falling from the sky; photo snapshots of missing loved ones are posted on walls; at one point, the space aliens even crash a passenger jetliner' (2005). Noah objects to a film that he perceives as all reference, no commentary. According to Noah, *War of the Worlds* teaches us nothing about 9/11, 'has nothing to say about 9/11', and 'has no meaning. It's merely an elbow in the side, reminding the audience of that day's awful events'. Noah's theory is that Spielberg's previous 'historical' films (*Schindler's List*, *Amistad*, *Saving Private Ryan*) rely upon a 'reservoir of collective memories' to move the audience emotionally.

Noah's argument begs the question, is there a 'collective memory' of the Amistad trial? Perhaps Noah is thinking of a larger frame of Civil Rights and the history of mistreatment of African-Americans, but until the film, few Americans had heard of the Amistad trial, outside of history classrooms. Most of the audiences for *Schindler's List* and *Saving Private Ryan* had not yet been born when the events they portrayed occurred. *War of the Worlds* re-presents 9/11 as a science fiction/horror film in order to domesticate and control it. Let us consider how those other three films ended: despite the horrors of the holocaust, Schindler saved over a thousand Jews. Despite the horror of D-Day and the sacrificial death of Captain Miller (Tom Hanks), Private Ryan (Matt Damon) is saved. The Supreme Court eventually freed the Amistad slaves and returned them to Africa. In all of these films, the ending is a redemption of sorts. That ending is what Spielberg's *War of the World* provides 9/11 – the possibility of survival and redemption in the face of mass destruction. Heroic films directly about 9/11 ring false or flat and fail to capture the experience of the day. *War of the Worlds*, by duplicating images and experiences of that day, albeit through the flimsiest of masks, allows Spielberg to change history's ending.

The film, we must also remember, was not made immediately after 9/11. Instead, additional events and situations are further reflected in the film. Kristin Moana Thompson reminds us that when Steven Spielberg's *The War of the Worlds* was released in 2005, the United States had already been in Iraq for two years with over 1,800 dead American soldiers and countless Iraqi civilians (2007: 145). *War of the Worlds* renders 9/11 as a national event. New York is attacked in the opening, but by the end of the film, the military is clearly fighting in New York, Connecticut, Massachusetts. Ray and Rachel approach Boston, clouds hanging over that city and fires burning, echoing Manhattan (figure 1.17). In *War of the Worlds*, all American cities are Manhattan and Manhattan stands for all American cities.

As noted above, the central image of Spielberg's film is Ray emerging from the basement to find a crashed jet in the living room. Spielberg literalizes the metaphorical situation of September 11. While those in New York and at the Pentagon experienced 9/11 directly, the rest of America experienced it though the television. The planes crashed into the living rooms of the United States. Every catastrophe, every tragedy since, has also entered the home through the television and the internet. Spielberg's film recreates 9/11 as a horror film for the purposes of moving past the crashed jet in the living room and returning to some semblance of normal family life.

As noted above, images from 9/11 dominate the film, as does a narrative resembling the experience of that day: an unexpected attack on American soil comes out of nowhere, killing inordinate number of civilians who are 'totally unprepared and unprotected', and destroying a cityscape (Gordon 2008: 261). The initial attack leaves empty clothing fluttering in the wind, buildings burning and human beings reduced to a powdery gray ash which coats Ray when he arrives at home, calling to mind what Tom Junod calls 'the throng of ashen humanity' in New York on 9/11 (2003: 178).

All of these images serve to reaffirm the film as a contained and controllable echo of 9/11. Ray's inadvertent heroism brings down a tripod. He manages to deliver his daughter safely to her mother and even his lost son safely finds his way to Boston. Spielberg gives us images of terror in order to transcend them. The only problem is that transcendence rings false. Perhaps Andrew Gordon captures the problem of the film: 'possessed by the images of 9/11, compelled to replay but not yet able to master them' (2008: 264). Spielberg offers 9/11 as summer blockbuster, attempting to interpret it through the framework of *Jaws*, *Poltergeist* or *Jurassic Park*: the threats may be terrifying, but a knowing father figure will guide the children safely home, stop the threat and preserve the community. Ray, a marginal father at best, cannot serve in the same capacity as Chief Brody, Steve Freeling or Dr. Alan Grant. We survive, but we are permanently scarred and not yet ready to deal with the trauma.

Cloverfield as 9/11

Like *War of the Worlds*, *Cloverfield* represents 9/11 as mainstream blockbuster, although it was an independent film, it has received the same amount of attention as Spielberg's film and has also been recognized by numerous critics as a film that reinvents 9/11 as a monster movie. As the above survey of images and elements clearly indicates, *Cloverfield* employs numerous visual and experiential references to 9/11.

Cloverfield begins with a series of images marking the video as government property, found footage, and containing images from 'case designate "Cloverfield"'. The text on the screen then states

Figure 1.22 The decapitated head of the Statue of Liberty, showing scars in *Cloverfield*.

that, 'Camera retrieved at incident site 'US-447' / Area formerly known as "Central Park"'. Although it only appears on the screen for a handful of seconds, this text immediately establishes Cloverfield as referencing the terror attacks of September 11. First, the reference to 'Central Park' establishes the film as taking place in New York City. The fact that 'Central Park' is now identified as 'US-447' resonates with the transformation of 'World Trade Center' into 'Ground Zero', and the repeated numbers 447 hint at 911. The renaming of landmarks in face of an attack in this film and the increased military presence in New York all suggest the experiences of 9/11.

The characters' farewell party for Rob is interrupted by an explosion in New York. They run to the roof and see another explosion happen. They run to the street just in time to see the head of the Statue of Liberty come flying through the air and crash into the street (see figure 1.22). Conservative commentator Jonah Goldberg sees the decapitated head of the Statue of Liberty as symbolizing 'the end of America, or at least the end of America as we know it' (quoted in Kenny, E3). The characters begin to journey across New York, first to escape and then to find a missing friend. Along the way, they begin to die one by one. Jason is swept off a bridge by the monster's attack. Marlena is bitten in the subway by one of the smaller creatures that fall off the large monster. As the group enters a sort 'green zone' military operating base in the city, she announces that she does not feel well and the camera pans to reveal her bleeding out of her eyes. 'Bite!' screams a woman, 'We've got a bite!'. Marlena is seized by soldiers, hustled into a lit quarantine tent, where her silhouette expands and explodes, spattering blood on the plastic (see figures 1.23a–c). She is a monstrous suicide bomber, exploding open to generate more terror among the doctors and soldiers.

Rob, Hud and Lily then must climb the Time Warner Center, a leaning skyscraper, to rescue Beth, who is injured, impaled on a piece of rebar and unable to move. As on 9/11, it is the building itself that harms her as much as the monstrous being attacking New York. She is unable to escape from one of the top floors of her skyscraper until rescued by her friends. Returning to the ground floor, the four make their way to Grand Central Station. Lily climbs aboard a helicopter and is seemingly taken to safety. The other three also climb aboard a helicopter and fly away over the monster, which

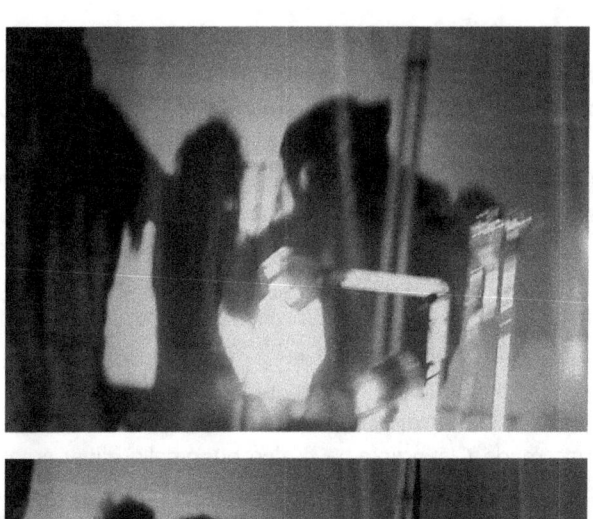
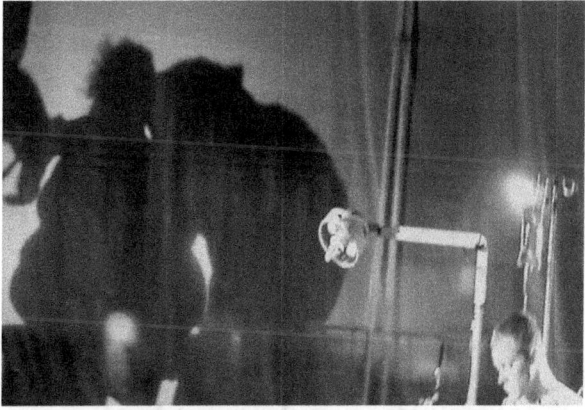

Figure 1.23 Marlena as monster suicide bomber. Inside the military post, she explodes.

knocks them out of the sky. The helicopter crashes in Central Park. Hud is then bitten by the monster and dies. The film ends with Rob and Beth proclaiming their love for one another while the bombs the military drops on the monster buries them under rubble in the park.

The film offers obvious parallels with 9/11. Emblematic and iconic locations in New York are attacked and destroyed. The characters must rescue a friend trapped on the top floor of a skyscraper. As noted above, the film replicates images and experiences of the attack on New York. Glenn Kenny concedes that Cloverfield is a 'commentary' on September 11 (E3). Like *War of the Worlds*, it attempts to understand and contain 9/11 through the use of its imagery in a monster movie. Yet, like *War of the Worlds*, the people who made *Cloverfield* have also been called 'just crass fear-mongerers and tragedy-exploiters' (quoted in Kenny, E3). Stephanie Zacharek, who despised *War of the Worlds*, also found nothing of worth in *Cloverfield*, asking in the title of her review, 'Do we really need the horror of 9/11 to be repackaged and presented to us as an amusement-park ride?' (2008). The short answer is that we do not need it, but when it does happen, how does it help us to understand 9/11?

The six main characters are all twenty-somethings, a few years out of college, living in New York. If *War of the Worlds* concerns families, especially parents and children, *Cloverfield* is 9/11 for the generations X and Y. The post-9/11 media tended to focus on families: lost parents, husbands and wives. Widows and widowers were left behind and had a voice with which to share their grief. The single urbanite was left out of the mourning of 9/11. These characters are disconnected from their families, but they have formed a new family with each other. In her testimonial on Rob's video Lily tells Rob she thinks of him as a brother. As he provides a testimonial on the camera, aware that he is going to die soon, Rob gives the names of his brother Jason, his best friend Hud and Marlena Diamond (the first time her whole name is mentioned). These people, including the woman he barely knew at the beginning of the film, are important to him and he wants others to know that they lived and died in New York during this crisis. *Cloverfield* contains 9/11 for those whose families do not live in or near the city. It reflects the experience of those who come to the city from far away to make their fortune and reinvent themselves. While others might privilege biological family, these people make each other their family, and their loss is as sincerely felt as those who lost family.

Mulberry Street as 9/11

Not as well known or celebrated as the previous two films, the next two films are smaller recapitulations of 9/11 as horror. *Mulberry Street* (2007) was one of the films selected for the second After Dark Horrorfest. It does not feature huge special effects. No buildings are destroyed in it, no crowds flee. It is a small film. Nevertheless, it is also an attempt to recreate 9/11 as a horror film, just as the previous two films did. Mulberry Street offers a view of how 9/11 affected the working class tenement dwellers who live near the World Trade Center.

Mulberry Street itself runs through the centre of Little Italy, bisecting Canal Street and ending in Chinatown. It is about a half-mile east of the World Trade Center. The film centres on an apartment building in which the lower working class residents have been given eviction notices as the building is due to be razed to allow for a redevelopment project. The main character is a former boxer named Clutch (Nick Damici) who is awaiting his daughter Casey (Kim Blair), who is returning from the military hospital at Bushkill, where she was recuperating from wounds received either in Iraq or Afghanistan. The tenement dwellers hear about rat attacks on the subways on the radio and television. Charlie (Larry Fleischman) scoffs, 'I bet it's Bin Laden, that rat bastard,' calling to mind the mastermind of 9/11. What they learn about through the media becomes the reality of their home as those bitten by infected rats devolve into zombie-like rat creatures (or rat-like zombie creatures). The individual characters all become trapped in various locations by the monsters. One by one, the residents of the building are attacked and killed.

Clutch leaves the building to rescue Kay (Bo Corre), a single mother who works in a nearby bar and who finds him attractive. He manages to lead her safely from the bar, but she is attacked and dragged from the truck they steal in order to get home. An infected and violent Kay arrives at the building and Clutch kills her in front of her son. Bitten by her, however, Clutch throws himself and the infected Coco (Ron Brice) off the roof, choosing to die by falling rather than become a rat monster.

Whereas *Cloverfield* shows iconic structures attacked and destroyed, *Mulberry Street* shows a lower working class building in which the residents are already trying to survive and get along and are forced to confront twin crises. First, they learn they are to be evicted. Second, the rat attack brings about catastrophe and death. All of Manhattan becomes the top floors of the World Trade Center in *Mulberry Street*. Residents watch the news to learn the truth of their situation, where the anchor solemnly intones, 'There are still an unknown number of survivors trapped on that island'. They may try to escape, but most die horrible deaths at the hands of the monsters. The protagonist becomes the Falling Man writ small, jumping off a ten-storey apartment building.

Although we witness the city falling apart and hear about the subway attacks and the expanding crisis on Manhattan from the media in the film, the New Yorkers who are not living the elite life, who are not part of the bridge and tunnel crowd, who live their lives in their neighbourhood where everyone knows one another, are the focus of this film. They pull together. They attempt to help one another. They, too, die in the attacks. They, too, see their building destroyed. *Mulberry Street* refocuses 9/11 from the epic scale of *War of the Worlds* to how it influenced 'the neighborhood' and does so through the metaphor of rat attacks and rat zombies. It is not coincidental that Bin Laden is referred to as a 'rat bastard'. In contrast, *Mulberry Street* offers Clutch as a self-sacrificing New Yorker, a heroic counterpoint to the survivors of *War of the Worlds* or the victims in *Cloverfield*. The smaller scale of the film allows for such heroism, which, as previously noted, rings hollow and false in larger epics.

2

Documenting the Horror

Two aspects of our highly mediated lives, not to mention near universal access to the tools of film, video and still photograph production, have resulted in an approach to horror that focuses on documenting horrific experiences as they happen. Many critics and scholars have observed that 9/11 was the most photographed and filmed event in history, recorded as still and moving images while it was happening. Furthermore, as noted in the introduction, Tom Engelhardt correctly perceives that only a relative handful of people experienced the terror attacks of September 11 directly; for most of the nation, it was a mediated 'on screen spectacle' (2006: 15). In other words, 9/11 was experienced as a real-time documentary about 9/11, a mediated experience of the events.

In one of the first episodes of *National Geographic: Ultimate Explorer*, entitled 'Witness 9/11', the program offered profiles of individuals living in New York City whose immediate response to the terror attacks was to grab a video camera and record the event. Many individuals initially ran to rooftops (as in *Cloverfield*, see figure 2.1). When buildings were evacuated, these amateur film-makers shot in the streets (also as shown in *Cloverfield*). Their footage was later used by local and national media, documentaries and by the 9/11 commission in order to construct an accurate timeline of events. This highly mediated experience of the terror attacks, through amateur

Figure 2.1 From National Geographic's 'Witness 9/11', amateur photographers and videographers record the burning and collapsing World Trade Center from the roof of their apartment building.

footage as well as security tapes, news footage and accidental recording of the events forms the first stream of influence on horrific pseudo-documentaries.

The second stream comes from terrorists themselves. Michael Ignatieff, in an essay entitled 'The Terrorist as Auteur', already drawing attention to the similarity between twenty-first century terrorism and film-making, has also observed that the terrorists are now 'using a video camera as a weapon' (2004: 50). With the technology to make videos and immediately upload them to the internet readily available anywhere in the world, we have seen a 'new kind of home video', in which hooded men with weapons and victims announce their existence and plans. The victims sit at the feet of their captors; 'They plead, they weep, they bow their heads, and then, more often than not, they die' (2004: 50). Ignatieff concludes, 'Terrorists have been quick to understand that the camera has the power to frame a single atrocity and turn it into an image that sends shivers down the spine of an entire planet' (2004: 50). In the previous century, westerners were kidnapped and murdered by terrorists, but the deaths were only reported, never witnessed by anyone other than the killers and their associates. Now the grotesque and violent murder of a single individual, such as Nicholas Berg or Daniel Pearl is then witnessed on video via the internet by anyone who wants to see it.

These two streams, the amateur video document of 9/11 and the terrorist-made, internet-dispersed video of real torture and death, combine into a major trope of post-9/11 horror: the pseudo-documentary / 'found footage' horror film. This subgenre is not a new one; it was not invented in the wake of 9/11, but it has risen to prominence since. The pseudo-documentary is an international phenomenon. There have been more than a few 'fictional documentaries' in the history of cinema, most notably *The War Game* (1965), which won the Academy Award for best documentary despite being a fictional film presenting life in Great Britain after a limited nuclear exchange with the Soviet Union, and thus hardly a documentary in the true sense of the word. The first horror pseudo-documentary was *Cannibal Holocaust* (Italy 1980), which claimed to be found footage. Part of the then-current cannibal film trend in Italian cinema, *Cannibal Holocaust* depicts an American anthropology professor discovering the footage of a documentary film crew that terrorized the indigenous peoples of the area in order to film them. It is then revealed that the indigenous people killed the film crew and ate parts of them. The Japanese film *Ginipiggu: Akuma no Jikken* (Guinea Pig: Devil's Experiment, 1988) is a shot-on-video pseudo-documentary, opening with a disclaimer identifying it as 'found footage' in which three men torture a woman, followed by sequels in the series, all of which imitate so-called 'snuff films'.

The most famous 'found footage' horror film is *The Blair Witch Project* (1999), although other pseudo-documentaries and found footage/first person preceded it, including *The Last Broadcast* (1998), which despite its nonsensical ending is actually a better, more interesting and disturbing film. *The Blair Witch Project* purports to be found footage from three students who were making a film about the Blair Witch, a colonial period legend in which a local old woman ostensibly killed several children and adults. The characters wander in the woods, hear strange noises at night, and eventually one of them vanishes and then the other two discover an old house. The film ends with the remaining two screaming, attacked by something in the basement of the house.

Although both incredibly popular and incredibly successful (in terms of both critical plaudits and box office receipts), *The Blair Witch Project* did not launch a series of pseudo-documentary horrors and the sequel was a straightforward narrative film that failed critically and at the box office. It was only after September 11 that an explosion of 'found footage', pseudo-documentary and 'mockumentaries' were created. In fairness, this phenomenon is not limited to horror. There have been mockumentaries in numerous genres, especially comedy, Christopher Guest and Sasha Baron Cohen perhaps being the best-known film-makers who specialize in comic pseudo-documentaries. But post-9/11, the visual influence of documentary-style film-making became prominent in horror in a way never before seen.

In the United States alone, *Behind the Mask* (2006), *Diary of the Dead* (2007), *Paranormal Activity* (2007), the American remake of *[REC]* entitled *Quarantine* (2008), *Cloverfield* (2008), *Paranormal Activity 2* (2010), *The Last Exorcism* (2010), *Paranormal Activity 3* (2011) and *Apollo 18* (2011), are all ether 'documentaries' or found footage, while films such as *Open Water*, which, although not purporting to be documentaries are filmed in a documentary style with handheld cameras. The phenomenon is an international one as well, with *[REC]* (2007, Spain), *Trollhunter* (2010, Norway), and numerous Japanese pseudo-documentaries also using the techniques of documentary to create horror. The overall effect of this subgenre, as David Roche indicates, 'aims at making "primary" and "secondary" identification overlap by including the camera and the camera operator within diagetic reality, but these films rely mainly on the sensations provoked by strategies relying on the off camera' (2011: 85). In other words, pseudo-documentaries use many of the same techniques to generate fear in an audience that straightforward horror cinema does. That fear is enhanced, however, but the indication that what one is watching is somehow 'real'. *Resident Evil* is just a movie. *The Ruins*, *Hatchet*, *30 Days of Night* and *The Exorcism of Emily Rose* are just movies. By framing itself as being filmed incidentally as part of the recording of other events, *Cloverfield*, as well as *[REC]*, *Quarantine*, *Diary of the Dead* and *Paranormal Activity* claim a greater connection to the real world. This effect is further enhanced by the casting of unknown actors. Megan Fox, famous for her work in *Transformers* remains a celebrity and in some sense herself when possessed in *Jennifer's Body*. Likewise, Anthony Hopkins remains Anthony Hopkins when possessed by the devil in *The Rite*. The unknown faces of the *Paranormal Activity* films, *Diary of the Dead* and *Cloverfield* make the performers seem less like actors and more like 'real people' caught in actual situations.

There are several key differences between the pre-9/11 and post-9/11 pseudo-documentaries. Those that came before usually feature film-makers discovering the horror that they were seeking. In *Cannibal Holocaust* the found footage is purportedly from a documentary film crew that went in search of cannibals, and was filmed being killed and consumed by cannibals. In *The Last Broadcast*, cable access paranormal investigative show hosts go in search of the Jersey Devil and are killed by another film-maker who then makes a documentary investigating their deaths. In *The Blair Witch Project*, student film-makers vanish while lost in the woods where the Blair Witch is supposed to have killed her victims.

Post-9/11 pseudo-documentaries are presented as inadvertent. One of the first structured, narrated documentaries about the day was Hanlon's *9/11* (2002). *9/11* was an accidental documentary, in the sense that the film-makers had originally set out to make a film about the transition of a probationary firefighter in New York City from recruit to professional. Film-makers James Hanlon and Jules and Gedeon Naudet followed Tony Benetatos from the academy to his initial assignment with Engine Company 7 in Manhattan. They happened to be down the street from the Twin Towers the morning of September 11 and caught one of only two video images of the first plane striking the North tower. As a result, the Naudet brothers' cameras were able to follow the fire fighters into the lobby of Tower 1 and capture the events of 9/11 as they happened to this single company of New York fire fighters. The documentary makers thus also became part of the narrative, as they find themselves running from collapsing buildings, uncertain if their friends and colleagues are still alive and unsure of what is happening.

This inadvertent horror documentary model is repeated in such films as *Diary of the Dead*, *Cloverfield*, *[REC]* and *The Last Exorcism*. In *Diary*, student film-makers from the University of Pittsburgh are working on a student's thesis film, a straightforward horror movie about a mummy that comes to life, when the dead begin reanimating. They then record their journey across Pennsylvania to reach the home of a friend. *Cloverfield* begins as the video record of a going away party that inadvertently captures the attack on New York City by a giant monster and the smaller creatures which fall off of it. In *[REC]* and its American remake *Quarantine*, a film crew documents an evening at an urban fire station, capturing horrific events when they follow the fire crew on a call, almost exactly like Hanlon's *9/11*. *The Last Exorcism* features an inversion of sorts. A film crew follows an evangelical preacher-cum-exorcist who invites them to film how he fakes exorcisms. The film then begins to give every indication of being real. *Paranormal Activity* features individuals who capture on film the supernatural events that take place in their home. They are not film-makers; they simply purchase a camera to record the increasingly threatening events, many of which seem to happen while they sleep.

Only *Behind the Mask* follows a pre-9/11 formula, and it is a pseudo-documentary/narrative film hybrid. In that film, a group of graduate student film-makers follow a real-life slasher on his killing sprees, but makes no attempt to maintain its documentary premise. The film keeps rolling when the documentary camera is put away. Tongue-in-cheek, the film is a true pastiche, but does not stay true to the documentary format. The scene in the library, for example, is filmed using standard narrative slasher film techniques. What is interesting in the film is the conflict between the motives and goals of Taylor the film-maker (Angela Goethals) and Leslie the serial killer (Nathan Baesel). The film indicts Taylor for being as craven and uncaring about the victims as Leslie, and for exploiting the pain and suffering he causes for her own benefit. The film ceases to be a pseudo-documentary fairly quickly. It features credits over its initial footage and when the documentary crew decides to warn the killer's victims, the handheld camera is gone and the film maintains a standard approach to narrative horror through the rest of its story. It is a narrative film about a documentary film, it is not a pseudo-documentary. Although, like *Scream*, it is a self-reflexive, self-aware slasher film, the documentary aspect begins to point towards the pseudo-documentaries that followed. Otherwise, every film discussed in this chapter is a pseudo-documentary that presents inadvertently recorded horrific events. In many ways *9/11* became the model for a new subgenre of horror film: the pseudo-documentary as horror film. Film-makers who set out to film something else inadvertently begin documenting the horrific unfolding events of an unusual phenomenon.

The pseudo-documentary simulates the experience of watching 9/11 footage, which is itself frequently an amalgam of professional and amateur shots, employs documentary techniques and direct visual references to 9/11 (as well as subsequent crises) to lend a verisimilitude to horror not found in straightforward fiction narratives. The use of hand-held digital cameras, commentary from cameramen or women, acknowledgement of the camera and a choppy editing style all signal that the footage is somehow 'real'. Pseudo-documentaries frequently employ text on screen as well. *Cloverfield*, as outlined below, begins with text on the screen. In *Paranormal Activity*, each night is indicated by a screen card that gives the date and what number night it is since they began filming. The sequel, *Paranormal Activity 2* also provides referential information through on-screen text. When Micah visits Katie's sister's family, the screen includes a text that says, 'August 9, 2006 – Sixty days before the death of Micah Sloat'. The use of such text makes the film seem more documentary and adds a veneer of factual information.

These films feature an awareness of the person behind the camera who is in danger as well. We are not concerned for the cinematographer or cameraperson on the *Friday the 13th* films or *Halloween*. The cameraman for *The Exorcist* never comes to mind while watching that film, and we are certainly not concerned that he or she might be in real danger. But Hud (T. J. Miller) in *Cloverfield*, Jason (Josh Close) in *Diary of the Dead* and Daniel (Adam Grimes) in *The Last Exorcism* are characters unto themselves who all die in horrible ways at the end of their respective films.

These films frequently feature an obligatory turn-the-camera-on-the-obsessive-cameraperson moment. Hud, Jason, Daniel, along with Angela (Manuela Velasco/Jennifer Carpenter, from *[REC]/Quarantine*), and Micah (Micah Sloat from *Paranormal Activity*) all insist the cameras keep rolling, even when asked to turn them off, even when their lives are threatened. At some point, someone else turns the camera on them. While the best known example of this is, of course, Heather's (Heather Donohue) iconic confession to the camera in *The Blair Witch Project*, in which only part of her face is visible in an extreme close-up as she apologizes for causing the

Figure 2.2 and 2.3 From *Diary of the Dead*: Jason films Debra who films Jason; an echo chamber of self-documenting and recording horror.

deaths of her friends, each pseudo-documentary features a similar film-maker as subject and object moment. In *Diary of the Dead*, Jason's girlfriend Debra (Michelle Morgan) turns the camera on him while he is filming her (see figures 2.2 and 2.3). They each have a camera pointed at them, hiding their faces, obscuring their identities. 'Tell us your name,' she asks him, echoing the question he has asked each of the other characters on camera. 'Gimme a break,' he stutters. 'Jay. Jason. Jason Creed,' as if unable to remember his own name. He does not exist when the camera is not on. He tries to remain the objective film-maker as the world falls apart around him and he therefore begins to lose his own identity.

The overall effect, however, is to remind the audience of the individual behind the camera who is experiencing the horror directly alongside all the other characters. The interaction with the camera and cameraman (or woman) by the other characters enhances sympathy, empathy and hence, the horror of the situation. Unlike in *Funny Games* (1997 and 2007), in which the fourth wall is repeatedly broken in a Brechtian attempt to break the illusion of narrative film and alienate the audience into thinking about what they are watching and why, the fourth wall is broken in pseudo-documentaries for the exact opposite reason: to reinforce the illusion that what one is watching is real. The self-reflexivity of *Funny Games* undercuts the illusion of narrative and reminds the audience that what they are watching is an artificial construct. The false self-reflexivity of *Cloverfield* or *[REC]* is designed to enhance verisimilitude and convince the viewer what he or she is watching is genuine.

The first type of post-9/11 pseudo-documentary purports to be 'found footage'. It is more or less 'unedited', presented as it was found in camera, with awkward, jerky editing that calls attention to the missing stuff. We never see inside the buildings on 9/11. No images came from the ninety-second floor, for example. In the final moments of *Paranormal Activity* we never see what happens to and between Katie and Micah. We only see what the camera records. We hear screams. Then silence. Then out of the darkness, Micah's body comes flying and hits the camera, knocking it over. The gaps, the edits become part of the story.

There is also 'unnecessary' footage and conversation. For example, *Cloverfield* begins with a video made by Rob (Michael Stahl-David) the morning after he slept with Beth (Odette Yustman) and then takes her to Coney Island. The time/date stamp on the bottom first marks this footage as being on a personal video camera and second records the date as 'Apr 27'. A jerky jump cut then shows a date of 'May 22' and features Rob's brother Jason (Mike Vogel) asking if the camera is on and arguing with Lily (Jessica Lukas), his girlfriend. 'I want you to go around with your brother's camera and get testimonials from everyone,' she tells him. On the camera we then see the evening unfold. By cutting back and forth between the two dates on the footage we are able to piece together what has happened between Rob and Beth. We also, however, inadvertently see the attack on New York by the monster and the subsequent deaths of all the characters. We also see conversations about the camera and how it works. At one point Rob realizes his brother and Hud are taping over his video of Beth and his day at Coney Island and grows despondent.

This reaction is also indicative of another impulse behind the documentary approach, which is that if an event is not on film then it somehow did not happen. Even if he never watched it again, Rob wanted the record of his and Beth's day together to exist somewhere. Videos are electronic memories which keep the events real and alive. Indeed, I write this as we approach the anniversary of September 11, and already the videos and images of that day are being played over and over again as part of the pledge to 'Never forget'. We need not forget so long as there is video to remind us. This is what Rob has lost to his farewell testimonial tape.

Cloverfield begins with a series of pre-video segments: colour test pattern, text identifying the video as government property and warning against copying it. Then, alongside a time code, the text on screen states:

Document #USGX-8810-B467
Digital SD Card
Multiple sightings of case designate
"Cloverfield"

A second text card appears, stating: 'Camera retrieved at incident site "US-447" / Area formerly known as "Central Park"'. Already, before a single foot of actual imagery is shown, the text identifies the images as coming from a digital camera recovered from the 'former' Central Park, both establishing New York City as the film's locale, as noted in the previous chapter, and that we are about to witness eyewitness coverage of something the government has now classified. This 'found footage' is marked, therefore, as being presented 'as is' and containing 'multiple sightings' of the title monster.

The sole perspective of the entire film is that of the camera and whoever is holding it. We begin with seeing Central Park and then Beth from Rob's perspective, then Rob from Beth's perspective, then Lily and the street from Jason's. Once the party begins, Hud becomes the dominant cameraman. He is interested in Marlena (Lizzy Caplan), which is established when Jason hands the camera to him and gives his own testimonial, and thus he records his own long conversation with her. He records the events on the roof; he records the events on the street – Hud keeps the camera rolling at all times. We see the characters attempt to flee through the subway. We see Marlena's death from a bite and Jason's death on the bridge. We see Hud, Rob and Beth climb aboard a helicopter, believing they are about to escape and we see the chaos as the creature then hits the helicopter, which crashes. We see the camera in the wreckage and Hud and Beth pull Rob out. The camera is set on the ground as they examine Rob to see how hurt he is, but Hud runs back to get the camera. The monster then arrives; Hud points the camera up, filming it. It notices him. The camera moves in and out of focus as the monster moves its head closer, finally opening up its mouth and biting Hud. The camera then moves in and out of focus again after it, and part of Hud's body tumbles out of the creature's mouth to the ground. Ron then takes the camera and, alongside Beth in the park, uses it to film their last moments. The film ends with Rob turning the camera on himself as the monster approaches.

> My name is Robert Hawkins. It's 6:42 a.m. on Saturday, May 23. Approximately seven hours ago, something attacked the city. I don't know what it is. If you found this tape, I mean if you're watching this right now, then you probably know more about it than I do. Whatever it is, it killed my brother, Jason Hawkins. It killed my best friend, Hudson Platt, and Marlena Diamond, and

many, many others. We've crashed here in Central Park and taken shelter under this bridge. The military has begun bombing the creature and we're caught in the middle.

From this monologue, several things are immediately apparent. Rob knows he will most likely die soon and wishes to document not only his last minutes but his existence and that of his friends. He wants those who find the camera to know what happened. What began as a party for him and a camera for testimonials ends in his last testimonial, an assertion that he was once alive and that this happened to him.

He then turns the camera on Beth, who does not know what to say or do. At his prodding, she states, 'My name is Elizabeth McIntyre. I don't know why this is happening'. An explosion causes the camera to be dropped and we see bricks and dirt falling. Rob and Beth tell each other that they love one another and the camera freezes. For one last time, the footage cuts back to Rob and Beth on Coney Island, with Beth asserting she had a good day.

The various moments documented on the tape individually are slices of life. Taken collectively, however, they form an inadvertent narrative of a group of friends experiencing an attack on New York that results in their deaths, almost entirely on camera. The entire story emerges out of a single camera capturing the events of an eight-hour period, plus flashbacks to the month before. The end of the film comes full circle not only to return the audience to Coney Island but to the idea that what they are watching is 'found footage'. The video testaments of Rob and Beth followed by the images and sounds that confirm their deaths reminds the audience of the opening, in which the camera was reported as 'found' in 'the area formerly known as Central Park'. The found footage of buildings being destroyed, people dying and crowds fleeing echoes the mediated, documented experience of 9/11. Other single-camera 'found footage' documentaries include the first *Paranormal Activity*, in which Micah and Katie record their haunting on a single camcorder, and *[REC]* and *Quarantine*.

Paranormal Activity uses many documentary techniques in order to establish itself as 'found footage'. The camera films standard images, but is also equipped with night vision, low-light filming, with which audiences have grown familiar. At night, although not always during the day, the film features a time-stamp clock in the lower right hand corner of the screen, where a home video camera would put it. Doing so allows the film-makers to speed up the clock (and the film) to show individual moments. The film employs a single camera, and, like Cloverfield, features extraneous conversations and 'unnecessary' elements that would not have been included in a straightforward narrative film.

[REC] and Quarantine both feature a television news crew following a group of firefighters, who then record the events in an apartment building, in which a mysterious virus transforms the residents into zombie-like killers. Rapid edits, unfinished conversations and promises of the camera being off when it is on (just as in Cloverfield and Paranormal Activity) add to the illusion that the footage is raw, unedited film straight from the camera as it was experienced. The change in titles reflects a bit of a change of focus. The title of the Spanish original refers to the word 'rec' that appears inside a camera when it is recording. The title of the American remake refers to the situation in which the firemen and the film crew find themselves. The original frames the focus on the recording of the events, on the inadvertent documenting of the situation. Interestingly, the Spanish film was not filmed on sets but only in real locations and was filmed chronologically with relatively unknown actors in order to increase the verisimilitude. The pseudo-documentary does everything it can in order to look real. In an era where computer generated graphics frequently dominate low-budget horror, the use of a naturalistic approach with only in-camera and on-set effects results in a film that resembles news footage.

Interestingly, like Cloverfield, there are strong echoes of the documentary 9/11 in [REC]/Quarantine, as both documentary and pseudo-docs follow a company of firefighters. In the horror films, a television crew is supposedly shooting a documentary about what the lives of firefighters are like. The documentary crew follows the company when they go out on a call. Both [REC] and 9/11 emphasize how the film crew knows nothing of what is going on inside the site when they arrive or outside the site once they enter. The documentary and pseudo-documentary both have a cinéma verité, watching-it-as-it-happens quality to them. Both films also feature the individuals involved watching television and seeing footage of themselves in order to understand the magnitude of what is happening. Just as in *9/11*, suddenly, a situation turns dire and the documentary crew becomes part of the story.

Unlike *Cloverfield*, *Paranormal Activity* and *[REC]/Quarantine* which present material as unedited in order to create a documentary-like verisimilitude, many other pseudo-documentaries involve multi-camera, multi-format perspectives, which also emerge out of 9/11 documentaries. *Paranormal Activity 2*, for example, is a blend of security camera footage, home camera footage, characters filming everyday activities and events with different cameras. The result is a mosaic of textures, colours, angles and formats which suggest, when blended together, a complete picture of the events. Individual points of view are provided in confessional moments when Daniel (Brian Boland) and Ali (Molly Ephraim) turn the camera on one another. Distanced moments occur when the footage comes from security camera footage.

George A. Romero's *Diary of the Dead*, for example, presents itself as a film within a film. After opening with footage allegedly found on the internet of a local television news crew being attacked by zombies, Debra voices over the introduction to the film within the film, called 'The Death of Death'. It is the product of her boyfriend Jason, which begs the question why he is not editing it. The film combines images from the internet, footage Jason and his friends have shot, security footage from a warehouse and security footage from the panic room of his friend's mansion. Debra admits at the beginning of the film that she has edited the footage together to show what has happened to the world at large as well as what happened to their own small group.

In presenting the material this way Romero offers a metacinematic critique of our highly mediated lives. He critiques his young film-makers for not connecting to anything that does not come through a computer or appear on a screen. They upload their footage of the crisis to see how many 'hits' they get. At one point, Debra observes, 'We don't stop to help. We stop to look'. Citizen journalists are also passive citizen observers. They do not actually do anything to change or relieve the situation; they are detached and disconnected from the events except to document them.

Romero, as I have argued elsewhere, equates the camera with a gun in its destructive power (Wetmore 2011: 217). When the group of student film-makers take one of their own to an abandoned hospital, seeking help for her since she shot herself in the head, Professor Maxwell (Scott Wentworth) uses a pistol to kill a zombie, then hands the gun to a student saying, 'Take this. It's too easy to use'. Debra, frustrated and outraged when she finds herself, like Jason, filming the death of their friend in the next scene, hands the camera to Maxwell, repeating, 'Take this. It's too easy to use'. Finally, when Jason lies dying, bitten by a friend who has turned, he groans to Debra, 'Shoot me,' an ambiguous request by this point in the film. She picks up a camera first and aims it at him. She then picks up a gun, conflating the two. 'Shooting' is a violent destructive act in *Diary*, regardless of whether one holds a camera or a gun.

The Last Exorcism is also an edited mockumentary. Although it is also clearly 'found footage', because of its use of a single camera and the fact that the producer, Iris (Iris Bahr), the subject of the film, Reverend Cotton Marcus (Patrick Fabian) and Daniel the cameraman all die at the end of the film, means that someone else has discovered the camera and edited the film. Like *9/11*, it begins as something else. Iris and Daniel plan to film Marcus showing the tricks he uses when he performs 'exorcisms', demonstrating that they are false. Marcus, who has been a preacher, healer and exorcist since he was a child has grown guilty and a newspaper article about a child beaten to death during an exorcism convinced him to 'come clean'.

He demonstrates for the camera crew how he manipulates his congregation, working his mother's banana bread recipe into a call-and-response prayer. He then drives them to the Sweetzer farm in rural Louisiana, where a father has requested his daughter be exorcized. The film crew comes to believe that the father is molesting his daughter and her 'possession' is her way of acting out against it. The son is sullen and threatening until he realizes it is all a sham, then he is all smiles. Cotton demonstrates how he performs the fake exorcism to the crew before setting up the tricks in Nell's (Ashley Bell) room. Cotton then encourages Louis, the father (Louis Herthum) to stop drinking and seek help.

The film crew stays at a local hotel and is woken up to find Nell in Cotton's room. They take her to a hospital and discover she is pregnant. They return her to the farm and another exorcism is carried out, as Nell grows more feral and dangerous and her father more unhinged. What began as a simple documentary about a preacher who fakes his powers is transformed into a dangerous situation in which a girl might actually be possessed. They finally relax her, believing that she is acting out because she is pregnant from a boy from church. The crew finally prepares to leave, but when they interview the young man in question, he reveals he is gay and has never slept with her. They return to the farm to find the family's minister and the rest of his flock holding some sort of sacrificial ritual, in which Nell's baby is cut from her and thrown in a fire, Cotton confronts a giant, demonic spirit and Iris and Daniel are killed by the devil worshippers, including Nell's brother. The overall effect of the film is of a single-camera documentary, but music underscores several scenes, designed no doubt to enhance their creepiness and chill factor. Likewise, given the ending of the film, someone had to find the footage and put it together.

Apollo 18 functions much more like *Paranormal Activity 2*. The text which opens the film indicates that what the audience is about to watch is edited from 84 hours of footage loaded to the internet from NASA's secret 'Apollo 18' mission (there were only 17 Apollo missions). The astronauts are given multiple cameras in order to record their mission. All footage is either from mission cameras, ship cameras or personal cameras. Three astronauts are sent to the moon and discover an alien presence. In terms of horror cinema, there is nothing original in the premise, except the claimed documentary, 'found footage' aspect of the film. As Mark Olsen observes in a review of the film, 'Footage from space missions is frequently slightly spooky and unsettling – the meditative fixed camera, harsh lighting and odd angles can make the images creepy or sad' (2011: D8) *Apollo 18* blends ship camera footage with motion-sensor camera footage (set up by the astronauts on the lunar surface) and handheld shots from the astronauts themselves to capture the experience of the growing paranoia in the face of 'something out there'. What might have otherwise been a run-of-the-mill alien invasion film uses the documentary format to generate fear that would not have been possible otherwise.

Furthermore, in its claims of both being edited down from '84 hours of NASA footage' and of being evidence of a government cover-up of both the mission itself and the deaths of the astronauts, it links Apollo 18 with the internet documentary *Loose Change 9/11: An American Coup* (2009). *Loose Change*, as it is commonly known, is actually a series of films, or a fluid text of one film, released between 2005 and 2009, edited together from images and footage from 9/11, with a voiceover from director Dylan Avery. The film posits that 9/11 was an 'inside job' and the American government covered up its involvement in the planning and execution of the attacks on the twin towers. Editing together footage of the attacks, archival footage of other supposed government conspiracies and cover-ups, and other images, the film argues for the 'controlled demolition' of the towers. Similarly, *Apollo 18* claims to show that the United States government, specifically the Department of Defense, sponsored a mission to the moon for the purposes of discovering if alien life were there and if the Russians had encountered it. Not even the three astronauts on the mission were told what the true mission was, and ultimately their lives were sacrificed in order to cover up the government's plan. *Apollo 18* functions, culturally and visually, as *Loose Change* does, asserting a government conspiracy to hide its illicit activities and relying upon archival and documentary footage to make its outrageous claims. The producers of *Apollo 18* go so far as to assert the film is real. At this point in cinema history, pseudo-documentary and debunked amateur documentary become indistinguishable. Both function the same way as films, rely upon the same cinematic and narrative techniques, and both claim to demonstrate a real government conspiracy and cover-up.

The filmic style and imagery of 9/11 is used even in films that are not pseudo-documentaries, but generate, develop and maintain horror through documentary technique. *Open Water* is not a documentary, but it is filmed with hand-held cameras, eschews many of the techniques of narrative fiction films and employs the same *cinéma verité* aesthetic in order to suggest that these things are actually happening, in order to document the horror. Post-9/11 documentary style and horror subject matter combine to create documentary AS horror. Whereas Michael Moore uses a highly stylized, edited approach in *Fahrenheit 9/11* in order to argue that the Bush administration used September 11 to pursue its own war-making agenda, to reward friends and punish enemies, films such as *Cloverfield*, *Paranormal Activity* and *The Last Exorcism* use the same techniques to generate fear.

    Another unique aspect of *Paranormal Activity* that reflects upon 9/11 is the repeated concern in the first two films that the presence of the camera makes things worse. 'Maybe we shouldn't have the camera,' argues Katie. The psychic they consult warns them against antagonizing the presence. The presence begins doing things that will only be seen on the camera. In *Paranormal Activity 2*, Katie tells her sister that she remembers that the more attention they paid to the events in their childhood home, the worse they got. As noted in the introduction, terrorism is a 'paratheatrical activity' aimed at an audience other than its direct victims. The purpose of the terrorist is to generate terror through spectacle. If one responds with notice, if a great deal of media coverage occurs, then the terrorist is rewarded with the desired attention. Underlying *Paranormal Activity* is the fear that when one pays attention to terrifying things, the terrifying things take notice and increase their activity. This fear holds true for demons and for terrorists. When we document the horror, in some small way we also provoke continued horror. This concept works within the world of the film; within the world of the film industry (the number of people who saw the first and second *Paranormal Activity* films, after all, have guaranteed a third); and within the real world, where the United States' immediate response to the terrorists attacks was that they would not change how we live our lives. We will be vigilant, but not fixate upon them.

Jigsaw's Jihad

Just as the fragmented and documentary nature of September 11 is recapitulated in horror films, so, too are the terrorist videos an influence on horror as well. Jigsaw from the *Saw* films is on a moralistic crusade. Like the Islamic extremists his work imitates, he sees Western society as decadent. Unlike the extremists, however, he does not engage in terror to attack the West collectively. Instead,

Figure 2.4 Jigsaw as terrorist: jihadist-style videos present the *Saw* killer's victims with their fate.

his 'traps' are moral tests, designed to force individuals to reassess their lives and priorities.

Although in the first film he is encountered primarily through audio tapes, Amanda (Shawnee Smith) receives a video of a grotesque ventriloquist doll which becomes the face of the Jigsaw killer (see figure 2.4). As in terrorist's videos, the quality is grainy, the focus is on a disguised person – while the terrorists cover their faces with scarves, sunglasses and bandanas, Jigsaw uses the doll – who issues a series of demands and threats (see figure 2.5). Amanda must kill the man in front of her or her head will be torn apart by the device on it. Throughout the series of films, the 'Jigsaw' video replaces the audio tape as the preferred means of telling the terrified victim what is about to happen.

Jigsaw also watches his victims on video, frequently resembling security videos. Several times in the first film, the audience watches the prisoners on Jigsaw's monitors. The image resembles both security camera footage, made familiar on the evening news, and videos of hostages presented by terrorists. Grainy, out-of-focus footage shows captive individuals held prisoner in dank and dirty

Figure 2.5 *Saw* as terrorist video as seen on the internet: The disguised 'terrorist' in close-up, making his demands.

surroundings, obviously in mortal peril (see figure 2.6). In *Saw II* (2005), Jigsaw tells the police to wait 90 minutes and they will find Matthews's son. They watch his latest subjects on video as the film transitions in and out of the poison-gas filled house on the monitors to Jigsaw's lair. It is not until the end of the film that it is revealed what was on the monitors was not concurrent with the police interrogating Jigsaw. The events had unfolded long before the police watched them on television. Detective Matthews (Donnie Wahlberg), believing he was watching events in real time, kidnaps Jigsaw and brings him to the location of the trap, where he himself becomes imprisoned, left to die in the same room that Adam was in the original film. Like terrorists, Jigsaw videotapes his atrocities in order to further terrorize his victims.

This trope has emerged in horror films in general as well. Although criminals who videotape their crime sprees and murders existed long before September 11 (*Henry: Portrait of a Serial Killer* immediately leaps to mind), the changing nature of citizen media combined with mediated terrorism has made the horror film within the horror film not self-reflexive, as in *Scream* and *Funny Games*, but indicative of the mediated nature of terror. In *Seconds Apart*, for example, the 'found footage' within the film comes from the protagonists, who film their atrocities, although the film itself is shot in a standard narrative style. The film begins with a group of teen jocks at a party filming themselves as they casually converse while playing Russian Roulette. When one dies, another picks the gun up as if nothing has happened and continues to play. As they continue to film their victims, one brother tells a young woman they are 'making a movie' and then asks her, 'Wanna be in it?' The brothers make the videos for themselves, but the terror of the film for the viewer comes from watching individuals casually kill themselves on camera. This phenomenon is not limited to pseudo-documentaries. Other horror films contain moments in which characters watch others undergoing horrific experiences, again reminding the audience of the mediated nature of horror. In *The Happening*, patrons of the diner in which the protagonists stop to eat and get information watch a cellphone showing an uploaded video of a man walk into a lion's cage at a zoo and get his arms ripped off by the lions before they attack and devour him completely. This trope is not just the mediated experience of 9/11 but also a sign of a highly mediated society in which almost everyone

Figure 2.6 Videos of hostages taken by terrorists: *Saw*.

has access to cameras and recording devices, often combined with personal phones which allow for immediate uploading to the internet. Between Twitter, Facebook, YouTube and email our every thought, our every impulse, every image we capture can be and is often put up on the internet for all to view. The very factors that allowed 9/11 to be such a heavily documented and heavily mediated event also infuse every event and every aspect of our society. This factor must also be included when considering the pseudo-documentary.

This impulse to document is driven by and shaped by the technology that allows us to do so. It is also shaped by the popular culture of reality television. Between reality shows that eliminate one or more contestants each week (the repeated use of the words 'eliminate' and 'elimination' in talking about people on such programmes is also highly suggestive of horror films, in which a group gets smaller each period with the 'elimination' of one of the group – there is a fine line between *Halloween* and *Hell's Kitchen*, between *Alien* and *America's Next Top Model*), and those that document the highs and extreme lows of celebrities, pseudo-celebrities and average people with interesting jobs, the culture currently has embraced the documentary-as-entertainment instinct, which also makes pseudo-documentaries much easier to accept and believe. The reality television technique of the confessional camera implies access to an individual's genuine beliefs, feelings and self-perception, even though we know these moments are also highly edited and juxtaposed with other images to create either the illusion of continuity or the illusion of hypocrisy.

This impulse to document is also reflected in numerous other films. In *War of the Worlds*, for example, when the first tripod begins to emerge from the ground, a man is shown holding a small camcorder, filming the event. As others move back, he moves forward to get a better shot. As the heat rays begin to activate and disintegrate people, the cameraman is one of the first to die, perhaps a comment on the dangerous nature of video journalism, but also a cautionary warning about the danger of privileging the image over one's own life. Spielberg reverses the angle of the shot and we see the camera clatter to the ground where, without an operator, it continues to film and document the atrocities (see figure 2.7). On the one hand, the fact that the camera is operator-less shows how

Figure 2.7 The screen within the screen: the camera makes the alien attack both more and less real, both safer and less safe in *War of the Worlds*.

the image is everything. No one needs to be filming, the events ultimately are filmed regardless. There is no longer a guiding intelligence behind the film, but the camera continues to capture images. On the other hand, Spielberg also gives the audience a view solely through the camera for several seconds. We do not watch the same events play out behind the camera monitor in 'real life', we focus on the screen within the screen: we know what we are watching is mediated, and we prefer it to reality. Paradoxically, Spielberg shows how the camera makes the image both more real and less real than reality. The camera keeps us safe in a way that it did not keep its operator safe. But by seeing the images on the screen, we know they are 'real' in a way that the special effects-driven actual film at that moment is not.

Thus, even when the film is a straightforward fiction narrative, more and more horror films are claiming a kind of reality. *The Strangers*, to give but one example, begins with on-screen text and a voiceover saying, 'What you are about to see is inspired by true events'. Although the actors are recognizable movie stars (Liv Tyler and Scott Speedman), the film is framed as a docudrama, that bastard cousin of the documentary. The next text states, 'On the night of February 11, 2005, Kristen McKay and James Hoyt left a friend's wedding reception and returned to the Hoyt family's summer home. The brutal events that took place there are still not entirely known'. The text is similar to the ones that begin *Paranormal Activity*, *Apollo 18* and *The Blair Witch Project*, giving the background for the images one is about to witness. The text and voiceover are then followed by the images of suburban houses being driven past in a car, the camera set to slow motion. The houses and the images grow darker as we hear the recording of a 911 call, setting into motion the discovery of the bodies as the film is then played out as a flashback. Even when not entirely in documentary style, horror films frequently claim a basis in reality and utilize documentary techniques to frame the world of the film as 'real'. That assurance of 'reality', of film coming raw out of the camera and on to the screen as it happened (or as it is happening) echoes the experience of September 11. Just as the filmed images from that day filled a nation with horror and terror, so, too, do the makers of these films hope the raw, documentary style generates a fear perhaps not possible in more polished films.

3

'Because you were home': Anonymous and Random Death

> We face an enemy determined to bring death and suffering into our homes.
>
> GEORGE W. BUSH, 2006
> FIFTH ANNIVERSARY OF 9/11

> Kristen: 'Why are you doing this to us?'
> Dollface: 'Because you were home ...'
> THE STRANGERS

Random and anonymous death and a sense of nihilism were present in horror long before 9/11. In films such as *Last House on the Left* (1972), *The Texas Chainsaw Massacre* (1974), *Natural Born Killers* (1994) and *Funny Games* (1997), ordinary people were killed not because they were engaged in illicit or forbidden activities but because of where they were. Indeed, the model for post-9/11 random death might be found in the pre-9/11 film, *Targets* (1968), directed by Peter Bogdanovich, itself inspired by an event that terrorized America: the shooting spree by Charles Whitman from the observation deck of the University of Texas's tower in August, 1966 that left 16 dead and twice as many wounded. In Bogdanovich's film, Byron Orlock (Boris Karloff, for all practical purposes playing himself), a horror film star, quits making movies, since real life is so much more terrifying than the gothic thrillers in which he performs. He agrees to make a personal appearance at a drive-in theatre where disturbed young Bobby Thompson (Tim O'Kelly) has decided to set up a sniper's nest behind the screen and begin shooting moviegoers. Isabel Christina Pinedo argues, 'The juxtaposition of these two figures dramatizes how the psychotic killer's inexplicable violent rampages had supplanted the traditional monster of castles and closed endings' (1997: 90). Similarly, the post-9/11 horror film supplants the ironic knowing and reflexive horror of the nineties. Post-9/11 horror presents *Targets* writ big and consistent. Whereas *Targets* opened the door for more nihilistic fare such as *Night of the Living Dead* and *The Texas Chainsaw Massacre*, but remained an outlier of late sixties horror, its heirs after 2001 began to dominate.

Our understanding of death changed significantly in the twentieth century. Lindsay Prior advocates the view that the attempt to quantify, qualify, measure and scientifically calculate death in all its aspects is a phenomenon of the last century (1997: 177). Between advances in medicine, advances in the insurance business, and technological advances in warfare, the human understanding of death has changed radically in the past century. 'The premodern portrait presents a vision of random, unpredictable and untamed death; of a death which can strike anyone, anywhere at any time whatsoever and with equal possibility' (1997: 178). Then the Holocaust and the Cold War brought about the scientific measuring of death: extermination camps meant to run at peak efficiency, cataloging and eliminating thousands of human beings per day, and nuclear war casualties, measured in 'megadeaths', i.e. one million people killed or dying simultaneously, casually discussed in the highest circles of government.[1] Likewise, thanks to medical technology, the development of hospice care and improved understanding of the human body combined with a more complex understanding of the cessation of life, death has become 'in many respects a technically controlled event' (Prior 1997: 189). Death became, in a sense, less random, more controlled and measurable.

In a sense, that mindset ends on 9/11 and we return in popular culture to Prior's 'vision of random, unpredictable and untamed death; of a death which can strike anywhere at any time'. As the terror attacks were unfolding, and over the weeks and months afterwards, the media focused on mourning the death and the horrible ways in which people died. 'The form of dying,' states Charles B. Strozier, was 'confusing and painful.' The immediate abjection of individuals, in Kristeva's sense, also created a troubling sense of death. 'The issue is the radical dismemberment of bodies that occurred in the disaster. The dying was not natural' (Strozier 2005: 268–9). Not only was the dying confusing, painful and 'not natural', even an abject state was not always possible as many bodies simply vanished in the debris. The people in the planes and towers died immediately and painfully, leaving nothing to mourn or even identify. Such an end to one's life is, for all practical purposes, an end of a world, if not the world. Slavoj Žižek states, 'the terrifying death of each individual is absolute and incomparable' (2002: 51–2). Every death on 9/11 was a horror narrative unto itself. What was ultimately terrifying, for those watching, was the randomness and the anonymousness of the death seen and experienced on that day, and in other disasters and terror attacks since.

Random and anonymous (but purposeful ... sometimes)

In the film *The Strangers*, Kristen (Liv Tyler) asks the three masked killers, 'Why are you doing this to us?' The killer known as 'Dollface' responds, 'Because you were home.' Death is random in post-9/11 horror – the result of being in the wrong place at the wrong time, as the cliché goes. Unlike in eighties slasher horror, for example, where engaging in negative behaviour such as drinking, doing drugs, having premarital sex are often forerunners to being killed by the killer(s); in post-9/11 horror death is random and unrelated to one's behaviour. Yet in some of these films the reason for the killings is purposeful, even if the individual victims are random.

In the National Geographic documentary *Inside 9/11*, pilot and journalist William Langewiesche posited 'if you were within these concentrated zones, basically within the footprint of the buildings themselves, you were going to die.'[2] Individuals many storeys up, rode the debris down and were rescued from the rubble. Others, much lower in the building when it collapsed, were killed. Many stories were told of two individuals on the same floor of the World Trade Center who went down different stairwells, or one stayed in what was thought to be a safe location and another left, or one person overslept and missed a vital meeting and in all these cases, one person lived and others died. To expand on this idea, many flights took off from the various airports on September 11, but only four were involved in the terror attacks. Someone headed to Los Angeles from Boston but on a different airline or on a later flight lived, while those on American Airlines flight 11 died. Likewise, those who missed the flight (most notably and best known being Seth McFarland, creator of *Family Guy*), which might have seemed like bad luck at the time, lived while those who were on time died.

This aspect is true of any air disaster, but the scope of death on September 11 brought home the reality and possibility of death at the hands of people who did not know you and were not targetting you specifically. Conversely, as Andrew Schopp states, the 'targets were not random even if the victims who suffered were' (2009: 262). The terrorists attacked specific targets of high symbolic value: the World Trade Center Twin Towers, the Pentagon, and, had the terrorists on United 93 succeeded, most likely the Capitol Building or the White House. Yet the specific victims who died on that day were random, and not only Americans. Christine Muller reports that while the attacks 'targeted American citizens or undifferentiated personifications of U.S. policy, nevertheless, they killed American and non-American citizens alike, as undifferentiated human beings' (2009: 45–6). In other words, while America and Americans were the targets, anyone on the plane, in the Twin Towers or the section of the Pentagon died, regardless of nationality. Individuals so targetted, not just on 9/11, but afterwards in Iraq, Afghanistan or anywhere in the world, were targetted not because of something they had done or their personal beliefs. They were and are targetted simply for being American. One dies not because of one's actions or behaviour but simply because one was the American that the killers caught. These ideas are echoed in numerous movies from the overt (such as in *Buried* where the man who has kidnapped Paul Conroy (Ryan Reynolds), insists that as a civilian truck driver in Iraq he is not a soldier, and tells him, 'You American? Then you're a soldier ... 9/11 was not my fault but you're still here,') to the covert (such as *The Final* (2010), which, while seeming like a film about bullies and school shootings demonstrates that while some students are targetted for torture and death because they are cruel bullies, others suffer simply for showing up at a party). Not everyone in the room 'deserves it'; some simply are part of the crowd that goes to parties and thus are now targets.

There is a history of horror cinema in one sense as always being about 'undifferentiated human beings', especially in high-number sequels. There are no real characters other than the killers in *A Nightmare on Elm Street 4: The Dream Master, Friday the 13th V: A New Beginning*, or *Saw VI*, just types of victims for the killers. The result, of course, was a simply lack of empathy for the victims and hence any sense of horror or fear at their demise. The higher the sequel number, the more likely the audience roots for the killer and not the victims or 'final girl'. After 9/11, we can no longer find such deaths amusing. If Slavoj Žižek is correct, above, then every death is terrifying.

Slasher films used to be inventive and humorous. The deaths demonstrate a variety of imaginative ways in which and with a variety of implements with which people can be killed. At various points in his career Jason uses a speargun, pitchfork, machete, weedwhacker, spear, harpoon, chain or rope, or smashes a sleeping bag against a tree. In *Silent Night, Deadly Night*, the psychopathic Santa impales a girl on the antlers of a mounted deer head. Michael Meyers strangles a nurse with her own stethoscope in. Freddy, of course, has his glove, but in later films he, too, grows inventive in his killing. Conversely, after 9/11, the inventiveness is gone, the humour is gone, the creative deaths are gone. In *The Strangers*, a knife is all that is needed. In *Funny Games*, a golf club, a knife and a 'hunting rifle', (as Paul calls it, though it is actually a shotgun) are all that is needed to slaughter innocent people.

This mixture of random, anonymous death and targetted death is one of the great paradoxes of September 11. The people who died were not specifically targetted, and their deaths were random and anonymous. But they still died, in a sense, because of who they were. Likewise, where they died is paradoxical. 9/11 demonstrated that public space is unsafe. 'Home' is sanctuary. Home, however, carries multiple connotations. When an American citizen passes through immigration and customs when flying back into the United States they are told, 'Welcome home'. Not since the War of 1812 has a foreign force attacked the continental United States. Yet 9/11 demonstrated that 'home' is no longer safe. In response, we created a Department of *Home*land Security. The United States as a whole as attacked at home.

Compounding this fear was the anthrax scare which immediately followed 9/11. Getting the mail can cause one to die slowly and painfully. Going to work can cause one to die quickly and horribly. Simply being somewhere ('the wrong place at the wrong time') can result in death. Previous horror tended to be more moralistic: behaviour causes death. Virginity and good behaviour were immunizers against death at the hands of serial killers, as a general rule. September 11 results in random and anonymous death in horror cinema, not because of what you did or who you were, but where you were.

The Strangers, or, why are you doing this?

After 9/11, a key question was 'why?' What would drive a group of people to commit this kind of atrocity? The motive for the attack was of great concern to the American people. Yet, paradoxically, the motive was irrelevant. The administration chose to frame it in terms of a conflict of values and civilizations: 'they hate us for our freedom', 'we love life and they love death'. But with the release of the identities of the hijackers and subsequent information on al Qaeda such simplifications were obviously insufficient. 'Why are you doing this?' is a central question of 9/11.[3] We know the hijackers on 9/11 had motives, but in the end, those motives are irrelevant to the majority of Americans. It does not matter why they did it. The fact that they did it is what matters. People died horribly, the reason does not matter. The seemingly random and anonymous way in which thousands of Americans were killed, therefore, evokes in horror cinema what Samuel Taylor Coleridge, speaking of Iago in Shakespeare's *Othello*, calls 'motive-hunting of motiveless Malignity' (1969: 315).[4] This phrase is often taken to mean that Iago lists a series of rationalizations for his actions because he actually has no motive. Iago is simply evil and therefore does evil. His malignity is without motive, it is simply a defining characteristic.

Until 9/11, the only true 'motiveless Malignity' is Jason Vorhees. Michael Meyers seeks to kill his sister(s), Freddy kills for pleasure and revenge, other slasher film monsters kill out of sexual confusion or frustration, revenge or to gain in some way. Jason kills because he kills. By the third *Friday the 13th*, there is no reason for his killing. There is no persona there, he simply kills. But even in the *Friday the 13th* films there is a moral universe. Jason might not have a reason to kill, but the universe allows him to kill the young people at Camp Crystal Lake and environs (not to mention Manhattan) because of their behaviour. Having sex, doing drugs, being mean or selfish, results in being killed by Jason. As Carol Clover demonstrates in *Men, Women and Chainsaws*, the 'final girl' survives because she is intelligent, resourceful and she does not engage in the negative behaviour that brings about the deaths of her friends. Horror, especially horror involving serial killers, exists within a moral universe in which death is not random or anonymous, but the direct result of one's choices and actions. Annie (Nancy Kyes) and Lynda (P. J. Soles) in *Halloween* are both killed because they act in immoral ways. Annie deserts her babysitting job to have sex with her boyfriend; Lynda has sex with her boyfriend in the house in which Annie is supposedly babysitting . Only Laurie (Jamie Leigh Curtis) survives, primarily because she does not even want to talk to Ben, the boy she likes, but babysits, watches the children on Halloween, and responsibly keeps her commitments while remaining sexually inactive. She lives. By the nineties, the moral code of horror films was so well known and understood it was parodied, undermined and deconstructed in *Scream* (1996). Sydney Prescott (Neve Campbell) has sex with her boyfriend, but still survives as the 'final girl'. Despite that, the film still gives answers to the question 'why?': Billy Loomis (Skeet Ulrich) wants revenge on Sydney because her mother broke up his parent's marriage and Stuart (Matthew Lillard) craves fame, but also argues for 'peer pressure ... I'm very sensitive' as a cause for his killings.

Post-9/11, motiveless Malignity in a universe with no moral justice becomes a trope in horror cinema. Motives are passé in the nineties, as *Scream* notes (and then immediately undercuts by providing motives), but by the oughts, they are irrelevant. Films such as *The Strangers* and the remake of *Funny Games* feature killers who kill because, as noted in the epigraph to this chapter, 'you were home'. The killers have no real reason to kill the couple in each film. They do not know them before the events of the film. The murders depicted are random and motiveless.

In *The Strangers*, three people arrive at night at an isolated house. A private tragedy of sorts is occurring within the Hoyt family summer home. James Hoyt (Scott Speedman) has asked Kristen McKay to marry him while they are at another couple's wedding. It is clear from the events which follow that she has declined to accept his proposal. Both of them are sad and regretful, and attempting to discern the next steps in their relationship. In a traditional Hollywood film, the experience of being attacked by killers would bring them together and result in their marriage at the conclusion of the film. Instead, they are both tied to chairs in formal wear and stabbed to death.

A small group of three highly organized, coordinated killers transform the Hoyt household into a realm of terror, first for Kristen, then for both Kristen and James. Wearing masks and armed only with knives, they manage to terrify their victims into panicking and then overreacting: James accidentally shoots Mike (Glenn Howerton) in the face, mistaking him for one of the attackers. After smashing the car they attempt to escape from, destroying the phone and a radio, and chasing them around the house, yard and barn all though the night, the three individuals stand in front of the bound couple, where the above question and answer about motive are given. What makes the moment especially chilling is Dollface's matter-of-fact voice. No other reason is needed to terrorize, torture and kill Kristen and James.

They have only enough time to tell one another they love each other before the killers remove their masks (although the audiences never see their faces), pick up knives and take turns stabbing James and Kristen. The killers then depart in an old pick-up truck, stopping alongside the road to talk to two Mormon boys delivering literature. 'Can I have one?' Pin-Up Girl (Laura Margolis) asks the boy, referring to their pamphlets. 'Are you a sinner?' the boy asks. 'Sometimes,' she replies, taking the pamphlet from the boy and returning to the truck. The boys then discover the house and the dead bodies within. The first boy reaches out to Kristen's seemingly dead body and her eyes open, she grabs his hand and screams. The overall effect of the film has been one of constant dread, building to unnecessary murders. Unlike slasher films, which feature a death every eight or so minutes, only three people die in *The Strangers*, but their deaths are far more horrific than anything Jason or Michael have ever done.

John Kretschmer, the production designer for *The Strangers*, refers to the film as not a horror film but a 'terror film'.[5] 'It's an absolutely new approach to the genre,' he asserts. Every aspect of the film is designed to provide no relief, no respite from the horror. Instead, the film serves as a constant reminder that those who want to kill you and who plot to do so can succeed despite your best efforts to stay safe. They do not need a reason to do so.

The same question is asked in *Funny Games*, both the original (1997) and remake (2007). The pre-9/11 original serves as a critique of American cinema and media that revels in violence. Writer/Director Michael Haneke claims his theme is 'the portrayal of violence in the media and in film' and 'the way violence is dealt with in movies'.[6] Self-reflexive and canny, in many ways it is an intellectual variation on *Scream*, a postmodern pastiche for the doctoral crowd. The remake, however, cannot be viewed with pre-9/11 eyes. The remake is almost entirely a shot-by-shot recreation of the original in English with new actors (I cannot say they are American actors because Tim Roth is English and Naomi Watts is English by birth but raised in Australia, though both are now based in Los Angeles and perform almost entirely in American projects). Even though director Michael Haneke intends the same cultural critique as the original, it is impossible to view the American remake of *Funny Games* without knowledge of 9/11.

In both versions, George asks Paul multiple times 'Why are you doing this?': the same question asked in *The Strangers*. The first time Paul answers, 'Why not?' The next time, Paul offers a variety of answers: Peter's father left his mother for another woman; Peter's mother dominated him, making him 'gay and a criminal'; Peter is 'white trash' from 'a filthy, deprived family'; Peter is a drug addict;

and Peter is a 'spoiled brat ... jaded and disgusted by the emptiness of existence'. Paul concludes, 'None of what I said is true. You know that as well as I do.' He then asks, 'You happy now, or you want another version?' Haneke's point is that there is no satisfactory answer. No answer could or would adequately justify, explain or excuse the violence these strangers have heaped upon this family. There is no motive. Nothing gives reason to what happens to this family. There are only the 'funny games', the psychological and physical abuse of this family until all of them are dead before nine in the morning and 'Peter' and 'Paul' move on to the next family they will terrorize.

Whereas Haneke himself states that he was inspired to make this film while researching a previous one,[7] and forced to read about motiveless crimes by bourgeois youth who kill or hurt others 'in order to feel something', the idea of motiveless, random death reads differently in 2007 than in 1997 and in an American film than in an Austrian.

The remake, like the original does not show the extreme violence, although the occasional slap, hit, kick, or blow from a gun or club is still seen. The violence is mostly heard, in an attempt to make it less exploitive. Its after-effects, however, are clearly seen. After Peter shoots Georgie, his body lies on the floor and Haneke shows a television screen spattered with his blood. As the camera pulls back, a larger blood spatter is on the wall. George's body is left on the floor after he is shot. Anne's death is almost an after-thought, pushed overboard into the water to drown off the back of the sailboat. All three family member's deaths are, in Žižek's terminology, 'terrifying ... absolute and incomparable' (2002: 51). The deaths are random, committed by malevolent men with nothing personal against those they kill.

Missing from remake is a significant moment in the original. Paul offers Anna a choice of how her husband will die. George tells her not to respond, that the situation is 'enough' and the young men will kill them anyway. In the original, but not the remake, Paul states, 'We're not up to feature film length yet.' Then he looks directly at the camera, and, by extension, the audience, and asks, 'Is that enough? But you want a real ending with plausible plot development, don't you?' Haneke critiques the Hollywood hero complex, the redemptive violence found in such films as *Straw Dogs* and *Last House on the Left* (both of which, it should be noted, have been remade since 9/11), in which the victims successfully fight back against aggressors, turn the tables and kill those who would have killed them. What seemed incredibly disturbing in 1997, by 2007 had become all too common.[8] The bad guys rarely have the tables turned on them, and when they do, everybody still dies.

It is quite telling that this moment is left out of the remake when all the other self-reflexive moments were retained. After 9/11 it is useless to ask if it is 'enough'. It is already apparent that the only 'plausible plot development' is the death of everyone. Both original and remake feature the same, horrific ending. The entire family has been killed in a meaningless orgy of violence. Haneke indicts the audience watching, for their desire to see such things, but the ending itself resonates much more strongly in the remake. Americans are terrorized, killed, and their killers move on to the next attack. While Haneke's indictment remains at the centre of the film, the audience's willingness to accept such an unremittingly bleak ending (despite the fact that it is indeed the most plausible scenario that the killers will succeed in killing and not be hurt themselves) is shaped and tempered by the experiences of a post-9/11 world.

Paul never gives a real answer to the question 'why are you doing this?', but the answer 'Because you were home' fits here as well. George and Anne come to the attention to Peter and Paul because they stopped at a neighbour's house on the way to theirs, asking for help. The young men were already playing their 'funny games' with Fred, Eve and Jenny, the neighbours. After killing George, Anne and their son, the young men move on to Betsy and Robert's house, as they had met them while playing with Anne and George, the implication being that the young men choose their next victims simply by meeting friends or neighbours of their current victims. George, Anne and Georgie die because they know Fred, Eve and Jenny, and live next to them. Betsy and Robert presumably die next because they knew Anne and George and just happened to stop by while Paul and Peter were there. Death is random. One is selected to die simply because the young sociopaths notice you.

Death itself wants you dead

Although the first *Final Destination* film was made and released in 2000, the sequels use the concept to embody the idea of random and anonymous death, with victims stalked by death abstracted and personified. The films offer the paradox of random anonymous death actually being part of a plan. As established in the first film, in which high school students, who get off a plane which subsequently explodes after one of them has a vision of it happening, die mysteriously in the order they would have died in the plane explosion. Death itself has a plan: people must die in order. If something upsets that order, death works to re-establish order by killing teenagers in visually interesting ways.

The first film concerned a plane (hence the title) exploding upon takeoff. To date, four sequels have followed since September 11. The title 'Final Destination' only really makes sense for the first film, which involved a plane flight. The second film concerns death's pattern with a traffic accident, the third a roller-coaster accident, the fourth film (called *The Final Destination*, for some reason) features an accident at a racetrack and the most recent one a bridge collapse, none of which have 'final destinations' (which is a commercial aviation term, and two of which – the third and fourth – simply involve riding in a circle, so that the 'final destination' is also the starting point). Titular inaccuracies aside, the films all follow the same basic premise: an individual sees an accident before it happens, removing several people from the site which would have otherwise resulted in their deaths. After those who did die are mourned and buried, the 'survivors' are killed one by one by death itself.

In the face of motiveless malignity, a killer is not even needed. Death itself seeks to kill those who are supposed to die in accidents according to some cosmic plan. When they survive the accident in which they were supposed to die, death provides new, random ways to die: being strangled in the shower, burning to death in a tanning bed, being decapitated by a faulty elevator, being diced by a barbed wire fence thrown by an exploding gas tank, etc. Death is nothing if not inventive.

The *Final Destination* films ultimately do not make sense. One person has vision, which spares some from horrible deaths. Death then stalks those that survived. The person sees the pattern, and apparently death playfully warns those about to die and sends cues that their demise is eminent. Death then uses Rube Goldberg devices to bring about horrible painful death to those marked to die. One wonders why the protagonist was given the vision in the first place and by whom. The only logical explanation (one is never offered in the films) is that death itself sent the visions, generating terror and fear in those about to die. The invention of Final Destination and its sequels is that death is not the result of a malevolent monster at work, death *is* a malevolent monster at work. Death is a terrorist, creating maximum fear, pain and trauma, not just in the one killed but in his or her friends and family.

Survivors of random death

Frank Furedi posits, after R. Coward, that 'risk-taking heroism has been increasingly replaced by stress-bearing heroism,' in which our culture celebrates 'being able to take it, rather than doing something about it' (2006: 178). The corollary being 'the ridicule directed at the aspiration of human control' (2006: 179). Furedi argues that 'survivors' and 'damaged people are celebrated' (2006: 91). Post-9/11 horror follows this model as well. Heroics change nothing. Despite their efforts, the victims in *The Strangers*, *Funny Games* and the *Final Destination* movies suffer greatly physically and psychologically before they are finally killed. In *Scream 4*, Sydney is referred to by the media as 'professional victim Sydney Prescott'. 'Stress-bearing heroism' becomes the model of the post-9/11 horror protagonist. We mourn those who are the victims of random and anonymous death and then celebrate those who survive.

Robert Jay Lifton posits, 'As a result of 9/11, all Americans shared a particular psychological experience. They became "survivors". A survivor is one who has encountered, been exposed to, or witnessed death and has remained alive' (2003: 137). Thus, we are all survivors. Those who are alive after September 11 are survivors of September 11. Horror film viewers, in that sense, are pseudo-survivors. We look upon death (as a special effect or an actor's performance) and remain alive. We celebrate our ability to bear the horrors that we witness on the screen.

The Strangers, *Funny Games* and *Final Destinations* two through five also represent a kind of containment. The deaths may be random and anonymous, but they are also limited. The three killers in the first do not harm the Mormon boys who are approaching the house. 'Peter' and 'Paul' can only play their funny games one house at a time. It will take them many years to reach the numbers killed on 9/11. And, despite twist endings, the *Final Destination* films at least suggest that death can be avoided for a while. Terrifying though all these films are, they also remind us of the limits of random and anonymous death. Frank Furedi accuses the media and politicians of inflating the abilities of terrorists: 'If, indeed, the terrorists can strike any place, any time and with any weapon, they must possess some formidable superhuman powers' (2007: 7). Not even the Nazis nor the Soviets have ever been seen as unstoppable super-monsters who could destroy everything and everyone at any moment.

Yet the reality is, the United States has been kept relatively safe since 9/11. As will be outlined in Chapter 8, the level of fear of terrorism is out of proportion to actual incidents of terrorism. Survivors are celebrated because they have survived that which killed others. We are survivors who recognize that we do not have control, but we can take certain measures to reduce random and anonymous death.

4

'Torture Porn' and What It Means to Be American

But [America] goes not abroad in search of monsters to destroy ...

JOHN QUINCY ADAMS
INDEPENDENCE DAY ADDRESS, 4 JULY 1821

We believe that the worst thieves in the world today and the worst terrorists are the Americans. Nothing shall stop you except perhaps retaliation in kind. We do not have to differentiate between military or civilian. As far as we are concerned they are all targets.

USAMA BIN LADEN
MAY 1998[1]

I always knew the Americans would bring electricity back to Baghdad. I just never thought they'd be shooting it up my ass.

AN ANONYMOUS YOUNG IRAQI
BAGHDAD, NOVEMBER 2003[2]

We don't kick the (expletive) out of them. We send them to other countries so they can kick the (expletive) out of them.

ANONYMOUS U.S. OFFICIAL QUOTED IN THE *WASHINGTON POST*, 26 DECEMBER 2006[3]

In 2006 in *New York Magazine*, David Edelstein coined the term 'torture porn' to describe a trend he saw in recent films such as *Saw*, *Hostel*, *Wolf Creek*, *The Devil's Rejects* and even *The Passion of the Christ*. Edelstein points out that *Hostel* begins as a teen sex comedy, with young American men headed for parties, inconsequential sex and perhaps even a little growth experience while travelling through Europe. 'The director, Eli Roth, captures the mix of innocence and entitlement in young American males abroad,' he writes (2006). Then we see one of the young men wake up in a filthy dungeon, tortured as he screams and pleads: 'he doesn't understand *why* he's in that place' (emphasis in original). Edelstein does not understand why we, the audience, are in that place either. He wonders why American filmmakers and audiences are so interested in torture.

Edelstein's answer is that such films are a form of masochistic sadism. We identify with both torture victim and, then, torturer. Edelstein asks what possible 'moral use' might exist for such extremes of prolonged, personal violence. He then reaches the conclusion: 'Post-9/11, we've engaged in a national debate about the morality of torture, fuelled by horrifying pictures of manifestly decent men and women (some of them, anyway) enacting brutal scenarios of domination at Abu Ghraib. And a large segment of the population evidently has no problem with this.' Edelstein thus sees two driving factors in the rise of 'torture porn': the wide dissemination of visual evidence of Americans torturing prisoners in Iraq and the fact that many Americans, including the administration (both then and now) find such practices acceptable. Quoting James R. Schlesinger's *Final Report of the Independent Panel to Review DoD Detention Operations*, Danner cites Abu Ghraib as a place where 'acts of brutality and purposeless sadism' were committed by Americans on Iraqis (2004: 41). The photos were seen all over the world, evidence of what Jane Mayer calls, 'a policy of deliberate cruelty' that was seen all over the world (2008: 228). Recent American use of torture neither began nor ended with Abu Ghraib. Mark Danner reports that by early 2004, from media reports it was an obvious truth known all over the world, 'that since the attacks of September 11, 2001, officials of the United States, at various locations around the world, from Bagram in Afghanistan to Guantánomo in Cuba to Abu Ghraib in Iraq, have been torturing prisoners' (2004: 10). The government used the euphemism 'enhanced interrogation', which many around the world took to mean 'torture'. In addition, the United States introduced a policy of 'Special Rendition' in which individuals would be seized and transported to an ostensibly allied country where torture was not against the law, allowing us to make the argument that 'we' did not torture, even though the person being renditioned was taken to their destination specifically for the purposes of torture, as indicated in the final epigraph above.

This book has thus far argued that popular culture and specifically horror films reflect the world as we perceive and experience it. 'Torture porn' thus rose to prominence as torture rose to prominence within our media and national debates. Yet horror films displaying scenes of extreme graphic violence are considered differently, perhaps given horror's history of already displaying such images. These films occupy a unique position and have, perhaps unfairly, been singled out by critics. Jeremy Morris observes that films such as *Syriana* (2005) and *Rendition* (2007) are not considered 'torture porn' despite containing lengthy scenes of torture (2010: 43). Morris advocates for four distinctive features that render a film 'torture porn', instead of merely a film containing scenes of torture. First, torture must be 'the primary vehicle of fear', second, the torture must be a 'realistic depiction', third, a rationale must be provided for the torture, and lastly, the victim must then be transformed into a torturer him or herself (2010: 45). We might also note that by referring to a film as 'torture porn', Edelstein and those who have followed imply that these images give some kind of pleasure, perhaps even a form of sexual gratification. We 'get off' on watching people get tortured on screen. In the films considered in this chapter: the *Saw* films (2004–10), *Hostel* (2005) and *Hostel Part II* (2007), *The Ruins* (2008),

Turistas (2006), *The Last Resort* (2009), *I Spit on Your Grave* (2010) and *The Final* (2010), these four elements are all present. Sometimes the torture is not presented as torture per se, as in *The Ruins*, where the application of knife to flesh without anaesthetic is presented as the best possible option for saving a life of those remaining. Yet each of them also provides insight into American torture and what it means to be American in its own way. In post-9/11 horror cinema we have become fascinated by the detailed terror of the calculated inflicting of pain and deconstruction of the human body, especially the American body.

We might also note that in addition to American torture and special rendition, the news was also full of Americans suffering grievous bodily harm. Perhaps W. J. T. Marshall summarizes it best:

> Then, in May of 2004, images of bodies began to proliferate in the mass media, and a new kind of photo op emerges: atrocity photographs and videos of the beheading of American hostages; the dismemberment of American contractors and the display of their mutilated bodies on a bridge outside the city of Fallujah; the flag-draped coffins of American soldiers, and the scandalous torture photographs from Abu Ghraib prison. (2011: 95)

As argued in Chapter 2, the terrorist video and the images of American torture, while not necessarily on a par (Americans were not beheading anyone), were nevertheless perceived in many parts of the world as being remarkably similar.

In this chapter, I consider how 'torture porn' domesticates and controls these images and provides a narrative which justifies them in context and in the world. Films such as the *Saw* series and the two *Hostel* films carry specific tropes: bodies are destroyed slowly, while the victim is alive and aware, someone purposefully inflicts the damage, frequently but not always in the same physical space as the victim. At the very least, the damage to the body is witnessed, if not in person then on video or closed circuit camera. Two possible outcomes result from the torture: a justifiable payback in kind in which the tortured becomes the torturer (in, for example, *Saw II*, *Hostel*, *Hostel Part II*, *I Spit on Your Grave*, but also in non-torture porn films such as *30 Days of Night*) or the individual dies from the torture with no escape (in, for example, *Buried*, *Martyrs* and even implied at the beginning of *Hostel Part II*). Torture porn is not about enjoying being grossed out by tortured bodies (although that may be true for some individuals). For Americans, it is about what we are doing to others, what is happening to us, in both cases why it is happening, and what it means to be American.

The *Saw* films show Americans paying the price for their lifestyle and individual life choices. John (Tobin Bell), AKA Jigsaw, does not directly kill anyone. In the first film the audience learns, 'Technically speaking, he's not a murderer. He's never killed anyone. He finds ways for his victims to kill themselves'. This statement is not entirely accurate, legally, as he places his victims in situations where they will die unless they harm themselves or someone else, which makes him responsible for murder under the law. This statement is accurate, however, in that Jigsaw ultimately does not want the victim to die but to complete the test and survive, learning to appreciate life and sin no more. In that sense, he is a moral scientist. He sets up a situation and observes. The situation he creates, however, his tests, or traps, or games, always involved the painful torture of the human body. In *Saw* a man must climb through razor wire and dies of exsanguination before reaching the exit. In *Saw II* a character must climb through a working furnace in order to reach an antidote and ends up burned to death. *Saw III* sees a man's limbs slowly twisted off his body and another man nearly drowns in pureed pig carcasses, and so forth down the series. The horror of *Saw* is that when Jigsaw decides to test you, you will be tortured; there is no choice and no escape. The only choice is whether you suffer a little, being left scarred by the experience, or you die. Torture becomes an ironic form of self-improvement. Amanda, the junkie, kills her dealer in order to get the 'reverse bear trap' off her head.

In the *Hostel* films, one is tortured because one is an American. Wealthy businessmen and women from around the world come to Eastern Europe in order to torture young people to death, and Americans are the most sought after. Interestingly, in the sequel, it is Americans doing the torturing. So Americans pay a good deal in order to torture other Americans on foreign soil. The next wave of horror after that was not body horror but specifically American body horror: in films such as *Turistas*, *The Ruins* and *The Last*

Resort, individuals are tortured, their bodies broken because they are Americans abroad, although the films also show locals suffering, too. Foreign countries have always been dangerous in American horror films, from *Dracula* (1931) to *Don't Look Now* (1973). After 9/11, however, there is an awareness of the American as target because he or she is American.

With the international revelation of Americans as torturers, however, the situation becomes more complex, especially since, as Edelman notes, above, some Americans approve of our use of 'enhanced interrogation.' Susan Sontag's *New York Times Magazine* article on the images from Abu Ghraib was entitled 'The Photographs *Are* Us'. Osama bin Laden released a video before 9/11 in which he argued that, 'U.S. democracy renders all American citizens morally accountable for the policies of their elected representatives' (Muller 2009: 45). After the pictures of Abu Ghraib were released, Americans began to wonder about our moral obligation and accountability for what was being done in our names. Deeply troubling for many was the idea that 'the U.S. government not only engages in torture but goes to great lengths to conceal such violations' (Welch 2006: 123). Horror cinema began to reflect this concern, the ambiguous relationship between Americans as victims, Americans as heroic defenders of freedom and Americans as torturers. 'Torture porn' was born in the media's presentation of Abu Ghraib and Guantanamo.

The Albert Gonzalez torture memo defined torture:

> Physical pain amounting to torture must be equivalent in intensity to the pain accompanying serious physical injury, such as organ failure, impairment of bodily function or even death. (quoted in 'The Torture Trail' A16)

The photographs, reports and later revelations by both perpetrators and victims revealed what was done: hooding, exploitation of phobias, stress positions, 'beatings with electrical cables', 'suspended by his arms', 'chained naked to a metal ring in his cell wall', and, in at least one case, 'sliced his penis with a razor blade' (Mayer 2008: 220–4). The last one is reproduced, of a sort, at the climax of *Hostel Part II* and in *I Spit on Your Grave*, but all of them are present in one way or another in the *Saw* films. The iconic image of Abu Ghraib was the Hooded Man, also referred to as 'Triangle Man', a hooded figure, standing on a box with his hands wired with electrical wires (Zimbardo 2007: 19). The image of a hooded individual being tortured is frequently repeated on screen as well, including in *Hostel*, when Josh (Derek Richardson) first finds himself in the torture room. What America has done to its alleged terrorist prisoners is repeated on screen, frequently done to Americans.

Philip Zimbardo, one of the creators of the Stanford Prison Experiment, defines evil as, 'intentionally behaving in ways that harm, abuse, demean, dehumanize or destroy *innocent* others – or, using one's authority and systemic power to encourage or permit others to do so on your behalf'(2007: 5; my emphasis). While Zimbardo's definition seems fairly accurate, the difficulty is the modifier 'innocent.' It is not evil to harm, abuse, demean, dehumanize or destroy those who, lacking innocence, deserve it. Zimbardo's concern, both in the experiment and in the book about it in the wake of Abu Ghraib, is that such situations allow for dehumanization, 'one of the central processes in the transformation of ordinary people into indifferent or even wanton perpetrators of evil' (2007: xii). One of the things that happens in *Hostel* and *Saw* and other 'torture porn' films is the transformation of ordinary people into perpetrators of atrocities. In these films, characters' actions are justified because of what has happened to them. When Paxton tortures, demeans and kills the Dutch Businessman (Jan Vlasák) in an airport restroom, the audience does not perceive this action as evil, as he deserves to die – he tortured and killed *first*, and thus is not innocent and therefore morally culpable and deserving of death. If someone deserves to be tortured and killed, then we do not object when they are.

Saw

The *Saw* films present a morally problematic situation. All Jigsaw's victims, in a sense, deserve what happens to them. They are liars, cheaters, adulterers, thieves, drug dealers and those who prey upon the innocent, yet his device for forcing them to come to terms with their own moral failings is to torture them. The films do not present Jigsaw as a moral hero, but he is the centre of the films, even after his death, and the films do present what he is doing in a noble light. In *Saw III*, his trap offers Jeff (Angus McFadyen) the opportunity to forgive those who wronged him, reunite with his wife and protect his daughter. Instead, Jeff's drive for vengeance kills Jigsaw, his wife and perhaps even his daughter. Jigsaw simply insists that just as one expects rewards for making the right choice, one must pay a price for making the wrong ones. But as always, 'the choice is yours'. Tapp (Danny Glover) and Sing (Ken Leung), the detectives in charge of tracking down Jigsaw in the first film, whose very names suggest they are 'song and dance men', giving a good show but not up to the task of actually doing anything, refer to the devices and situations Jigsaw creates as 'traps'. He calls them 'games', but technically, however, they are not traps or games but tests.

The title of the first film, repeated in the sequels, carries multiple referents. Obviously, the initial reference is to the hacksaws he provides Adam (Leigh Wannell) and Gordon (Cary Elwes) ('He doesn't want us to saw through the chains. He wants us to saw through our feet!'). The title also refers to the name he has given himself, 'Jigsaw', after the puzzle piece he leaves as a calling card, either by drawing it on paper or cutting it into the skin of those who do not survive his traps. A jigsaw puzzle is a picture that is then cut up into component parts that individually make no sense. It is only when all the pieces are seen together that the grand design of the image is finally seen. The *Saw* series functions in the same way. Each subsequent sequel reveals that the previous films have only shown small pieces of the puzzle, which expands with each new entry in the franchise until finally Saw *3D* reveals that after he escaped, Dr Gordon joined forces with Jigsaw and has been working with him ever since, unknown to all the other people and former victims (Amanda [Shawnee Smith], Hoffman [Costas Mandylor], and Jill Tuck [Betsy Russell]) also working with him, even after his death.

The title, however, also carries a secondary meaning: the past tense of the verb 'see'. Victims of Jigsaw became his victims because he saw them. And, once he sets a trap, he continues to watch. Established almost immediately in the first film is that Jigsaw always has 'a front row seat' for his victims in his traps, whether via a hole in the wall, a camera recording, or even his actual presence in the room, as in *Saw III*. Jigsaw is not just a cutter, he is an observer. The film concerns watching people being tortured to see if they change their ways, or if they reveal information. Jigsaw looks at larger pictures, which his victims are unable to see, focused on small details instead of the much larger web he is weaving. Even those above-mentioned assistants are not above being tested again, as Jigsaw observes. When his previous test subject seems to be backsliding, as Amanda does in *Saw III*, he again creates a new test in order to observe. *Saw* is about watching as much as it is about torture.

It is in this way that *Saw*, the heart of the 'torture porn' subgenre, is actually about post-9/11 America. It concerns bodies being broken for a moral reason. If the person undergoing the torture makes the 'correct' choice, he or she might be scarred, but he or she will live and will hopefully change their erroneous ways. The films, especially the first, however, make a point that Jigsaw is always watching his victims, whether in person, through a peephole in the wall or via video. It is significant that Jigsaw saw how his victims were living and chose to test them. It is significant that he watches them as they are tested. It is significant that he continues to watch the successful ones.

Jigsaw's victims are chosen for specific reasons. 'Most people are so ungrateful to be alive', he states. Tapp tells Amanda, 'You are, in fact, a drug addict. Do you think that's why he picked you?' Seeing that she must cut open the body of her dealer in order to find the key that will free her head from the 'reverse bear trap' that he has installed on it, thereby literally cutting off her supply, it seems that Jigsaw creates poetically appropriate situations. One must redeem oneself, but in doing so, one will be scarred and perhaps more than a little broken.

Saw 2 even features a 'ticking bomb' scenario in which the clock is counting down, but in reverse. The justification frequently given for 'enhanced interrogation' is that if a terrorist knows a bomb is about to go off, it is morally justifiable to torture him in order to learn where the bomb is and save lives. Jigsaw tells Detective Matthews (Donnie Wahlberg) that if he does nothing for the next 90 minutes, everything will be fine and nothing will happen. Only if he acts will tragedy occur, and he will not be reunited with his son. In other words, the bomb situation is reversed here: by not doing anything, the situation will resolve itself. Matthews refuses to wait past a certain point, tortures Jigsaw, beating him and causing him grave physical harm. Jigsaw agrees to take him to the house on the video feed. The son is, of course, completely safe, appropriately in a time-lock safe with an oxygen supply, which opens after 90 minutes right next to where they were sitting. Because Matthews forced Jigsaw to leave, he finds himself trapped in the house, wounded and locked in a room full of a slow nerve gas.

Like the United States, Jigsaw rarely if ever tortures people himself. He works through surrogates. Zep the orderly (Michael Emerson) is forced to trap Adam and Dr Gordon in the original, charged with killing Gordon's wife if he does not kill Adam by the deadline. After Adam kills Zep, Adam discovers another tape on Zep's body in which it is revealed that he, too, is a victim of Jigsaw. A slow-acting poison has been put into his body: 'Will you murder a mother and child to save yourself?' The use of surrogates to torture suggests America's policy of special rendition, in which third parties do the actual torturing. Yet the question Jigsaw asks is at the heart of America's torture policy: will you harm others, perhaps even innocents who have done no wrong, in order to protect and save yourself? While we may judge Zep for becoming Jigsaw's pawn, the question is answered 'yes' by official United States policy, drafted at the highest levels and approved by the American president. We will torture and murder in order to keep ourselves safe.

Hostel

Hostel functions on a variety of levels and has been read in different ways by different critics. Andrew Schopp argues *Hostel* 'satirizes the American economic exploitation of poorer European countries' (2009: 259). Schopp concludes, '*Hostel* indicts American capitalism by showing exploited countries literally turning the tables by turning Americans into commodities sold for the hunt' (2009: 282). Yet that indictment is undermined by 'inviting the viewer to indulge in the excessive gore and extreme torture scenarios' (2009: 282). Ross Douthat sees *Hostel* as evoking 'al Qaeda execution videos' (2008: 55), while Stephen Prince compares the *Hostel* films with the documentaries *The Ghosts of Abu Ghraib* and *Standard Operating Procedures*, which 'emphasize the stench and appalling filth of the prison' (2009: 284). In a sense, one's reading of *Hostel* is also coloured by one's own ideology and political views.

The name of the film is a play on the homonyms 'hostel' and 'hostile'. The former is an inexpensive hotel for young travellers and the other is feelings of aggression and anger towards another. In both the original and the sequel a small group of young Americans (men in the first, women in the second) go to a hostel in Slovakia where they are kidnapped, imprisoned and sold to the highest bidder to be tortured to death. The hostel, we learn, is run by an organization called 'Elite Hunting', which runs the torture for profit organization. We might compare Elite Hunting with corporations that profit from the war on terror. Former military personnel make better money and have better benefits by working as out-of-uniform mercenaries. There is something of Halliburton, KBR and Blackwater in Elite Hunting. In much the same way, there is something of special rendition in *Hostel Part II*, where American men go to Europe in order to torture and kill their fellow citizens. What would not be legal in the United States is acceptable business in Eastern Europe.

The first film engages the fear of being tortured and the fear of torture in general. The second film engages the fear of becoming a torturer and the ambiguity of rendition, enhanced interrogation and the 'ticking bomb' justification for torture. *Hostel* and *Saw* series are also both a part of a motif of proactive monster fighting, what might be termed 'preemptive violence', echoing President Bush's doctrine of preemptive war. In *28 Days Later*, Mark (Noah Huntley) is not given the opportunity to 'turn'; the second Selena (Naomie Harris) believes he may have been infected she attacks and kills him with a machete. Self-defence now includes killing those who might later become dangerous.

In Hostel, *Paxton* (Jay Hernandez) called Pax for short by his friends, which ironically means 'peace', and Josh, college friends from the United States, tour Europe with Oli (Eythor Gudjonsson), an Icelander travelling with them. They are belligerently American, bringing about a whole series of images and ideas in the film's first 15 minutes on the nature of Americans. 'Kiss my American ass', they tell a club bouncer. They demand to be let into their hostel in

Amsterdam even though the doors are locked since it is after curfew. In response to the ruckus they make, the neighbours begin throwing beer bottles at them. Alex (Lubomir Bukovy) invites them into his flat, saying 'Not everyone wants to kill Americans.' As it turns out, Alex's job is to guide Americans to the Slovakian hostel where everyone pays to kill Americans. Additionally, the Americans themselves do not like Americans. 'Kind of over Amsterdam,' Josh tells Alex, 'Way too many Americans.' The Americans do not like to be around other Americans. The men are tempted to go to the hostel Alex recommends because there are no Americans, but the Slovakian girls supposedly go crazy for Americans. The young men are privileged, self-centred, and in many ways the stereotypical 'ugly Americans'. They want to indulge in a sybaritic pleasure tour of Europe without consequence or responsibility.

In Slovakia, Josh and Oli are the first to be kidnapped and tortured to death. Pax is also sent to a torture room, but escapes. The torture provided by Elite Hunting visually suggests Abu Ghraib, where 'physical mistreatment is combined with humiliation, sexual taunting and sadism' (Anonymous 2007: 60). A former prisoner recounts the use of restraints, a bag over head, being kept naked and receiving physical beatings. The torturers themselves hide their identities (2007: 61). Two American women, he reports, 'were hitting me with a ball made of sponge on my dick. And they were taking pictures of me' (2007: 62). In *Hostel*, the young men are restrained, tied to chairs, bags are placed over their heads. They are kept naked and subjected to beatings and physical abuse. Part of the torture is also psychological: Josh and later Pax are shown the tools that will be used to torture them. Josh's torturer cuts his Achilles tendons and then tells him he can leave. Josh crawls almost all the way to the door before the torture begins again and continues until Josh is dead.

Pax, too is tortured by a European man, but manages to escape. He attempts to free a Japanese girl who is being tortured as well, but when she sees herself in a mirror, she commits suicide rather than live on deformed. Pax escapes and the film ends with him finding the Dutch Businessman at an airport and killing him in the men's room by drowning him in a toilet. Pax is killed at the beginning of the sequel, as Elite Hunting tracks him down and decapitates him for escaping and for killing one of their clients.

The horror of *Hostel* comes from supposedly civilized, educated elite human beings paying for the ability to torture to death their fellow human beings. While the national concern for torture is in this film, two significant factors emerge. The first is that the rest of the world is hostile to Americans, even when they claim not to be. The world is a dangerous place, especially for Americans. The second is that Pax's torture and murder of the Dutch businessman is presented as justifiable and acceptable. Although no one is in any further danger from the man, after all, he killed Josh in Slovakia and is now simply on his way home, Pax is presented as not only justified in seeking revenge but righteous for doing so. Morris's elements of torture porn show that Pax is justified in torturing another man to death because of what he did to his friend (2010: 45). Pax ('Peace'), like America, must use violence and torture in response to violence and torture in order to achieve some sense of justice in the world.

Hostel Part II is the more interesting and more complex film. In the first film, young American men are tortured by European men in a secret prison in Eastern Europe. In the second film, young American women are tortured by American men in a secret prison in Eastern Europe. At home, in suburban United States, Stuart (Roger Bart) is emasculated. He cleans up after breakfast while his wife drives the children to school in hostile silence. His family does not even speak to him. When Todd (Richard Burgi) invites him to Europe for the adventure offered by Elite Hunting, he jumps at the chance. Only outside of the United States may be behave in truly barbaric, masculine fashion. He represents a sense of lost American masculinity that can only be found by leaving the country and performing atrocities that would land him in jail at home.

The final girl, Beth (Lauren German), is a young, independent wealthy woman who literally emasculates Stuart at the film's climax. She is a literal *femme castratrice* in Barbara Creed's sense (1993). Stuart goes to Europe in order to torture and kill someone, hoping it will capture his sense of manhood. Although he initially offers to help Beth, he changes his mind and decides to torture and kill her in order to get revenge on his wife and his children and all the others who have made him feel like less of a man. Beth, however, does not survive by her wits. It is her money that saves her. 'I can buy and sell everyone in this room,' she announces, and she can. Her parent's death left her independently wealthy, whereas Stuart is desperately attempting to pay off a second mortgage. The film, thus offers no possibility for true justice. Beth is allowed to leave because she pays for the privilege of killing Stuart by cutting off his manhood and feeding it to dogs, and gets the Elite Hunting tattoo on her lower back (popularly known as a 'tramp stamp', indicating that she is sexually active and sexually available). Elite Hunting has literally marked Beth: she has no choice in the matter. Elite Hunting is not shut down. Its activities are not exposed to the world. It is her position of privilege that made her an expensive victim, but it is also her position of privilege that allows her to extract herself from the hostel situation (pun intended), get revenge on the man who would have harmed her, and walk free. No other victim is able to do so. Indeed, both of Beth's companions are slaughtered mercilessly.

In the final scene of the film, Beth succeeds not only in surviving but in getting revenge on Axelle (Vera Jordanova), the young woman who brought them to Elite Hunting. There is no sense of sisterhood in this film. Mrs Bathory (Monica Malacova) kills Lorna in order to bathe in her blood, behaving like and named after the historic Countess Elizabeth Bathory. There is no sense of shared nationality in this film. Americans kill Americans in the most painful ways without a second thought. When the head of Elite Hunting demands that one of the pack of feral children from the village must be killed, the others push one forward and watch his death emotionlessly. This is a film in which human life is literally bought and sold and no other social relationships are honoured.

Linnie Blake sees in the American victims in these films a dangerous mindset. Speaking of *Cabin Fever*, she writes that the characters 'claim freedom as a right, yet display no awareness whatsoever as to the responsibilities of liberty' (2008: 140). These privileged, young Americans wander the globe, 'unequivocally proclaiming their own class and regional superiority' (2008: 140). Blake is writing of 'hillbilly horror' in which wealthy urban college students (or recent grads) head to the rural areas for some 'deserved' recreational time, resulting in a conflict with locals that itself results in the urban dwellers being hunted and killed. I extend her analysis to the various torture porn films which feature the same characters in a third-world country. Whether rural America (*Wrong Turn* and

Cabin Fever, for example), rural Mexico (The Ruins, The Last Resort), rural Brazil (Turistas), or provincial Slovakia (Hostel, Hostel Part II), privileged Americans assert their right to do what they want when they want, and pay the price, frequently with their lives. Hostel itself begins with Pax, Oli and Josh being kicked out of a nightclub in Amsterdam for fighting. As the bouncers push them out, Josh screams, 'I'm an American! I got rights!' and Pax flips them off. This single exchange captures this sense of aggressive privilege lacking any sense of responsibility simply because one is an American, regardless of context. The characters of Hostel are belligerently American.

American ignorance is on parade in these films, specifically the ignorance of the educated elite of the younger generation (who are also, paradoxically, the target demographic of these films, not to mention of this volume). Blake writes, again of Cabin Fever, that it 'can also be viewed as an extremely forceful indictment of the ignorance and complacency of a generation that has managed to graduate college without learning a single thing about the world, their country or themselves' (2008: 141). This observation holds true for all of the films listed in this chapter. Beth in Hostel Part II is not saved by her resourcefulness, her knowledge or her self-awareness. She is saved by her bank account. She buys her way out of trouble abroad.

Some Americans abroad

A major motif in torture porn is the idea of young Americans abroad being tortured and exploited for a variety of reasons. The cautionary tales seem to suggest that if foreigners could get their hands on Americans they would do far, far worse than we have done to them. Films such as Turistas, The Ruins and The Last Resort all show young American tourists enjoying themselves in Latin America and being tortured and killed as a result.

The Ruins, based on the novel by Scott Smith, sees young Americans, recent college graduates, visit Mexico for a final hurrah before separating for their professional lives. They meet a German and some Greeks and agree to visit some Mayan ruins in the nearby jungle, which are being excavated by the German tourist Mathias's (Joe Anderson) brother and his girlfriend. As they approach the pyramid, they are initially warned off by the indigenous people until they step on the vines covering the pyramid. Dimitri (Dimitri Baveas), the Greek, is then shot by the Mexicans, driving the others up the pyramid.

Attacked by vines, the young Americans and their German associate find themselves trapped on a Mayan pyramid by the indigenous Mexicans where they are injured, slowly dehydrated and forced to tend to each other's injuries with rudimentary medicine at best. Interestingly, much of the body violence in this film is thought of as a positive and even necessary thing to cope with the unpleasant situation they find themselves in. After Mathias breaks his legs falling down a shaft in the ruins while looking for his archeologist brother, he implores the American medical student, 'Cut off my legs.' Later, when the vines enter Stacy (Laura Ramsey), she cuts herself to get them out and then tells the others to 'do it' when they want to finish the job. Eventually, one by one, the characters are killed by the vines and their bodies consumed until Jeff (Jonathan Tucker) sacrifices himself so that Amy (Jena Malone) can escape. In the original theatrical ending Amy escapes in a jeep and returns to the resort, which is different from the novel, in which everybody dies. In the DVD version, Amy escapes, but the vine is in her body and she takes it with her back to 'civilization'. In an alternate ending, Amy's funeral is held in a cemetery in the United States. The final shot is of the 'evil' flowers and vines now growing on Amy's grave.

The Ruins features two dangers: the Mexicans and the vine. The Mexicans first try to warn people away from the ruins but must then prevent anyone from leaving the ruins once they enter. Not only do they kill Dimitri and threaten to kill the others, they kill a Mexican boy who is struck by a piece of vine thrown by one of the Americans. The multiple nationalities complicate things. The Europeans and Americans are vacationing in Mexico. They are wealthy and privileged. They go to visit local ruins and ignore the warnings of the indigenous people who then must kill them or watch them die. It becomes clear that the pyramid's defenders do not want to kill or enjoy killing the foreigners, but must do so in order to prevent the vine from spreading.

The vine itself is the worst danger. It is intelligent and cunning. It can mimic sounds (such as pretending to be a cell phone or a human voice). It is insidious in that it can lull an individual to sleep, enter their body surreptitiously and begin devouring from within. The goal of the vine, confined as it is to a rural area in a third-world country, is to escape from this place and spread around the world, hence the terror of the alternative ending, above. The Americans themselves are innocent and naïve and believe that their incursion onto the pyramid is nothing serious. Unaware of the threat of the ruins, they blindly walk all over them and are completely unprepared for the attacks by both the vines and those charged with preventing the vines from ever leaving the pyramid.

The Americans in this film, and their European associates, are not evil. They are self-centred, self-important, privileged and unaware of how their behaviour will impact the local population, but though such ignorance is no excuse, it is not malevolence. The film, however, depicts the very ground, the plants, the nature found in this third-world country as being hostile to Americans. We might interpret the murder of the boy in a less charitable light, if it is viewed as the shooting of a local who has been contacted and corrupted by the Americans. The twenty-somethings of *The Ruins* are hardly an occupying force, but they are Americans in a third-world country where they do not speak the language, do not know the customs and are in constant danger from the threats around them, which they remain blissfully unaware of until it is too late.

Along the same model are films such as *The Last Resort* (2009), in which a group of young American women, a bride-to-be and her four bridesmaids travel to Mexico for a final hurrah before the wedding. While one of them meets a young American man and stays in town, the others take a tour of the countryside where they are robbed, beaten and left for dead at a haunted resort. Just as in *The Ruins*, where graduation from college serves as cause to leave the country and visit a nation that claims to be an ally, but is not as safe as it seems. *Turistas* (2006) also features a group of twenty-something American backpackers stranded in Brazil where they are captured by bandits who harvest organs for profit. In all of these films, Americans roughly the same age as those fighting in the Middle East travel to a nation where they are not safe. The young people are then set upon by the dangers of the foreign land, in the form of evil foreigners, natural and supernatural terrors and their own naiveté. Being an American does not protect them. Being an American, as in *Hostel*, in fact, makes them targets.

Ambiguously justified torture

Barbara Creed identifies the original rape/revenge film *I Spit on Your Grave* as 'still misogynistic' (1993: 129). Jennifer Hills's revenge on the men who raped her is 'deliberately eroticized' and she becomes a female monster 'defined in terms of her sexuality' (129; 3). As a *femme castratrice*, quite literally, she emasculates the leader of the men while seducing him in a bathtub. In the 2010 remake, no such erotic revenge takes place. Instead, Jennifer (Sarah Butler), like Paxton and Beth, turns the tables on her torturers and justifiably tortures them.

As in the original, Jennifer Hill, a writer, travels to a remote cabin in the woods to finish her book. She is set upon by a group of men, five in this case, and raped and tortured. They film the rape. They hold her head down in a puddle while violating her. Finally, the most sadistic one, who is also the local sheriff (Andrew Howard) anally rapes her. They carry her body further into the woods, in order to kill her, but she leaps from a bridge into a river and is carried away by the current.

In the original, she then uses her body to seduce the men and once they believe she is no threat, she kills them. Not so in the remake. Dressed in clothing more suggestive of the military than suggestive of being suggestive, she begins to stalk and terrorize the men who did this to her. One awakens to find himself tied up and suspended on wooden planks over a half-filled bathtub. She removes one of the planks, causing his head to drop into the tub, simulating drowning. While meant to serve as poetic justice, as he was the one that pushed her head into the puddle while raping her, the entire scene suggests waterboarding, as the man is strapped to boards and drowning. She then adds lye to the water, so not only does he drown, but the flesh on his face and head is eaten away and he dies slowly and painfully. The garage mechanic and ostensible leader of the group (Jeff Branson), is tied up naked, abused and finally castrated and left to bleed out. Until the end he displays aggressive masculine bravado, but he is unable to punish her in any of the ways he threatens to. He simply dies painfully, emasculated and abused. Finally, the sheriff who anally raped her is first terrorized by threats to his daughter and wife and then trapped and rendered unconscious. When he wakes up, he discovers himself tied to a table, bent at the waist, with a shotgun inserted into his anus and the trigger tied to the hand of his unconscious friend. When the man wakes up, he lifts his hand, pulling the trigger and killing both of them.

All of the images in the film are lifted directly (if, perhaps presented more extremely) from Abu Ghraib and Guantánamo. Naked men, suspension in chains, waterboarding, stress positions, beatings, chokings, all designed to humiliate and cause pain are present. The woman does not use her sexuality or her sensuality to lure the men into a false sense of security, she brutalizes them, rendering them incapable of resisting before she finally kills them. It is a standard rape-revenge film, but the extremes of violence on both parts make one wonder whether or not we should be supporting Jennifer either. The audience is clearly on her side, but she does not just get revenge: she humiliates, violates and terrorizes them as much as they did her. Therein lies the justification. At heart, the rationale behind *I Spit on Your Grave* is, they did it first. The satisfaction one derives from watching the film emerges from knowing that the men 'deserve' everything that happens to them. Torture, humiliation and terror are justified if one is using them in response to the same. Like the end of both *Hostel* films, it is acceptable for an American to do this to those who did this to Americans.

The Final (2010) ostensibly echoes school shootings, in which bullied students take revenge on their tormentors, but it is actually a study in the making of torturers and in how far one will go in torturing others in order to avoid being tortured oneself. A group of bullied students plan a party for the popular kids at their high school and spike the punch. When the popular kids wake up, they are all chained to the floor and threatened with death. Very few people are actually killed in this film, and most of them are suicides or murders within the circle of the bullied. Instead, the popular students are tortured: a football player has his knee destroyed with a device used for killing cows, another is paralyzed and tormented with acupuncture needles.

The bullied then reveal themselves to the bullies and the games begin in earnest. A girl is offered the opportunity to cut fingers off another football player in order to go free and escape the same fate. She declines initially, saying, 'I could never hurt anyone,' to which her daily victim responds, 'You hurt me. Every day.'

In *The Final*, there are echoes of 9/11 and of Americans using torture. A small group takes a large group hostage using its own culture against it (partying, drinking, etc., causes the popular kids to lower their defenses). Dane (Marc Donato), the leader of the bullied, tells his victims, 'Some of you will be spared, but you will all bear witness to the horror.' The bullies get hurt, but they are only part of the target. The audience is everyone chained to the floor, forced to watch the football players and cheerleaders get tortured and then torture one another, just as they 'stood idly by in the hallways and did nothing to stop the bullying'. One football player has his fingers cut off, a cheerleader has her face covered in an acid paste which deforms her. Several of her fingers are also cut off. Lastly, a football player has his spinal cord severed, so he can neither play football nor have sex ever again. The torture is, as in *I Spit on Your Grave*, ironically appropriate – the popular kids have the things that make them popular (beauty, athletic prowess, etc.) taken from them, so that they are now the freaks and outcasts. Those who watched bullying and did nothing must now watch torture and cannot do anything. Yet, as in *I Spit in Your Grave*, while we sympathize with the bullied, their methods are extreme, violent and difficult to watch.

'Now it's your turn to ask, "why us?",' Dane tells the captive crowd. 'Where did all this evil come from?', he rhetorically ponders. The point he, and the film, make is that the torture is justified in the face of the bullies' behaviour and in the face of the indifference of the crowd to the violence done against those who have done nothing wrong, committed no sin. This is a vision of America as underdog, using techniques it would otherwise abhor against an enemy that respects nothing else. The violence is necessary in response to the situation. The torture is unfortunate, even appalling, but it is justified by the actions of those who are being tortured now.

Yet, at the same time, the audience is not encouraged either to enjoy the torture or empathize too much with either group of victims. Instead, the audience realizes that bullies and bullied, both of whom have been shown to be mean-spirited tormentors encourage us to reflect upon a situation in which torture seems like a reasonable answer. Jeremy Morris advocates:

> The enjoyment of torture horror is not necessarily immoral. The prevailing theme of the torture horror genre is the attempt to share the purposes, intentions and feelings behind realistic torture. By putting the audience on the side of the torturer in some way or other, the audience is disturbed in a way that goes beyond the fear generated by bare depictions of torture. (2010: 55)

The hope behind such films is that while we are disturbed by the torture, and fear is generated by its depiction, we are not the complacent, accepting audience that Edelstein fears. We do not find 'such practices acceptable', but we go the cinema to come to terms with the fact that this is being done by Americans, in our name, to keep us safe. As such, the films disturb the audience but give us an out: the torture is necessary, vital and will make a difference. Torture porn is disturbing, not only for its depiction of torture, but because it frequently justifies 'our' use of it. The saving grace is that even in the face of regressive messages, it is still impossible to make actual depictions palatable.

5

Hopeless Bleak Despair, or How I Learned to Stop Worrying and Love *The Mist*

I never knew what everybody meant by endless, hopeless bleak despair Until one day when I found out ...
They Might Be Giants
'HOPELESS BLEAK DESPAIR'

Numerous nihilistic horror films were made before 9/11 featuring bleak endings with the death of many or all the main characters, including, but not limited to, John Carpenter's *The Thing*, *Night of the Living Dead*, *Deathdream*, *Children Shouldn't Play with Dead Things*, and *Se7en*, to name but a few. In the underrated *Halloween III: Season of the Witch* (1982) ends with Daniel Challis (Tom Atkins) begging a television station manager to turn off a commercial that will cause the heads of all children wearing Silver Shamrock masks to dissolve and release venomous spiders, snakes and insects, which will subsequently attack and kill parents, siblings and anyone else nearby, an act of terror planned by Conal Cochran (Dan O'Herlihy), an Irishman and toy maker who wishes to return Hallowe'en to its Celtic roots as Samhain. The film ends ambiguously with the suggestion that it is too late and many, many children are dying hideous deaths as the credits roll.

Post-9/11 horror did not invent the bleak ending. It did not feature the first films in which all the protagonists die. The cultural shift after 9/11, however, has greatly increased the number of films which end bleakly, which display a nihilistic world view, or which clearly demonstrate that sometimes death is not the worst thing that can happen. Sometimes those who survive catastrophe experience greater anguish than those who die. Films such as *The Mist*, the *Saw* Series, *Drag Me to Hell*, *Buried*, *The Last Exorcism*, *Paranormal Activity* and its sequel, and *Insidious* all demonstrate a nihilistic core, an ending that offers only hopeless, bleak despair in the face of death, anguish and torture. Post-9/11 horror, more often than not, spells the death of hope. These are films which offer the audience a portrait of hopelessness. Douglas E. Cowan refers to this trend as the 'denial of catharsis' (2008: 261). The narrative does not allow for the purging of pity or fear, in an Aristotelian sense. This chapter explores exemplary films that deny catharsis and promote nihilism and despair.

9/11, nihilism and despair

Both on the day itself and in subsequent reports of the events, such as in documentaries, books such as *102 Minutes* and even the 9/11 Commission Report horrifying situations are and were presented in which there was no good choice. For example, on the top floors of the North Tower, some theorize that in the face of certain death, the only thing left was a choice: burn to death or jump to death (Flynn and Dwyer 2004: A1). Even worse were individuals who found conference rooms or offices 'protected from fire by walls' who called loved ones and were on the phone up until the moment the buildings collapsed

(Flynn and Dwyer 2004: B8). Many believed that they would be saved or that they were safe until the very end. Those on the phone with loved ones on United 93 heard everything, including the sound of the plane hitting the ground, signifying the death of the person on the other end of the phone. Many of the experiences of 9/11, both on the day and recounted afterwards are tales of hopeless, bleak despair, of nothing to be done, of helplessness in the face of a tragedy one knows is coming but powerless to prevent, of dark nihilism.

While popular culture often focuses on heroics and the positive stories (it is no coincidence that the two major narrative films directly about September 11 are both heroic films, in which actions have efficacy: *World Trade Center*, in which firefighters rescue their own from the smoking debris, and *United 93*, in which passengers fight back against terrorists, heroically sacrificing their lives to save others and possibly themselves), the bleak stories, the nihilistic narratives, have been displaced into genre cinema, into horror, thrillers and science fiction. Characteristic of this nihilism is the impossibility of rescue. There are no more 'final girls', or heroes, or authority figures who know what is going on and can stop it. In post-9/11 horror cinema, there is no God, there is no authority figure that can fix the situation, nothing saves us and everybody or almost everybody dies. Those left behind are forever scarred and haunted by what they have endured. Susan Faludi reminds us that 9/11 represents a massive failure on the part of every major institution in the United States (2007: 12). The military, elected representatives, the airline industry, the police, the FBI and everybody in between failed to protect, to keep us safe, to prevent the tragedy and to respond effectively. While the attack on the Twin Towers was spectacular and terrifying, and the number killed exponentially higher, much more disturbing to my mind at the time was the ability of the terrorists to crash a plane into the Pentagon, the headquarters of the entire Department of Defense and our armed forces. If our military could not even protect its own nerve centre, what hope was there for the rest of the nation? 9/11 represented a failure of the administration to heed warnings that came in the form of Presidential Daily Briefing entitled 'Bin Laden Determined to Strike in US', delivered on 6 August 2001, slightly more than a month before the attack. Even with a warning, the government failed to act, to protect, to do its job.

A dominant trope of post-9/11 horror, therefore, is the failure of leadership and authority figures to protect, the inability of the things we believe in to stop catastrophe (whether that be prayer, the police, God or government), and the resultant death and destruction which follows. Combined with this despair at being rescued or saved is a deeper despair of having to watch loved ones die (or even directly or indirectly causing their deaths) and/or suffer great pain before doing so. 9/11 did not invent the bleak ending, but it made it not only believable but probable. The rewind moment in *Funny Games* is designed to directly demonstrate to the audience that Hollywood conventions of the hero or heroine getting a lucky break and getting a weapon away from the villain, or escaping from the situation or even stopping the monsters in time is just that: a convention. In reality, the likelihood is that everybody dies. *Funny Games* and *The Strangers*, both explored in Chapter 3, are excellent examples of the post-9/11 nihilist horror film. The example I wish to carefully consider in this chapter, however, is an adaptation of a Stephen King novella that offers one of the bleakest visions of a post-9/11 America.

The Mist

The Mist is a 2007 film based on a novella by Stephen King first published in an anthology entitled *Dark Forces* in 1980 and circulated widely in a slightly different form in King's 1985 collection *Skeleton Crew*. A storm has knocked out the power in a small Maine town, and so David Drayton and his son Billy go to town to get supplies. As they wait in the supermarket, the town is covered in a mist, which hides monsters. Various creatures, both giant and small, imperil the denizens of the supermarket. It is suggested that the mist may be the result of 'Project Arrowhead', a top secret government experiment being carried out at the military base outside of town that has possibly opened a hole to another dimension. As characters begin to get killed by the creatures, the survivors band together, but begin to fall into two groups. One remains rational but wary, the others are the followers of Mrs Carmody, a fundamentalist Christian who sees the mist as part of the last days and judgement of humanity as outlined in the book of Revelation. She has her followers sacrifice a young soldier, since he serves at the military base where 'the demons' were unleashed. After David has a sexual liaison with Amanda, a young woman trapped in the supermarket with them, Mrs Carmody raises up her followers against 'the fornicators' who will bring God's judgement upon the supermarket.

Taking the gun from store manager Ollie Weeks (who is killed as they try to escape out to David's car), David, Billy, Amanda and Mrs Reppler (a kindly retired school teacher) escape the supermarket and drive away. David, who narrates the tale, tells the reader that there are three bullets left in Ollie Week's gun. 'There were four of us in the Scout, but if push came right down to shove, I'd find some other way out for myself' (1985: 147). They drive south, out of Maine, the mist now blanketing everything as far as the eye can see. Eventually, stopping at a Howard Johnson's, they rest and David writes the story and then relates that he thinks he hears a word on the otherwise static-filled radio. He then whispers two words in his son's ear as Billy sleeps:

Two words that sound a bit alike.
One of them is Hartford.
The other is hope. (1985:154)

The story then ends with that word. Although the world seems to be covered in the mist and the creatures it has unleashed roam free, this small group has escaped the dangers of the fundamentalist society forming at the supermarket and now have a plan and a destination. Also, they were able to safely move from the car to the Howard Johnson's, not to mention presumably refill the gas tank along the way, so the immediate dangers seem to have lessened. The novella ends in hope and a potential respite from the terror.

The film is a very different story, so to speak. Adapted and directed by Frank Darabont, who also did *Shawshank Redemption* and *The Green Mile*, both hopeful in their endings, *The Mist* follows much of King's original story, but offers a much bleaker ending. The Mist is a film without heroes, where action is punished and inaction is punished and those with deep religious beliefs cause death and destruction. *The Mist* is also about how we narrate disaster to ourselves.

The Mist begins with a catastrophe – an enormous storm that pushes a tree into painter David Drayton's (Thomas Jane) studio, ruining the painting commissioned by a publisher. He then discovers that a neighbour's tree has fallen on his boathouse, crushing it. Just then his wife (Kelly Collins Lintz) notices a mist across the lake. While Drayton states it is nothing unusual, she observes that the mist is coming off the mountains into the lake, instead of the other way around. Both the storm and the mist are markers of something wrong, the natural world rebelling against something happening in the mountains.

That something is 'The Arrowhead Project', which Norton (Andre Braugher), David's neighbour from New York, asks about when they pass a military convoy on the way into town. Drayton tells him it has something to do with 'missile defense research'. Although the men laugh at local rumors about the base, they grow uneasy at the sight of so many military vehicles moving so quickly. Upon arrival at the store, David makes small talk with locals like Ollie (Toby Jones), Sally (Alexa Davalos), Mrs Reppler (Frances Sternhagen) and Mrs Carmody (Marcia Gay Harden). The film establishes a small community coping with a major storm: nothing life-threatening but 'damn inconvenient'.

Then a siren sounds, suggestive of both fire alarms and cold war civil defence alarms. Darabond shows the faces of the concerned townspeople as a bloody and terrified Miller (Jeffrey DeMunn) runs into the store screaming, 'Something's in the mist!' A panic is sparked and the supermarket doors are shut as other run to their cars. The ones who ran are heard screaming in the mist. As on 9/11, those in the supermarket wait and watch and guess at what is happening. An earthquake strikes the building, further terrifying the trapped people. Thus far, images from 9/11 have been subtly deployed: the mist itself rolls through the town in a greyish cloud like the smoke, dust and debris on 9/11, the earthquake suggests the building is being struck by something, crowds watch and scream as the first deaths occur. Unlike *War of the Worlds*, *The Mist* is more subtle in its echoes of September 11.

A woman (Melissa McBride) must leave to get home to her children. The others try to convince her to stay, but she cannot. Her eight-year-old daughter is watching her infant son and she cannot leave them for long. She begs someone to go with her. No one will.

'Isn't anyone going to help me?' she asks. 'Won't somebody here see a lady home? You? You?' The men she specifically asks cannot make eye contact with her. Drayton, holding Billy, tells her 'I got my own boy to worry about.' She walks out angrily, saying, 'I hope you all rot in hell.'

It is a powerful moment that adequately summarizes the conflicting needs of the moment. The woman wants someone to help her, but what she is asking is for someone to sacrifice their own life, perhaps needlessly. Because she must go home, she wants someone else to go with her and most likely die horribly. The others do not want her to go. The fact that she leaves alone confirms their own fears and cowardice, although one might ask by what right she asks others to die so that she can leave. The irony, of course, is that at the end of the film, we see the same woman, with her children, alive and well among a group of survivors in a military convoy. Drayton by this point has just shot his own son. Had he and Billy left with the woman, there is a good chance they, too, would have been rescued by the military. This shot of the surviving family confirms the randomness of death in the mist as well. Although all those who ran for their cars seemed to die, Norton's group was seemingly attacked and killed, and even Ollie Weeks eaten just as he had reached the car, this lone woman and her two young children survived. They did not survive because of her courage or because she proved to be resourceful. The film never shows how or why she (and they) survived. Just that they did.

The moment when she departs the supermarket also demonstrates the loss of heroics discussed in Chapter 3. Initially, at least, there are no 'risk-taking heroes' in the supermarket. The men beg the woman not to leave, as much for their own sake as hers, so they do not have to feel guilty for not helping her. Instead, the supermarket is filled with Furedi's 'stress-bearing heroism', people whose defining characteristic is that they can keep 'taking it' (2006: 78). It is only when the situation inside the supermarket grows more dangerous than the monsters in the mist, primarily through the efforts of Mrs Carmody and her followers that Drayton, Amanda and Ollie decide to leave. Their decision to go is not a heroic one; it is a simple matter of self-preservation.

After the woman leaves, the people in the supermarket are confronted by an increasingly terrifying series of attacks by the creatures in the mist. As the group tries to figure out what is happening, and different explanations are offered, Mrs Carmody proposes that it is 'judgment day'. At first ignored by the group, she begins to gain adherents as hers is the only narrative that matches the facts and offers an opportunity to escape the situation. She promises that they will be saved if they offer expiation. She also accurately predicts a death and then the subsequent period when the group is left alone, lending credibility to her knowledge.

After Drayton hears a noise in the back store-room, a group of men go to investigate. They do not believe him that there is any danger in opening the delivery door, which is odd, considering what they all just saw a few minutes before. The men argue about which one of them will go out and David says, 'You guys ... you, well, you don't seem to understand or you're tryin' real hard not to.' This accusation, which angers the men, is also a major theme of *The Mist*. The situation is very dangerous, but most of the people in the supermarket choose not to understand, or to change their understanding of the situation in order to carry out the actions they want to do anyway. Drayton is incredulous: 'You guys are going to let this kid risk his life over a generator we don't even need?' The men threaten to beat him up if he does not shut up. His warning, which is merited based both on what they have seen and what he has heard, is met with aggressive denial. Ollie correctly observes, 'They've lost their sense of proportion.'

A trope of the horror film is the person in denial about the reality or depth of the threat which the community faces. After September 11, however, this trope is expanded, showing the unbeliever as militantly and aggressively unbelieving, even in the face of evidence that he, she or they is wrong. It is not coincidental that *The Mist* was made in 2007, four years into the Iraq war, although Frank Darabont had planned on producing it much earlier. Aggressively religious and nationalistic individuals use the central crisis of the film to push their own agendas and to attack anyone who disagrees with them.

When bagboy Norm (Chris Owen) is attacked by a tentacle, only Drayton tries to save him. The men who were mocking him a moment ago stand frozen with fear, unable to respond. Though Drayton begs for help, they do nothing. Aggressive posturing and ignoring danger, the film suggests, is worse than bravado or false heroism, it gets people killed. Again and again in *The Mist* Darabont shows members of the group wilfully ignoring the real dangers and embracing inaccurate hopes. Norton ('an important attorney from New York. That fellow could be on the bench one day,' states Ollie, framing him as both New Yorker and a powerful person in the social structure, suddenly rendered irrelevant by the mist) believes they are playing a trick on the out-of-towners, and despite the screams he heard earlier refuses to accept that the others are genuinely afraid of what is in the mist. He wilfully believes that other people are using the situation to prank him, rather than understand the actual danger, and decides to leave. In one brilliant series of shots, while the majority of people attempt to pile things in front of the window, Norton argues that the evidence is flimsy (and is repeatedly called 'Mr Lawyer' for his trouble), Carmody argues that judgement is at hand. Both are in denial. Carmody wants people to 'prepare to meet their maker', Norton wants people to 'discuss this rationally' and the only option left open to the others is to pathetically pile bags of dog food in an attempt to protect themselves. Religion does not help. Rationality does not help. Denial does not help. Despite the evidence, Norton chooses to believe his own paranoia, that this is 'a pathetic attempt at a joke' and leads a group out into the mist. At least one member of their group, who agrees to have a 300-foot clothes line tied around his waist, is cut in half and killed. The implication being that everyone else is also lost. Later, in the pharmacy, some of the missing people's bodies are found, serving as incubators for monstrous spider eggs. While Norton and Carmody both believe they have the answers and are doing the right thing, both are clearly doing damage and bring death to themselves and others as a result.

With each incursion, either of humans into the mist or mist creatures into the supermarket, people die painfully and horribly. Others must watch as bodies are dissolved, broken apart, eaten or otherwise destroyed. There are no quick deaths in *The Mist*. Interestingly, there is also little to no humour. The horror is bleak and unrelenting, with no opportunity to relax or laugh. Even during quiet moments of seeming safety, such as when the storeroom door is closed again and the men escape back into the supermarket, the depth of the danger is suddenly highlighted. 'We shut the loading door,' argues Jim (William Sadler) when Ollie says they must create a strategy for preventing the thing 'that those tentacles were attached to' from entering the store. With a grim look Ollie responds, 'Yeah, but the entire front of the store is plate glass.' The camera captures the reactions of the other men as they realize the depth of their vulnerability. 'It appears we may have a problem of some magnitude here,' the supermarket manager (Robert Treveiler) announces, employing the traditional euphemistic language of the politician. As noted above, the only defence is to pile bags of dog food.

Wilful ignorance of the danger, exploitation of the danger in the service of religious fundamentalism, personal agendas and blind panic become the dangers within the supermarket, just as the monsters in the mist form the dangers without. The second half of the film then builds the tension, the despair and towards the not-inevitable conclusion (which is what makes the film more heartbreaking – the ending was not inevitable). As the small group that has gone to the pharmacy gathers supplies, they discover the bodies of the group that went out before. These individuals are all cocooned and hanging from the ceiling or attached to the walls. The group then discovers they are alive. The M.P. from the beginning of the film (Amir Joseph) begins screaming and twitching and then his body begins hatching small, spider-like monsters, which brings their much larger parents, which are capable of shooting webbing that disintegrates human flesh. Bobby's (Brandon O'Dell) leg is destroyed and another man is killed by the spiders. The horror of the scene comes not only from the potential death from the monsters but that the death is not quick but slow and painful. The M.P. is aware that he is being consumed from within by the spiders. He tells the others, 'I can feel them' right before they burst out of his face and chest.

The other soldiers hang themselves when Private Jessup (Sam Witwer) tells them that the M.P. claimed that 'we' (i.e. the military and Project Arrowhead) brought about the situation. Carmody then whips the crowd up and has them believing 'she has a direct line to God'. She demands 'expiation', a sacrifice which will appease God and make Him call off the monsters. She commands the crowd to sacrifice Jessup, as he stands for the scientists, the military and all those who 'go against the will of God'. 'Walking on the moon, or splitting His atoms or stem cells and abortions', are the examples she gives of how science has defied God. 'The fiends of hell have been let loose,' she tells the crowd and calls Jessup 'Judas'. The crowd beats Jessup, stabs him repeatedly and then throws his still-living body outside the store to be consumed by the monsters. Jessup tries to explain that he was merely stationed at the base, a mere private with nothing to do with the experiments, but she tells him he must die for his sins. As his blood smears the doors of the supermarket, he is quickly seized and pulled away.

The horror now comes not from (or at least not only from) the monsters outside but the crowd inside and their fundamentalist leader. We are horrified at how easily the citizens in the supermarket are led astray and encouraged to kill one of their own. The small group of rational people remaining, decide to leave. Interestingly, in the novella, Carmody turns upon Drayton and is able to convince the crowd to join her because David has a brief but adulterous tryst with Amanda. No such tryst happens in the film, nor is it needed. Carmody does not need a reason to turn on David, the fact that he does not follow her religious agenda is enough. Conversely, David in the film is a good family man whose first stop upon leaving the store is his own home, in order to rescue his wife.

As David, Billy, Ollie, Amanda, Dan, Cornell (Buck Taylor), Bud, Myron (David Janssen) and Mrs Reppler attempt to flee, Mrs Carmody stops them and demands that the crowd kill Billy, telling them that these people 'who refuse to bend to the will of God', who 'mock us ... mock our God, our faith, our values, our very lifestyle, and our humility and piousness', and who 'piss on us and laugh' have 'brought this down on us'. Carmody uses the crisis to advance her own religious agenda and get revenge on those who dared to challenge her beliefs. Just as the night before, she blamed Jessup, now she blames this small group and demands human sacrifice in the form of Billy. As the crowd begins to riot, she screams, 'Kill them! Kill them all!' The fundamentalist Christian has taken over the society of the supermarket and is driving them to fight and kill in the name of God, demanding the sacrifice of soldiers and children. It is fairly easy to read into this a larger metaphor for the American condition, in which leaders who claim to be deeply religious demand the sacrifice of our soldiers in order to drive their own agenda. Likewise, one can also read a metaphor for al Qaeda in this situation, in which religious fundamentalists drive others to commit violence in God's name, killing innocents, ostensibly to please God but actually to continue to satisfy the leader's twisted agenda.

Mrs Carmody's terrorism in the supermarket ends with two bullets from Ollie Weeks, leaving her in a cruciform position with blood spreading out around her head like some sort of murderous halo. The group flees the supermarket, but only David, Billy, Amanda, Dan and Mrs Reppler reach the car. Ollie is snatched and consumed by some giant monster. The other men get lost in the mist and find themselves confronting the spider-creatures, who kill Myron and Cornell. Only Bud makes it safely back to the supermarket. As with any horror film, the group of survivors is limited to a very few. Some of the horror arises out of the slow shrinking of the group as individuals die or get left behind (in *Aliens*, or *Hatchet* or *Night of the Living Dead*, for example). The group is now down to five people, who drive off past the supermarket, seeing the faces of those now left behind.

It is from this point on where the movie differs most from King's novella, in which although David knows he can use Ollie's pistol, he will drive on in hope to Hartford. Likewise, in the novella, we never learn what happens to David's wife. Upon leaving the supermarket, David drives home to see his house covered in the webs that the spider creatures make. His wife's body is mounted in the window, witnessed as a monster roars in the distance. 'I told her I'd fix it. Front window... . broken open,' he laments, blaming himself for her death. He weeps while Amanda holds the sleeping Billy. Then he drives on.

They pass a school bus with some dead bodies in it, overturned cars on the freeway. At one point, a giant creature, so large it cannot be seen completely from below in the mist, passes over them (another moment taken directly from a single line in the novella). The film clearly demonstrates that the mist is seemingly endless. There is no Hartford, there is no hope. The car falters and runs out of gas. Through a series of close-ups and two-shots, Darabont shows the realizations of the people in the car. Amanda begins to weep quietly, Dan resignedly says, 'We gave it a good shot. Nobody can say we didn't.' Then the noise of roaring and something approaching is heard. The adults in the car make eye contact and nod. David sighs, looks in the gun and finds four rounds left. As he re-loads it, the gun is in the foreground and the sleeping Billy on Amanda's lap comes into focus. Darabont draws out the moment by panning across the adults with a close-up of each face, ending on Amanda, tears quietly streaming down her face. The last shot inside the car is of Billy, slowly waking up, seeing the crying Amanda and then looking at his father, recognizing the gun and his eyes grow wide as fear washes over his face.

We are then shown the outside of the car through the mist and witness four muzzle blasts with the sound of four gunshots, followed by the sound of David screaming The camera cuts to back inside the car. Behind him, Dan's corpse is visible, but no other body is. He does, however, have his son's blood spattered all over his face. He continues to scream and pound the dashboard, placing the now empty gun in his mouth and pulling the trigger repeatedly. In a suicidal fit, he leaves the car and begins screaming 'Come on! Come on!' to the approaching roar. As he stands in the road waiting to be killed by the monsters, the mist begins to part and the low rumble he has been hearing is revealed to be an army convoy. In slow motion, a tank emerges out of the mist two minutes and five seconds after he begins firing. Soldiers wearing bio-warfare units walk past, followed by a civilian transport holding the woman and her two children from earlier. A soldier with a flamethrower burns cocoons and kills some of the monsters as the sound of helicopters passing overhead is heard.

Drayton sinks to his knees and asks, 'They're dead. For what?' and then begins screaming uncontrollably while two confused soldiers stand over him and the camera then pulls back to reveal the mist completely dissipated and a large military force moving through the area, cleaning it of threats. He shot his son, thinking he was saving him from a fate worse than death, but instead there was no reason for his son or any of the others to die. He killed them and then he lived to see the pointlessness of it, how unnecessary their deaths were. As horrifying as the first hour and 50 minutes of the film are, the last two minutes are what fills the viewer with a bleak despair. It is bad enough all the other characters died. These last four, including a child, died needlessly at the hands of one of their own who thought he was helping them, and who thought he was being heroic by not shooting himself, since there were only four bullets left.

The film makes clear in virtually every scene that heroics and bravado are useless and get people killed. Yet even David must be taught this lesson again at film's end.

The title of the film is *The Mist*, referring to that which obscures the actual things attacking. The title might also tangentially refers to the blinding aspect of fear that cripples the community in the supermarket, forcing it to look for easy answers, especially those provided by Mrs Carmody. The mist is a marker of a changed world, but it is not the actual threat itself. The mist is not dangerous, but what it hides is. These sentences thus far could refer to either the film or the book, but *The Mist* on screen takes on an additional aspect. The mist never dissipates in the novella, but it does vanish at the end of the film. When it does, it reveals that what is in the mist is not always dangerous. The real danger is in overreacting to threats because of recent experiences. The real danger is in acting at all without all the information. David kills his own son to spare him a horrible death in the mist, but the thing that was approaching was not a monster, but rescue. Billy Drayton should be alive, but was killed by his father in a panic without all the information.

In the end, *The Mist* is about two things: how we interpret disaster and how we choose to respond to threats, especially when we do not fully understand them. *The Mist* shows the danger of denial. *The Mist* shows the danger of retreating into fear or fundamentalism. *The Mist* shows the danger of wilfully ignoring the evidence and what those who have witnessed the danger tell you. But at the end, *The Mist* shows that even those who know, who are not in denial, who have acted as best they can under the circumstances and placed the welfare of others at the highest priority can still make the wrong choice, leading to deadly consequence that they must then live with. The film ends with the woman who begged for help and received none united safely with her children and David kneeling in the mud, screaming in pain and despair, knowing he killed his own child just as they were being rescued. The film closes not only with images of despair, but with a bleak nihilism. Every choice was wrong and the only person for whom the situation resolved satisfactorily was simply lucky. She could have just as easily died, or returned home as David did, to find her children consumed by monsters. Perhaps that is the final takeaway from *The Mist*: life is unfair. Some live, some die horrible deaths, some kill their children seconds before they are rescued and must live with the consequences and the knowledge, and there is no reason for any of it.

'I need you hopeless': films that end in despair

Saw (2004) ends with despair. The final 15 minutes is a cascade of death, torture, self-mutilation and the final revelations, all of which indicate that none of it was necessary, as in *The Mist*. Zep (Michael Emerson), whom the film has framed as the Jigsaw killer, kills Tapp (Danny Glover), the police officer obsessed with catching him. Gordon (Cary Elwes) saws off his own foot, and, in an attempt to save his wife and daughter even though the deadline has passed, shoots Adam (Leigh Wannell) in the shoulder. Ironically, neither of these actions were necessary. Gordon's wife and daughter are safe by this point. Adam then beats Zep to death with a toilet tank lid when Zep arrives to kill them. Adam is still chained and Gordon is bleeding to death when Gordon crawls out of the room, promising to go get help and 'bring someone back'. Later sequels confirm this does not happen: Adam's dead body is found in the room, and a footless corpse is also seen, although Gordon shows up in *Saw 3D*, in yet another reversal and indication that all is not what it seems.

Adam discovers that Zep was not the Jigsaw killer but yet another of Jigsaw's victims. As he learns this, in the background, the body that has been on the floor for the entire film then stands up and removes its head wound, revealing it to be makeup. The 'dead' body is the real Jigsaw, who tells Adam that the key to his chain was in the tub he woke up in, and that it went down the drain when he emptied the tub. Adam begins screaming as Jigsaw turns out the lights, closes the door behind him as he leaves, telling Adam, 'Game over.' This ending then set the model for every subsequent sequel, which relies upon a montage of flashbacks to show the full 'picture' of the Jigsaw puzzle, set to a building soundtrack which emphasizes the horror of the situation. In each subsequent film, it is revealed that the protagonists have failed the test Jigsaw has set, and they are either dead, left to die, or horribly mutilated for the rest of their lives. The *Saw* series is, at heart, a group of films that ultimately offers no redemption, no hope, no expectation that 'we're going to be OK', as Gordon tells Adam in the original film. Instead, all *Saw* protagonists, just as they believe they are safe, find themselves in anguish, both physical and psychological, and trapped in a situation that will only end in their agonizing death. While audiences might find such endings satisfactory, the ultimate result is a bleak nihilism. In the average *Saw* film the audience watches half a dozen people die painfully in hopes that the protagonist will successfully complete his or her test. Instead, at the conclusion of the film, all deaths were in vain, as the protagonist also perishes despondently.

Paranormal Activity and its sequels are continued exercises in helplessness and hopelessness. In the first film, Micah (Micah Sloat) believes he can stop the demonic infestation that has troubled Katie (Katie Featherston) on and off since childhood. After an increasingly terrifying series of events, she tells him, 'You are absolutely powerless.' No one else can help her. The psychic (Mark Fredrichs) she consults initially offers some suggestions, but as the seriousness of the problem becomes apparent (she is troubled not by a ghost but by a demon) he cannot and will not help her. The demonologist he recommends is unavailable for several days. No one can help her. Micah finds a website that tells the story of Diane, a name that the oiuja board he borrowed spelled out. Diane had all the same events happen to her in the sixties. Initially, Katie thinks that the website will then give a solution. Instead, it reveals that Diane sought out an exorcist, whose work only made things worse and she died horribly. In other words, the very thing that solved the problem in other films such as *The Exorcist* did not work. Eventually, Katie is possessed, kills Micah and vanishes. The film closes with a text that states her whereabouts are 'currently unknown', implying that a demon-possessed Katie is still running about Southern California.

The first sequel offers additional information on the back story. Katie's ancestors made a deal with a demon that allowed it to take the first-born male. The first male in two generations is the son that Katie's sister Kristi (Sprague Grayden) has brought home from the hospital. When Kristi's husband Daniel (Brian Boland) discovers the terrifying reality of the situation, he carries out a ritual which will send the demon to the nearest living relative. This explains why the demon returned to pursue Katie in the first film. His effort to sacrifice his sister-in-law to save his son and family backfires, however, as the now-possessed Katie kills him, his wife and takes the child, leaving his daughter Ali (Molly Ephraim) an orphan and the sole survivor of the family line.

A major theme of the horror films of the last decade is that exorcism does not work. For every film such as *The Rite*, in which the exorcist himself is possessed, but then exorcized through the power of faith held by a formerly faithless clergyman (very similar to *The Exorcist*, one might note), there are many films in which faith, ritual and prayer offer no hope or help. *The Exorcism of Emily Rose* ends in the death of the title character. Though she willingly accepts death, believing it will bring others to believe, before she finally dies she is repeatedly terrified by apparitions, physically abused (jury members are shown turning away from the autopsy photos of her face), and made to undergo numerous painful experiences. Her family must watch her slowly deteriorate, eat insects, transform into an unrecognizable, diabolical stranger and then die painfully. Father Karras (Jason Miller) may die at the end of The Exorcist, but Regan (Linda Blair) did not. Father Moore (Tom Wilkinson) lives in *Emily Rose*, but Emily (Jennifer Carpenter) does not. *The Last Exorcism* carries this trope further by ending with the death of every major character. The rituals offered by various psychics in *Drag Me to Hell* are unable to rid Christine (Alison Lohman) of the Lamia after her, which eventually does indeed drag her to hell. Similarly, *The Last Exorcism* ends suddenly with the deaths of the camera crew and the exorcist himself. No one is saved, no one is rescued, no one even really knew or understood what was happening at the Sweetzer farm.

The family does not fare well after 9/11. *Insidious* (2010) features a family whose eldest child Dalton (Ty Simpkins) goes into a coma just as the parents begin to believe the house is haunted. They move to a new home only to discover that it is not the house that is haunted, but the boy. He is not in a coma but astral projecting, and a demon has imprisoned his soul in 'The Further', a spiritual borderland where disincarnate spirits attempt to take over the bodies of the living. When psychic Elise (Lin Shaye) is called in to help, she reveals that

Dalton takes after his father, Josh (Patrick Wilson), who could also astral project as a child, but was in danger of being possessed by the ghost of an old woman (Philip Freidman). Josh enters The Further, finds and frees his son, despite being under assault by numerous ghosts and spirits, and leads his son back to his body. Josh, however, is confronted by the old woman and stops to scream at her that he is no longer afraid of her. Dalton wakes, to his mother's and grandmother's delight. Lin, however, uses a digital camera to take a picture of Josh, who then strangles her to death. Renai (Rose Byrne), Josh's wife, finds the body and wonders why he killed her. She then looks at the camera and realizes her husband's body is now possessed by the spirit of the old woman. The last image of the film is Renai's terrified face.

Pre-9/11 this might have simply been a twist ending, but the film sets up the entire situation from the beginning, with a pre-credit sequence showing the old woman outside Josh's childhood home. The entire film is thus framed as a sceptical man who learns to believe in the reality of the supernatural in order to rescue his son, but he was also a target for possession all along. The old woman now possessing him kills the one woman who might have been able to exorcize her. Though the boy has been rescued, the family is now in great danger from the old woman in his father's body. Like *Paranormal Activity*, an enmity that began long ago manifests in the present and results in someone being possessed and killing those they love with no hope of redemption or release.

In *Buried* (2010), Paul Conroy (Ryan Reynolds) wakes to find himself in a coffin buried somewhere in the Iraqi desert. The film identifies itself as taking place on 23 October 2006, near Baqubah, Iraq. Conroy was a civilian truck driver who has been kidnapped and buried in the hope that his company will pay ransom money. He calls 911 in his hometown of Youngstown, Ohio, then his employer. He speaks with his captors who tell him to get the money or he will die. His employers inform him he was terminated that morning for an inappropriate relationship with a co-worker, although it is clear this is their excuse to not pay the ransom or expend resources to rescue him. He speaks with his wife as the casket fills with sand. Initially, he thinks he might die, but he is reassured by 'Dan', a man who is coordinating the rescue effort, that they think they know where he is.

Paul tells his wife, 'The Americans are coming for me ... It's going to be OK.' He listens to the sounds of the rescue on the phone and Dan tells him that they have opened the casket. It is clear from the film that the American forces have rescued another kidnapping victim. Paul's coffin is almost full of sand. One of the last things Paul hears is Dan's voice on the phone saying, 'I'm sorry, Paul. I'm so sorry'.

On the one hand, this ending resonates in the wake of 9/11, especially when one learns of the phone calls made on that day. Betty Ong, a flight attendant on one of the hijacked planes was the first to call her airline and let them know of the hijacking. Calls were also made from the passengers on United 93 and the people trapped in the Twin Towers. Heartbreaking messages were left on answering machines and voice mail of those who did not answer the phone that morning. The echo of those calls is heard in a variety of horror films in which people say goodbye to loved ones over the phone or by using a camera or camera phone to record their last moments.

On the other hand, this ending is very nihilistic. Paul thinks he will be rescued at the end, even believes his rescuers are nearly there, just inches from the coffin lid, and instead hope is dashed away just as he begins to suffocate to death. In the last seconds of film, the audience watches knowing that Paul knows he is about to die horribly. Paul is not a victim of a slasher; he is not trodden upon by a giant monster; he is not eaten by zombies. He is the only character we have seen in this film in person (others have been heard on his phone), and we have come to know him. He is not particularly admirable or heroic, but we recognize him as a human being, a scared, human being all alone in a box under the Iraqi sand. Unlike the victims mentioned above, where the audience is aware that the frightening thing is not real, *Buried* presents a plausible scenario, brings us to be concerned about its flawed protagonist and then lets us watch as he is given hope and has it taken away and then begins to slowly die.

Conclusion: no catharsis

As Jennifer (Megan Fox) tells Colin (Kyle Gallner) just before she kills him and partially eats him in *Jennifer's Body* (2009), 'I need you hopeless.' For the demon possessing her, it is not enough to kill or for her victim to die, the victim must also feel hopeless and lost. She tells Chip (Johnny Simmons) that his girlfriend was cheating on him before she bites him. The negative emotions feed her, but they also serve as emblematic of the post-9/11 sense of horror. Before the characters die, the film must also demonstrate the hopelessness, bleakness and desperation of the situation. The urge driving someone to jump out a window on the hundredth floor of a burning building is reflected in a man sawing off his own foot in *Saw*. We are not just going to die – we will be literally dragged to hell in front of the ones we love (*Drag Me to Hell*). We will be possessed by dark forces and made to kill those we love (*Paranormal Activity*, *Paranormal Activity 2* and *Insidious*). After the devil has killed everyone else in the elevator, (s)he will kill the remaining person in front of the person they love the most (*Devil*). The situation is not only horrifying, it is bleak and despairing.

Father Karras (Jason Miller) dies at the end of *The Exorcist*, but Regan (Linda Blair) is freed of demonic influence. Buffy might lose a few friends along the way, and others will be scarred, but in both the film and the television series *Buffy the Vampire Slayer*, she is triumphant in defeating the evil and driving the 'big bad' out of her community. Nancy (Heather Langenkamp) defeats Freddy on more than one occasion, as Laurie Strode (Jamie Leigh Curtis) does with her brother Michael Meyers. Even Rosemary felt maternal stirrings for her baby. After 9/11, her possessed sister would simply take the baby, kill her and disappear, never to be seen again.

I close then, returning us to Cowan's 'denial of catharsis' (2008: 261). The narrative does not allow for the purging of pity or fear, and instead we leave the cinema or turn off the DVD with no sense of relief. When the film is over, the evil is still present in one's mind, undefeated and victorious. Parents have killed children for no reason, everyone dies regardless of the choices they make, demons win and the coffin fills with sand. There is no hope, no small solace, no cause for limited comfort. Indeed, hope is only offered in order to be taken away at the last minute so as to increase the despair. We are left lonely, isolated, despondent and without the possibility of redemption of any kind. Endings in post-9/11 horror cinema are, by and large, just that in every sense of the word: the end. There is no redemption, no catharsis, no final girl who will live and perhaps even be spared a sequel, allowing others to encounter the killer. There is no happily ever after. There is only death, despair, hopelessness, anguish and misery. Everybody dies. Or worse.

6

Fear of/from Religion

> *In a country where almost two-thirds of the population believes in the devil, Bush was identifying Osama bin Laden and his gang as literally Satan.*
>
> DAVID FRUM
> THE RIGHT MAN[1]

> *There are no more dangerous people on earth than those who believe they are executing the will of the Almighty.*
>
> ARTHUR M. SCHELSINGER, JR.
> WAR AND THE AMERICAN PRESIDENCY[2]

In her fascinating *The Age of American Unreason*, Susan Jacoby notes that religious fanaticism was 'critical to the motivation of the attackers' on 9/11, yet 'everyone was busy denying that "real" religion had anything to do with terrorism' (2008: 200). In the media and particularly in the academy, an effort has been made to separate the very real faith and religious beliefs of the terrorists from Islam itself, often mentioning that the terrorists do not represent what Muslims actually believe and that the term jihad, 'religious war' is misunderstood in the west. Conversely, the War on Terror has frequently been cast in religious terms, especially by those fighting it. Lt. General William G. 'Jerry' Boykin, the Undersecretary of Defense for Intelligence, in a speech to evangelical Christians, delivered while wearing his dress uniform, stated that Islam was a false religion created by the devil, and that, 'The enemy is a spiritual enemy. He's called the principality of darkness. The enemy is a guy called Satan' (quoted in Cooper 2003: A1). Boykin added, 'Satan wants to destroy this nation, he wants to destroy us as a nation' (Cooper 2003: A1). Boykin insisted that God put President Bush in the White House so that he could fight Islamic terror and lead the United States to being a Christian nation. Boykin described his fighting the militia of Osman Ali Otto, a Muslim warlord in Somalia, in religious terms: 'I knew my God was bigger than his. I knew my God was a real God and his was an idol' (Cooper 2003: A1). Although there was public outcry at Boykin's understanding of the war and his terminology, others agree with him and continued to cast the wars on terror and in Iraq and Afghanistan in religious terms.

Twin streaks regarding religion have existed in the United States since its inception. The first is a deeply religious one that sees the United States as both exceptional by grace of God and having a special destiny, as exemplified by John Winthrop's characterization of it in 1630 as a 'city upon a hill'. The challenge of this streak is the reality of what Cotton Mather called 'the invisible world'. In his 1693 book defending his conduct during the Salem witch trials, Mather saw the witches as genuine tools of Satan, out to destroy the young colony. While Susan Faludi argues that the Salem witches threatened to 'disrupt male control' (2007: 234), and thus large numbers of women (and a few men) were accused and executed, we must also remember that to the Puritans, the genuine fear of the devil in their midst is not to be discounted. The invisible world is real to the Puritan mindset, as it is to the contemporary American evangelical. Satan is real; angels and demons are real; and their actions have efficacy in reality.

Furthermore, central to the Calvinist theology of the Puritans is the belief in the innate depravity of all human beings. As children of Adam, we are all born in sin and doomed to hell. God has allowed a precious few elite to be saved by grace, but nothing one does can or will save one's soul. We are innately corrupt, wicked and decadent, our bodies and minds prone to give into temptations to sin that further degenerate us. America has, in short, always been concerned with the devil(s) in our midst, and with perceived spiritual decline and genuine spiritual warfare, both internal and external to humanity. The devil is real and we are inclined to weakness and wickedness. America is deeply religious and believes in the reality of devils, witches and principalities and powers of evil and we should fear the weakness of the sinners who have given themselves over to the devil, as they will further weaken this nation.

The second streak is a deep distrust of public religion, exemplified by Nathanial Hawthorne's 1850 novel *The Scarlet Letter* and Sinclair Lewis's 1927 novel *Elmer Gantry* (which, parenthetically, was also made into an Academy Award-winning film with Burt Lancaster as the eponymous clergyman in 1960). In the former, the village clergyman is revealed to be the man who had an adulterous affair with Hester Prynn and is the father of her illegitimate child, resulting in her having to wear the title letter. In the latter, Gantry is evangelical preacher who is also a hypocritical voluptuary and epicurean. He is the opposite of everything he preaches, yet despite causing a great deal of pain (including death) to those around him, engaging in adulterous affairs and destroying a genuine holy man, Gantry becomes minister to a large congregation in the Midwest. The novel ends with Gantry demanding his parishioners believe he is innocent of the charges leveled against him in the media. As they 'thunder' their assent, he prays for 'the domination of the Christian church throughout all the land' and asserts 'We shall yet make these United States a moral nation' (1970: 416). He cloaks his own degeneracy in the language and culture of evangelical Christianity. Twinned with its deep abiding religious belief, the United States also distrusts public religiosity and suspects clergy of hypocrisy. The past three decades have witnessed numerous scandals, both financial and sexual, that have highlighted this hypocrisy in American religious culture: Jimmy Swaggart, Jim and Tammy Faye Bakker, Ted Haggard, Bob Moorehead, John Paulk, Lonnie Latham, Paul Barnes, George Alan Rekers and Marcus Lamb, among many others, not to mention dozens if not hundreds of Catholic priests have fallen from grace in sexual scandals.

Lastly, religion has always been a presence in horror cinema. This presence is overt in *The Exorcist*, *The Omen* and many other films, particularly in the late sixties and seventies when the counter-culture prevalent in Hollywood distrusted all traditional forms of authority. Multiple pre-9/11 films feature preachers, priests or deeply religious people as the villains. The danger of fundamentalist belief is present in characters such as Margaret White (Piper Laurie) in *Carrie* (1976). Religion and dangerous clergymen formed the background for many millennial horror films such as *End of Days* (1999), *Stigmata* (1999), *Bless the Child* (2000), *Lost Souls* (2000), or even the *Prophesy* series of films (1995, 1998 and 2000) which feature angels turned evil, most notably in the form of Christopher Walken as an evil Gabriel. The passing of the year 2000, in theory, should have ended the millennial film cycle. Instead, the terror attacks of September 11 were rooted in an extreme version of Islamic fundamentalism. They were intended by their authors to begin a religious conflict between Muslims and the West. They have also had the unintended effect of bringing the horror of fundamentalism and religion to the forefront again. Yet, almost no American horror films are rooted in Islam. There are very few straight horror films rooted in Iraq and Afghanistan. In fact, *Red Sands* (2009) is the only horror film of which I am aware that is actually set in Afghanistan. There was actually more Middle Eastern-based horror before 9/11 in films such as the *Wishmaster* series (1997, 1999, 2001), in which the monster is a demonic *djinn*, or the original *The Exorcist*, which begins at an archeological dig in Iraq and in which the possessing entity is not, in fact, the devil but Pazuzu, an Assyrian wind demon.

After September 11, the fear of religion and of those who hold fundamentalist beliefs again rose to dominance in horror cinema. There are two streams of religiously based horror that emerge in the last decade. In the first, fear is generated because the religious teachings about evil are correct. There is a devil, there are demons, evil does exist and it can and must be fought and exorcized. By means of example, films concerning exorcisms and exorcists began to proliferate after 9/11: two prequels to *The Exorcist* (*Exorcist: The Beginning* (2004) and *Dominion: Prequel to the Exorcist* (2005)), *The Exorcism of Emily Rose* (2005), *The Unborn* (2009), *The Last Exorcism* (2010) and *The Rite* (2011), not to mention films such as *Drag Me to Hell* (2009), which in addition to positing in its very title the reality of hell also employs a New Age exorcism which goes awry. In the second, the fear is of religion itself, especially fundamentalism. In other words, religion itself is the problem. There is a subcategory of this stream in which fundamentalist Christians are revealed to actually be Satanists, as seen in such films as *The Reaping* (2007), *The Last Exorcism* and hinted at in *House of the Devil* (2009). We might consider these films the descendants of *Rosemary's Baby*, in which upper middle class Manhattanites are revealed to be Satanists. In this case, however, Satanism is not merely hiding behind the façade of middle class respectability, it is the driving force hiding behind fundamentalist Christianity. The very individuals one would presume would despise Satan are, in fact, in his diabolical service and out to kill or destroy 'regular' Americans. A more recent combination of these streams are films which feature warriors for God who have grown tired of killing in His name, but are confronted by real evil and must combat it, as exemplified by *Black Death* (2010), *Priest* (2011) and *Season of the Witch* (2011). This chapter examines these tropes of post-9/11 horror.

'The enemy is a guy called Satan'

Given General Boykin's pronouncements, it is not unusual that films such as *Devil* (2010), *Insidious* (2010), *The Exorcism of Emily Rose*, *The Reaping*, *The Last Exorcism* and *Drag Me to Hell* all take the reality of the devil, demons and hell seriously. They show a world in which evil is real, in which hell is real, and in which Satan and God are actually battling for control of the world. Both have agents among humankind. Even in graphic novel adaptations such as *Constantine* (2005), in which Keanu Reeves plays a Los Angeles-based supernatural detective who has literally been to hell and back. The audience is told, his is the only soul Lucifer himself (Peter Stormare) would come from hell to take, and the conclusion of the film confirms this supposition. The film reveals a conspiracy between the son of Satan and the angel Gabriel (Tilda Swinton) to bring about a war between heaven and hell, carried out on earth. Not only is hell real, but the forces behind Christianity (Gabriel, after all, was the angel that announced the birth of the saviour to Mary in Luke 1. 26–38) are aligned with the forces of hell to bring about hell on earth.

Horror cinema has, perhaps more than any other genre, always acknowledged the reality of evil, as well as its personification in devils, demons, monsters and spirits. As I argue in Chapter 9, the decade before 9/11 was dominated by human monsters. The nineties was the era of the serial killer, who is evil morally but not supernaturally. The sociocultural shift under the Bush administration after the terror attacks returned supernatural horror to the forefront. George W. Bush made religion a centre of his presidency, introducing government partnerships with 'faith based charities' and injecting religion into major decisions. During the 2000 campaign, he noted his favourite political philosopher was 'Jesus Christ' and he subsequently used his own religious beliefs to limit stem cell research. As W. J. T. Mitchell notes, until 9/11, cloning and stem cells were a central concern of the Bush administration, in its focus on the 'culture of life' (2011: 1). Even before 9/11, the government had publicly embraced religion and used Christianity as a guiding principle in making policy.

After 9/11, the Bush presidency became obsessed with 'evil'. In fact, from his inauguration to 16 June 2003, President Bush gave 319 speeches in which he spoke about 'evil', in which 914 uses of 'evil' was as a noun and 182 were as an adjective (Singer 2004: 2). Just three days after a 9/11 memorial at the National Cathedral in Washington, D.C., Bush claimed a mandate from God to 'rid the world of evil' (quoted in Welch 53). 'We are in a conflict between good and evil, and America will call evil by its name', he asserted, implying by the contrast that America was 'good' and the terrorists and those who sheltered them were 'evil' (1 June 2002, Bush's speech to West Point Commencement, quoted in Welch 2006: 52). Peter Singer surmises, 'This suggests that Bush is not thinking about evil deeds or even evil people, nearly as often as he is thinking about evil as a *thing*, or a force, something that has a real existence, apart from the cruel, callow, brutal and selfish acts of which human beings are capable' (emphasis in original) (2004: 2). Terrorists were evil, after 9/11, but evil itself was the enemy.

Supernatural evil, or, more accurately, evil personified, returned with a vengeance after 9/11. Michael Welch argues that Bush's religious rhetoric was problematic, as it was Manichean and messianic, among other things (2006: 53). The world is to be battled over between the principles of good and evil (and the humans that supposedly manifested these qualities) and it was the role of the United States, as the manifestation of the good, to deliver the world from evil. This Manichean duality, however, was embraced in horror cinema. The horror of Islamic extremists and terrorism was displaced onto devils, demons, monsters and other personifications of evil, which could be combated by good men and women.

Part of this trend is the assertion that the horrors depicted are 'based on a true story'. *The Exorcism of Emily Rose*, *The House of the Devil* and *The Rite* all claim to be based on true stories. The epiphenomena that surround the films, including press releases and cast interviews, DVD extras and television specials all emphasize the 'real' nature of the story. *Emily Rose* is based on the story of Analiese Michel, a young German girl who died in 1976 while being exorcized by two priests, discussed within the DVD extras (see Goodman 1981). *The Rite* is based on the experiences of Father Gary Thomas as represented in the book *The Rite* by Matt Baglio. Upon the release of the film, Father Thomas stated in an interview, 'I believe in the personification of evil' (quoted in King 2011: D3). The films posit the reality of the devil and then the film-makers state that these pronouncements represent their genuine beliefs. The films show the reality of Satan; the film-makers believe it.

Concurrent with this trend is the post-9/11 trope (again present pre-9/11, but brought to the foreground in the past decade) of the unbeliever brought to belief. *The Exorcism of Emily Rose* centres on a skeptical defense attorney (Laura Linney), charged with defending Father Moore (Tom Wilkinson), a priest charged with negligent homicide since the titular girl died while he was performing an exorcism on her. Erin Bruner, the lawyer, begins to encounter the supernatural while defending him and comes to believe in the reality of genuine evil. In *1408* (2007), Mike Ensiln (John Cusack), a writer specializing in debunking and explaining hauntings, finds himself a believer in the afterlife when he encounters the eponymous hotel room.

A variation is the former believer brought back to belief by a confrontation with genuine evil. Reverend Graham Hess (Mel Gibson) in *Signs* (2002, which was in production when 9/11 occurred) quits his job as a clergyman after his wife dies in an accident, forbids prayer in his house and asks his former parishioners to stop calling him 'Reverend'. After confronting an alien invasion in which his wife's dying words are revealed to be prophetic, allowing his son to be saved by asthma and the personality quirks of his brother and daughter, the final shot of the film is Graham putting his clerical collar back on. In *The Reaping* (2007), Katherine Winter (Hilary Swank), an ordained minister and former Christian missionary to Africa whose daughter died there, has become an academic and professional debunker of religion. She has investigated 48 miracles and discovered the scientific explanations for them all, telling her class, 'The only miracle is that people keep believing.' Yet, when confronted with the supernatural events plaguing a small Louisiana town, plagues echoing the biblical ten commandments centred on a little girl with supernatural powers, she becomes a believer again. *The Last Exorcism* follows Reverend Cotton Marcus (Patrick Fabian), a preacher who only plays at exorcism and agrees to show a film crew how he fakes the elements of possession and demonic presence and ends up confronting an evil cult and a real demon.

Conversely, the films also show the failure of exorcism, or at least that its efficacy is questionable. *The Exorcism of Emily Rose* and *The Last Exorcism* both end with the deaths of the young women being exorcized. In the former, the exorcist is on trial; in the latter he is most likely killed. Exorcism fails as often as it succeeds in film after 9/11, reflecting the bleak nihilism dominant in horror cinema but also the reality brought home by the terror attacks: sometimes evil wins.

Douglas Cowen has demonstrated that religious horror films are not mere exercises in mythology as psychology, but represent the exploration of genuine spiritual fears and concerns. *The Exorcist* may be read in terms of its concerns about single parents, lonely children entering puberty and the invasion of the home by foul-mouthed, masturbating pubescent teens, but it also represents a genuine concern (for some) about the reality of demons and possession. After 9/11, American religion asserts, and many believe, that evil is real. Confirmation can be found both in the footage of the terror attacks and the films that confirm the power of God and the good and the reality of Satan and evil.

Executing the will of the Almighty

For the film industry, religion itself, not its individual iterations, became scary and a source of horror in the wake of the terror attacks. Horror cinema displaces fundamentalist Muslims into fundamentalist Christians. The individual faith is not significant, the fact that a believer is a fundamentalist is an indicator of their potential to commit acts of terror. 9/11 demonstrated the ability for those who believe they act in the name of God to commit atrocities and believe it is the right thing to do.

In the Canadian film *End of the Line* (2007), fundamentalist followers of 'The Reverend' (David L. McCallum) eat hallucinogenic-laced muffins, and, when their individual pagers go off, use daggers hidden inside crucifixes to kill everyone they see in order to 'save' them and send them to heaven. Much of the film involves the young protagonists fleeing from followers of 'The Reverend' who cheerfully and gleefully stab to death everyone they meet. The second time the pagers go off, the Christians apologize to those they were about to kill, telling them 'it's too late'. They then commit mass suicide by giving one another cyanide pills.

This film demonstrates several concerns about religion and fundamentalism. The first is the seemingly inordinate power of holy men and women to order their followers to commit atrocities and even suicide. The fundamentalists literally begin killing when the pagers they have been issued go off and tell them to. The second involves the concern that fundamentalists, when committing such atrocities are not only doing the will of God, they are actually helping and saving those they are killing. Third, the religious justification of violence, in this case in order to start the Apocalypse and save as many people as possible before demons begin to walk the earth, is profoundly frightening, as it allows for the worst of terror acts to be justified. The mindlessness of the fundamentalists, their unwillingness to entertain any other explanations or ideas, the closed mindedness when presented with other options is presented as inimical to freedom and modern society. The sole fundamentalist who expresses doubt is convinced to continue with the plan every time, including killing himself. Even those who have doubt eventually carry out the atrocities.

That fundamentalism is dangerous is a central tenet of these films. The evil may or may not be real, but the cause of death is brought about by people who believe it is. Evil may or may not be a threat, fundamentalism is:

> We didn't have to look far to see where such an attitude toward belief can lead. Those who planned and brought about the deaths of 3000 innocent Americans on September 11, 2001, were people of *deep* religious faith who prayed frequently and, before they died, commended their souls to God's care. One of the ironies of American life is that these attacks by religious fanatics brought about even more public displays of religious belief than is usual in American public life. (Singer 2004: 99)

This attitude is embodied by Mrs Carmody (Marcia Gay Harden), in *The Mist*. She interprets the events unfolding inside and outside the supermarket through her own rigid scriptural worldview. It is one of paranoia, resentment and delusions of vengeance against those who mock her. 'You'll all be on your knees to me' she tells the others in response to their scoffing at her prophesies.

She prays alone to God in the bathroom, on her knees in front of a toilet. It is an odd location to offer up prayer and is a visual comment on what she is actually doing. When Amanda (Laurie Holden) offers to be her friend, Mrs Carmody tells her that if she 'need[s] a friend like you, I'll just have myself a little squat and shit one out'. While Mrs Carmody reveals herself to be remarkably profane and perhaps hate-filled with this comment, it is a directly related to what she was just doing by praying in front of a toilet. Her scatological insult also reflects that her faith is a toilet, seeing only the worst in humanity and hoping for death and destruction. She is irrational. She sees people as 'shit', but she prays where others defecate. Later, as the biker (Brian Libby) leaves with Norton's group, he tells Carmody, 'Hey, crazy lady, I believe in God, too. I just don't think He's the blood-thirsty asshole you make him out to be'. The biker's choice of words is not accidental, Mrs Carmody's God is a bloodthirsty asshole whom she worships in a toilet while despising the 'shits' he has created.

Mrs Carmody is able to convince the others of the need for 'expiation', killing first a soldier and then demanding the death of Billy

Drayton, a child. Her Christian faith is, as Amanda herself observes, 'a little too old testament'. Gone is the idea of loving one's neighbour as one's self or taking care of the poor and less fortunate. Gone are the ideals expressed in the Sermon on the Mount. Replacing them, in Mrs Carmody's theology, is a vengeance-filled God, out to destroy the world and demanding bloody human sacrifice in order to save a small group. 'Kill them all!' she begins screaming when Ollie Weeks finally shoots her, first in the abdomen, then in the head. He stops her 'gut' and then he stops her thought. It is an apt ending, as she chooses not to think but to live by her emotions, by what she knows is right. If many horror films demonstrate fear of evil, others demonstrate fear of those who misguidedly pursue what they believe is evil. Religion teaches us the devil exists; but religion also gives those who desire it an excuse to commit the worst kinds of acts.

Sympathy for the devil

In a variation on the dangerous fundamentalist theme, some films show deeply religious Christians who are revealed to be actual Satanists. Like Boykin's assertions of Islam, there are those who pretend to worship God, but they in reality worship Satan. *The Reaping* and *The Last Exorcism* both feature evangelical, bible-believing communities that are revealed to be Satanic cults. *The House of the Devil* offers an elderly couple advertising on a college campus for a babysitter for his mother. As in *Rosemary's Baby*, they present themselves as models of middle American respectability and belief, but they are, in fact, along with their son, members of a Satanic cult that plan to sacrifice the girl during that night's lunar eclipse.

The Reaping shows Haven, a small town in Louisiana, presented as a Southern bible-belt community. One of the first places Katharine visits is the local church, which is in the centre of the community. She has been brought in as her specialization is debunking religious phenomenon and the town has been suffering the biblical plagues of Egypt. Her investigations, aided by local Doug (David Morrissey), uncover a local girl (AnnaSophia Robb) with supernatural powers whom the locals believe is a servant of Satan. They encourage Katharine to kill her.

Father Costigan (Stephen Rea), however, who has been having visions, warns her that there is something terrible happening. A prophesy that 'predates Christ' warns of 'an ancient Satanic sect' will work great evil through breeding. 'Their first born are branded and left unharmed to carry on the genetic line. But all the second born thereafter are to be sacrificed ... to satisfy Satan'. Should the instructions be carried out, 'For their sacrifice they shall reap a perfect child, a second born, who upon coming into adulthood shall be reborn with the eyes of Satan'. The townsfolk claim that the girl is the child of Satan. The final part of the prophesy is that 'At the height of their power, God will send forth an angel to destroy them'.

Katharine finds the child, who does indeed have powers. She realizes, however, that she has been manipulated. It is the child who is the angel sent to destroy the town and the townsfolk are the members of the 'ancient Satanic sect'. Through flashbacks it is revealed the girl's brother, the family's first-born, attempted to sacrifice her, but he turned to dust when he stabbed her. Her entering the local river turned it to blood, which brought about the request for Katharine to investigate. The girl escapes the second sacrificial attempt on her life and, as Doug attempts to kill Katharine, she calls down the fire of God's wrath to destroy the town, God apparently liking blowing up Satanists with giant explosive special effects.

The film confirms the existence of both God and Satan, and alleges that not all who claim to be of God are good people. Some religious serve as a mask for 'ancient Satanic sects'. Just like the hillbilly horror discussed in Chapter 1, *The Reaping* employs fundamentalist Christianity in order to comment on fundamentalist religion in general and fundamentalist Islam in particular. A backwards, simple people living in a rural area with primitive beliefs sacrifice the lives of their children in order to gain power in this world.

Similarly, in *The Last Exorcism*, also set in rural Louisiana, believing that Nell (Ashley Bell) has been molested by her father (Louis Herthum), Cotton goes to see the family's pastor, Pastor Manley (Tony Bentley), who agrees to visit the family and welcome them back into the flock. He is the very picture of a southern preacher. His wife welcomes Cotton and the film crew to the church. The film presents the minister as an elderly man of God who is deeply concerned about his flock.

At film's end, when the crew and Cotton return to the farm, knowing that the boy Nell claimed was the father of her baby did not impregnate her, they discover a Satanic ritual underway. The baby is cut from Nell and thrown into a fire, wherein a giant demonic presence immediately registers. Leading the ceremony, chanting and throwing the foetus is Pastor Manley, who is also the head of a Satanic cult that brings about the deaths of Cotton, Iris (who is chopped to pieces by the cultists) and Daniel (who is beheaded by Nell's brother), just as Nell predicted in her drawings. Cotton had grown suspicious of Manley, since he said he had not seen Nell in three years and Logan (Logan Craig Reid), the purported father, said he only saw Nell once at a party at Manley's the previous year. When they encounter Manley again, he is dressed in a hooded red robe and leading the ritual to the demon Abalam. As he tosses the baby in the fire, he cries 'Hail, Abalam!' Though the film is ambiguous about Nell's possession, the reality of the demon and what is in the fire at the end, it is unambiguous that the local Christian minister leads a Satanic cult. These films posit that evil is real, but it is in the service of organized religion. The local pastor pretends to be Christian, but he is actually evil.

Warriors for God

More recently, religion has played a role in films that show tired crusaders who have grown weary of fighting in God's name, but who must face down supernatural evil in the face of the plague. *Black Death* and *Season of the Witch* are similarly set in medieval Europe, and the latter is specifically set during the crusades. Its protagonists are Christian knights who have fought and killed Muslims for years. The former is set in a land where pagans opposed to Christians seem to live a life free from the plague. *Priest*, on the other hand, is set in a future where the plague of vampirism has ravaged the land. The Catholic Church has trained a group of warrior priests to combat the vampires. All three films depict religious wars in which violence is done in the name of religion.

In *Black Death*, the Christian knights are told by the pagan villagers that unless they renounce Christianity's 'vengeful God', they will be tortured and killed one by one by their captors. 'When the Christian soldiers and paganesque townsfolk meet, their opposing – yet startlingly similar – ideologies clash spectacularly' (Kuebler 2011: 17).

Both Christian and pagan kill in order to enforce their religious beliefs, while both are motivated by a need to stop the plague that is ravaging the land. Director Christopher Smith asserts, 'It's about the way that religions can be manipulated and used by bad people for their own good' (quoted in Kuebler 2011: 18, 20).

'Vengeance is mine,' states Ulrich (Sean Bean), quoting the Lord and scripture, and who is already infected with plague by the time he reaches the village. As the villagers attempt to draw and quarter him, his robe tears, revealing plague buboes in his armpits, like a biological weapon suicide vest. Though his arms are torn off, he has already infected everyone with whom he has come into contact. He is a form of medieval Christian bio-warfare. His death results in plague coming to the village and the pagans finally dying from Bubonic death. *Black Death* 'is a dark parable about how things haven't really moved on in the last 600 years' (Kuebler 2011: 18).

In *Season of the Witch*, a prologue shows the execution of three witches who are hanged and then drowned. A priest begins to say prayers over their corpses and one of the witches reanimates, kills him and burns the prayer book. Although the village is remote, this action by a demon has repercussions: the destruction of the book will prevent demons from being exorcized. The credits are followed by scenes of an extended crusade – a religious war between Christians and Muslims that extends for years in different areas and nations. Two soldiers, Behman (Nicholas Cage) and Felsen (Ron Perlman) finally grow tired of war, violence and especially the killing of 'innocents'. They refuse to fight and, facing excommunication, leave the crusade.

In their travel home, they arrive at a city suffering the plague. While they will not fight innocents who are not the enemy of God (including Muslim women and children) they will fight genuine evil: witches and demons. They become outsiders aiding in the fight against an internal threat that can and will become a global threat if not stopped. They must transport a witch (Claire Foy) to a monastery where the monks can exorcize and execute her, thus ending the plague. She manipulates the men, assuring them she is not a witch, but they have numerous supernatural encounters on the road and upon their arrival at the decimated monastery, they learn the girl is possessed by a demon. The young priest (Stephen Campbell Moore) attempts an exorcism with the final surviving copy of the book destroyed in the pre-credit sequence, but he and the knights must sacrifice themselves in order to destroy the demon and return the girl to normal. The film ends with the girl and the last surviving knight bringing the book back to civilization, in order to fight both plague and demon.

Priest, set in an apocalyptic future, also distrusts the institutional church and places its faith (no pun intended) in the actions of a heroic individual priest (Paul Bettany), who tracks down his niece, who has been kidnapped by vampires. He is assisted by another warrior priest (Maggie Q) and a sheriff (Cam Gigandet). As in the other films, this small band of religious warriors fights the embodiment of actual evil, a vampire ruler (Karl Urban). As in all these films, institutional religions can be oppressive, manipulative and employed in the service of dark agendas. Religious belief can be employed to fight against others, to kill large groups of innocent people, and to reinforce the social and political status quo. Individual belief is fine; warriors for God must be careful, however, as they can be used to kill God's children.

9/11 created 'an opportunity to shape a remarkable global consensus against religious violence', in Jon Pahl's words, but instead, officials of the United States framed the war on terror in religious terms as well (2010: 167). In fact, the war on terror is frequently constructed as 'quasi-Manichean', as noted in Bush's statement above, that 'good' would defeat 'evil' (Bernstein 2005: 48). Interestingly, al Qaeda uses the same rhetoric when describing the struggle.

I began this chapter with a discussion of the twin and conflicting streams in American culture: that which sees America as a special nation blessed by God and that which fears the cynical use of religion for selfish reasons. These twin streams are reflected in horror films which confirm the reality of God and the devil, but fear fundamentalists who would justify violence through religious belief. The tension over religion in American culture in the wake of the religiously motivated terror attacks is made manifest in these films.

The Last Exorcism in many ways embodies the post-9/11 ideological tension over religion and over horror films as well: either psychology is correct and everything is rooted in shame, repression and hidden sexual power dynamics (because the father has been molesting his daughter), or religion is correct and regardless of the psychosexual situation, Satan is indeed walking the world (and his followers are out to kill us). Either way, the film ends in the same manner. The effect of belief in this world is real, regardless of whether or not the object of that belief is.

7

They Won't Stay Dead: The Ghosts, Zombies and Vampires of 9/11

Ghost stories are to do with the insurrection, not the resurrection, of the dead.

GILLIAN BEER
'GHOSTS'

One need not be a chamber to be haunted.

EMILY DICKINSON

The dead returned with a vengeance after September 11, literally in horror cinema. 9/11 resulted in a transformative period for traditional monsters of cinema. Nick Muntean and Matthew Thomas Payne write, speaking of zombies, that, 'in a culture suffused with a heightened sense of imminent terror and incalculable dread, meaningful fictional monsters must not only respond to the form of the prevailing cultural anxiety, they must also equal or transcend the depths of its possible horror' (2009: 244). In other words, post-9/11, traditional monsters must transform to equal the horror of terrorism otherwise they fade into irrelevance. Traditional monsters such as ghosts, demons, vampires, werewolves and other shape-shifters, zombies and giant beasts must somehow find relevance in a world in which the events of 9/11 are possible. One possible stream has been to construct such monsters as being sympathetic. *Twilight*, *Underworld* and *Fido*, for example, all feature sympathetic, even heroic traditional monsters. The other possible route is, paradoxically, to remove any sense of sympathy or empathy for the monsters, who, in turn, are constructed as malevolent, angry and destructive without potential for redemption. This chapter is not a comprehensive survey of post-9/11 ghosts, zombies and vampires. Nor does it argue that all movies involving the returned dead follow the same tropes as a result of the events of the past decade. It is, however, a study of why the dead are returning, how they are returning, and how it reflects a post-9/11 world.

Elias Canetti compares various religious texts and concludes:

> The first thing that strikes one is the universal *fear* of the dead. They are disconcerted and full of envy for those they have left behind. They try to take revenge on them, sometimes for injuries done them during their lifetimes, but often simply because they themselves are no longer alive. (1962: 262).

Several things emerge from Canetti's analysis. We are afraid of the dead. The dead envy the living. The dead seek revenge, for both general and specific things. In short, the dead are angry.

In the days after 9/11, envy was cited as a chief reason for the terror attacks: they envy our 'freedom' and our way of life. The terrorists, like the dead, seek revenge simply because they are not like us and do not have what we have. Films about the dead show a marked increase in angry dead after 9/11. In particular in this chapter I will briefly consider the angry dead in the form of ghosts, zombies and vampires, all of which have risen in prominence since 9/11, although, in fairness, none of the three have ever truly gone away and all of the three have been presences since the first days of cinematic horror.

For the purposes of this study, a ghost is the non-corporeal spirit of a dead human being, traditionally tied to a single location, which haunts for a reason, often, though not always related to its death. A zombie is a reanimated human corpse, usually unintelligent, often driven to consume human flesh. The zombie is enjoying the biggest renaissance right now across the arts, with fiction, drama, film, graphic novels and even pop phenomenon such as zombie crawls and zombie walks dominating horror culture for much of the past half-decade. A vampire, like the zombie was once a living human, but now is undead and feeds off human blood. Immortal, the vampire is still vulnerable to several things: sunlight, crucifixes, wooden stake through the heart and silver. Ghosts have changed, since 9/11, but even more than ghosts the corporeal dead in cinema have changed. A ghost is a memory, a vampire or a zombie is a physical presence. We are haunted by ghosts, but they are memories of tragedy. Zombies and vampires cause catastrophe by being present in the same space. If, as I will argue in Chapter 9, the nineties was a decade dominated by human monsters and, as I argue here, after Katharine Fowkes (2004) by the sensitive dead (who, like President Clinton, 'feel your pain'), the past decade has been dominated by angry dead, returned to fight the living in order to either destroy them or to make the living the same as the dead.

Ghosts

Jessica O'Hara's remarkably insightful essay on television ghost-hunting programmes observes that since 9/11 our culture has developed 'a collective interest in the nature of evil, haunted spaces (such as the destroyed World Trade Center towers), enduring trauma and mourning, and the debt the living owe the dead in seeking justice and reparation' (2010: 81). Such programmes as *Ghost Hunters*, *Ghost Hunters International*, *A Haunting*, *Ghost Adventures*, *Paranormal State*, *Most Haunted*, *The Haunted*, *The Haunted Collector*, *Haunted History*, *Celebrity Ghost Stories* and *My Ghost Story* purport to objectively and scientifically investigate, document and/or recreate genuine hauntings, and are year-round series, not merely Hallowe'en special fare. O'Hara argues that what all these shows have in common is a belief that truth has been somehow hidden, that historical trauma is causing a physical location to have a negative effect on its current inhabitants, and that there is a danger in not mourning. Over the course of a typical episode for many of these programmes, the possibility of a haunting is confirmed though evidence and research, heretofore unknown histories are revealed, and the ghostly presence is laid to rest, if possible.

O'Hara ties all this to the unofficial motto of the United States after 9/11: 'We will never forget' (2010: 82). But 'not forgetting' is not an active choice, and as actors say, one cannot perform a negative action. One cannot 'not forget', one can only remember. The challenge is, what to remember, for what purpose and why. Jeffrey Andrew Weinstock argues, 'We value our ghosts, particularly during periods of cultural transition, because the alternative to their presence is even more frightening: if ghosts do not return to correct history, the privileged narratives of history are not open to contestation. If ghosts do not return to reveal crimes that have gone unpunished, then evil acts may in fact go unredressed' (2004: 6). Ghosts are about truth and justice. 9/11 haunts the United States. We seek to exorcize its demons, remember and mourn the dead, and seek justice for them. Each programme from the list above represents what might be termed a 'mini-9/11': historic trauma has happened. It demands to be remembered and to be given justice. Once memory and justice have been served, the haunting ends.

It is the unmourned dead that haunt the living, which is the challenge of 9/11. All of those who died were memorialized, but many did not leave remains behind to be buried. Charles B. Strozier argues that on 9/11, for many who jumped or were incinerated or were in the towers when they fell, 'the form of dying radically impaired mourning' (2005: 265). Similarly, we use the language of hauntings to discuss 9/11. The terrorists themselves were not ghosts, but the memory of the events haunt us. We are angry at the haunting, at the need for the memory in the first place. As a result, the ghosts in horror films change after September 11.

Katherine Fowkes reminds us that in the nineties, spirits did not need an exorcism, they needed a therapist (2004: 195–6). Films such as *Ghost* (1990), *What Dreams May Come* (1998) and *The Sixth Sense* (2000) feature 'sad and frightened, not frightening' entities that need help in passing on (195). Like the president at the time, they 'feel your pain' and hope you can feel and understand theirs. After 9/11, the sensitive spirit goes into serious decline and many spirits become overtly evil and in need of stopping. In *The Sixth Sense*, one of the most popular horror films at the end of the last decade, Cole (Haley Joel Osment) has a role to play in the world: to comfort those who lost someone, to caution those left behind, and to encourage the dead to move on once their concerns have been met. A girl poisoned by her mother in Munchhausen-by-Proxy Syndrome is able to warn her father through Cole and spare her younger sister the same fate.[1]

The spirits after 9/11 would not gently warn or comfort. They are angry, vengeful and without mercy. I have argued elsewhere that it is not a coincidence that American remakes of J-horror rose to prominence after September 11 (2009: 73). Although the American remake of *The Ring* was in preproduction before September 11, its success and the numerous other remakes of Japanese (and subsequently Korean) ghost films was made possible by the cultural climate after 9/11. In *The Ring*, Samara is a vengeful ghost who curses those who watch her videotape. She leaves her victims alive for seven days, then kills them horribly. When she is freed from the well by Rachel (Naomi Watts), the traditional ghost film would end. Instead, as her son Aidan (David Dorfman) tells her, it was a mistake to free her. She is now unconstrained to wreak vengeance against the world. Although Rachel does not die, Aiden's father (Martin Henderson) does, most horribly. Rachel realizes the only way to prevent death is to copy the tape and show it to someone else. Samara's ghost wants to be replicated and passed along so she might continue to kill. Freeing her did not put her to rest, it allows her to kill more efficiently.

In *1408*, cynical sceptical paranormal writer Mike Enslin (John Cusack) checks into the eponymous room in the Dolphin Hotel in New York. He has been told that there have been 22 natural deaths and 56 unnatural deaths in the room. Gerald Olin (Samuel L. Jackson) also tells him that it is not a traditional haunting. While apparitions appear in the room, it is not haunted by a ghost. Olin asserts, 'It's an evil fucking room.' The malevolence in the hotel is simply evil. The supernatural presence has no sympathetic or empathetic attributes.

It simply exists to destroy those individuals unfortunate enough to stay in the room.

Enslin, who seeks for proof of life after death due to the loss of his daughter to an aggressive cancer, begins to investigate the room. He runs a black light over various surfaces, while talking into a tape recorder about how inherently creepy hotel rooms are. The film is literalizing a metaphor here: the stains and fluids left by previous occupants haunt us, reminding us of the people who were in the room before us. The space is not really ours, even if it feels private. Others have occupied the space and something of them is left behind.

In the case of room 1408, that something results in an increasingly eerie series of events. The radio continually plays the Carpenters' 'We've Only Just Begun'. The digital clock sets itself to count down from 60 seconds. When he looks through the peephole in the door, Mike sees an eye looking back at him. He witnesses ghosts jumping out the window. Considering that he is on the fourteenth floor of a hotel in New York City, the falling bodies also suggest 9/11, as does his own foray out onto the ledge, in which he almost slips and falls. The building remakes itself in response to his actions. Other rooms vanish, the room becomes freezing, paintings come to life and flood the room. The haunting literally destroys the entire room before resetting it to happen all over again. The only solution Mike arrives at is to burn the room and hotel down. Nothing else can stop the haunting but to completely destroy the site of it.

In *Insidious*, the chief entity is a demon, but the phenomena the family is experiencing are jealous, angry ghosts that want to take over Dalton's (Ty Simpkins) body. The premise of the film is that surrounding us at all times is a dimension called The Further in which aggressive, angry, belligerent ghosts watch and wait and seek to possess us, take our bodies and live our lives as we wander in the astral dimension. Even though a loving father can rescue his son from the demon, the ghost of an angry dead old woman possesses Josh (Patrick Wilson), who then kills Elsie (Lin Shaye), a psychic who knows the truth, and then turns upon his wife. The film ends with her look of horror. Insidious clearly demonstrates that surrounding us at all times are hostile and malevolent spirits that would take over our bodies and kill our loved ones if we ever give them an opportunity to do so. Ghosts after 9/11 are angry, envious and violent. We must be on constant guard against them.

Zombies

Although George A. Romero had introduced the zombie as social commentary in *Night of the Living Dead* (1968) and amplified the idea in *Dawn of the Dead* (1978), the post-9/11 period has seen an abundance of overtly political zombie films: *Homecoming*, *ZMD: Zombies of Mass Destruction*, *Zombie Strippers* and *Zombieland* all contain overt political and/or social metaphors. A key change from pre-9/11 zombie films as exemplified by the traditional Romero zombies in his trilogy (the two films mentioned above and *Day of the Dead* (1985)), is the transformation of the zombie into a fast, angry creature. Romero's zombies appear sad and are slow moving. They shamble and are slow to react. In the 1990 remake of *Night of the Living Dead* Barbara (Patricia Tallman) states that the zombies are 'so slow, we can move right past them'. Zombies are only dangerous in larger groups, although if one is incautious one can be bitten by just one and then suffer a horrible death.

Muntean and Payne refer to the post-9/11 zombies as 'enraged corpses' that individually are 'a swift, powerful and ferocious predator that makes direct, purposeful beelines towards the living' (2009: 246). In the 2004 remake of *Dawn of the Dead*, the first thing one notices is the speed of the zombies. The first one we see is Vivian (Hannah Lochner), a child, who kills Luis (Justin Louis), the husband of the protagonist by tearing out his throat. She is tossed down the hall and immediately leaps to her feet and comes running to attack. The next zombies seen are all runners, screaming as they attack their former friends and family members.

Often included in surveys of zombie films are *28 Days Later* and *28 Weeks Later*, although the hordes in those movies are technically not zombies. They are living humans infected with the 'rage virus', which drives them to attack other human beings. The effect is the same, though: all those so infected become mindless, rage-filled killing machines. Both the infected and the zombies represent complete depersonalization. Once one is zombified there is no 'I' anymore. Zombification represents a loss of Self, a loss of social self and a loss of all relationships that existed with that person. Similarly, Zombies cannot be reasoned with, cannot be negotiated with, they seek only to replicate themselves, which also makes them an excellent metaphor for terrorists.

In *Back from the Dead: Remakes of the Romero Zombie Films as Markers of their Times*, I argued that the remake of *Dawn of the Dead* is a post-9/11 zombie film for a number of reasons (2011: 144–9). The opening credit sequence visually links zombies with praying Muslims and Middle Eastern mobs. The film opens with a ten-and-a-half minute pre-credit sequence in which emergency room nurse Ana (Sarah Polley) returns home after working a 12-hour shift to watch reality television with her husband, only to wake up the next morning to her child neighbour killing him and then his reanimated corpse attacking her. These two are the first of hundreds of angry, vicious zombies shown in the film. No longer the slow, pathetic, shambling former humans of Romero's original, these dead are fast and dangerous. Her crash after escaping her dead husband is followed by the credit sequence.

Johnny Cash's apocalyptic folk song 'When the Man Comes Around' begins to play as the screen shows Muslims bowing in prayer. Credits, taking the form of streaking red liquid suggesting blood, then begin to intercut with rapidly edited, indistinct images of something falling in the water, a bloody screaming face and more crowds. As the credits run, other images include rioting crowds (both in the West and the Middle East), burning buildings, screaming people and attacking zombies. Snowy screen shots and confused and conflicting news reports interspersed in the credits both simulate the experience of ongoing reporting during a crisis and literalize the metaphor of media breaking down. Lastly, the final credit image is of a reporter standing on a hotel balcony in what appears to be the Middle East, beginning to give a field report when the camera rapidly whips to the side, showing a crowd of running zombies entering the space, attacking nearby soldiers, and a Middle Eastern-looking zombie attacking the camera. The visual link is made: while this crisis is world-wide, the images begin with Muslims praying and end with Middle Easterners attacking Western soldiers and journalists. 'America and the American way of life are particularly at risk,' I wrote, 'We are under assault from without and within, just as on 9/11. The zombie is a terrorist' (2011: 146).

After the credit sequence, the film follows the basic plot of the original: a small group of survivors hides out in a mall, but with some radical shifts that reshape the narrative and the meaning of the film in order to reflect the contemporary world. The original *Dawn* featured four working professionals (two S.W.A.T. team members, a television producer and a helicopter pilot) who secure the mall, slowly grow bored there and then defend it from a motorcycle gang. The remake features over a dozen blue-collar, working class people: a beat cop, an emergency room nurse (both, we should note, 'first responders'), a truck driver, three mall security guards, a retail clerk, a church organist, a student, a petty thug and his pregnant girlfriend. Only one upper middle class person arrives at the mall, Steve (Ty Burrell), we do not know his occupation, but he wears expensive clothes, looks down upon the others, owns a boat and prefers to film himself when he is having sex. The others might not always get along, but they understand and begrudgingly respect one another. Steve is just a selfish jerk whose death is the only one treated as justice instead of a tragedy.

No motorcycle gang invades the remake. Whereas in the original, the survivors grow bored and begin to find life tedious and meaningless, they are shocked out of their ennui by the arrival of a motorcycle gang. Peter (Ken Foree) puts his S.W.A.T. uniform back on, picks up his rifle and begins to find a purpose in life again. In other words, an outside threat returns meaning and purpose to those in the mall. In the remake, there is no such threat. Instead, two factors come into play. The mall hints at a looming crisis of supplies (they must go down to the generator room and refuel, recognizing the power will not stay on forever. There is also a hint of dwindling food supplies in that the mall coffee cart runs out of vanilla flavouring. There is no imminent crisis at all when it comes to supplies. The bigger threat in this mall is the ennui itself. The characters amuse themselves by having the nearby gun shop owner shoot celebrity look-alike zombies, play chess, watch movies, make love, spray-paint stairwells, stargaze, hit golf balls off the roof and indulge in other regular pastimes. Whereas the original film's mall-life montage clearly show-cased the growing boredom and ennui, the remake's mall-life montage (carried out to Richard Cheese and Lounge Against the Machine's cover of 'Down with the Sickness') is cheery and happy. All of the characters seem to be enjoying themselves. This is the least stressed or threatened that we have ever seen them. They are not bored by the mall, they are endlessly distracted by it and each other.

The group, however, decides one day that though they are comparatively safe and still have everything they need and, with careful conservation of resources and rationing, might be able to remain at the mall indefinitely, they should head somewhere else. The best plan they can come up with is to head to the marina, get Steve's boat and 'head for an island'.[2] They leave relative security for the unknown. The only reason Ken (Ving Rhames) gives for this is that he does not wait to 'wait to die' in the mall. A third factor becomes Andy (Bruce Bohne), the gun shop owner down the street who is out of food. Interestingly, he is the closest thing beat cop Ken has to a best friend in the mall.[3] Andy is starving and so the group sends food to him using Chips the dog as a courier. When zombies get into the gun shop with Chips, Andy is bitten. Nicole (Lindy Booth), who cares more for the dog than she does for any of the people in the mall, steals a truck and goes to rescue the dog, and in doing so imperils herself. An impromptu rescue party is organized, running through the sewers to get both girl and dog back. After Ken kills the now-zombified Andy, the group returns to the mall, losing Tucker (Boyd Banks) along the way. Zombies are able to follow them into the mall, so they must leave immediately, resulting in more deaths.

What is remarkable about this scenario is that they did not need to leave. They did not need to do much of anything. Nicole's panicked overreaction to rescue the dog (who would not have been hurt by the zombies), the group's rescue of Nicole (which causes losses greater than what was saved) and the subsequent need to then abandon the mall were all driven by selfishness and panic. In the original, the survivors (perhaps unnecessarily) defended the mall against the bikers, but the threat was at least real. Here, Nicole's actions directly led to the deaths of several of her friends and associates. On the one hand, the group was fortunate that they had already converted the mall's parking shuttles into armoured vehicles, allowing them to escape when the zombies had breached the mall, but on the other hand setting up good defences would have been easier and allowed them the time to leave when they chose to, instead of out of necessity. This scenario echoes the post-9/11 situation in Iraq, where American troops had been for over a year before *Dawn* was released. By panicking after 9/11, and by choosing to attack a nation that was not a genuine threat, America perhaps placed itself in greater danger and made a situation that was bad but contained, even worse.

The film offers an interesting critique of the United States and how it handles threats and crises. When the survivors first arrive at the mall, they are stopped by security guards who disarm them and take them prisoner. In a mall appliance store, the group watches a wall of televisions, showing them the crisis unfolding. As on 9/11, this is a mediated crisis. The survivors know what they know solely from television, even if what the television is telling them differs from their own experience. Head Security guard C. J. (Michael Kelly) observes a sheriff (played by Tom Savini) barking orders on television and shooting a 'twitcher' in the head. Gun in hand, grinning, he tells the others, 'America always sorts its shit out'. The film then proceeds to demonstrate how wrong he is. A military helicopter passes overhead, while the survivors are on the roof putting up 'Help us' and 'Alive inside' signs (in a scene eerily prescient of what would later happen during Hurricane Katrina), but the helicopter neither stops nor returns. The army does not appear. No police arrive (other than Ken). The media is gone the next morning. Instead, the mall survivors are left alone with a world full of zombies. 'America' did not sort this shit out.

The very real sociophobia in the wake of 9/11 being seen here is a fear of an ongoing war on terror in which 'America', by which we mean the government, the military and all authority figures, is unable to protect its people or solve the problems. It was not until nine and a half years after 9/11 (and six and a half years after *Dawn*) that Osama bin Laden was located and killed. Ten years after 9/11 and America is still fighting in Afghanistan and Iraq. The 'war on terror', I have argued elsewhere, is problematic at best because it is unwinnable by definition (2011: 146). It is a war declared on a tactic, not a particular group, nation or individual. Anyone can use terror. Success can only be measured, therefore, by how well the terror has been eliminated, or by how well terrorist attacks are prevented. In other words, the only measure of success is a negative: nothing has happened (yet). One is left, however, in a state of fear, as the terrorists can attack again at any point in the future. As Condoleezza Rice remarked to the 9/11 commission: '[T]hose charged with protecting us from attack have to be right one hundred percent of the time. To inflict devastation on a massive scale, the terrorists only have to succeed once' (quoted in Wetmore 2011: 146). Once the dead begin to walk, a cascading effect makes it impossible to 'be right one hundred percent of the time'. One of the dominant traits of zombies in all these films is the ability to pass along the condition, whether caused by virus, chemicals, magic or other means. Stephen Price points out that in *28 Weeks Later*, 'as in Iraq, the "friendlies" turn on the Americans' (2009: 285). The same holds true in Dawn: when Steve dies, he rises and must be shot, as must Frank (Matt Frewer), Luda (Inna Korobkina), and Andy. Michael (Jake Webber) shoots himself after being bitten, so that he will not turn and attack his friends.

Vampires

Despite the vampire renaissance of the past 30 years, the romantic aristocrat model is gone. Just as in the late fifties and the sixties Hammer Studios reinvented Dracula from the gothic romance of the 1931 Universal film to a series of much bloodier, much more violent confrontations with the count, and as the eighties brought us suburban, urban and rural working class and middle class American vampires in films such as *Fright Night*, *Lost Boys* and *Near Dark*, so, too, has the current decade produced vampires that reflect the times.

Two models of vampirism emerge in the new millennium. The first is a continuation of a previous model, the sensitive, lonely lost outsider, still romanticized, but updated to contemporary culture. The *Twilight* series may be the best-known manifestation of this trope. These are the children of Anne Rice, descended through Buffy and her boyfriend Angel, coping with teen angst by occasionally draining blood. These vampires are simply trying to survive in a world that occasionally tries to kill them. There are good vampires and evil ones. The vampires of *True Blood*, partly the heirs to *Near Dark* and its celebration of vampire as literal Southern gothic, also fall into complex categories and negotiate a highly politicized world. Most significantly, the vampires of this motif look 'normal'. They drink blood, have superhuman strength and unique weaknesses, but they are, for all practical purposes, a different religion. It is too much of a stretch to suggest that vampires are metaphors for, say, Muslims, in American society, but they do stand for outsiders with their own rules, codes, traditions and behaviours, and they also carry an element of danger with them.

The second stream is the exact opposite: the angry, violent vampire who is obviously a different being. These vampires have no intention of fitting in. They exist to be eradicated, as they only seek to destroy us. The vampire as terrorist is present in such films as *30 Days of Night*, *Priest* and the sequels to *Blade* (coincidentally, all graphic novel adaptations!) These vampires are not 'normal looking' – the physical differences are obvious. Some of the vampires, for example those in *Priest*, are barely humanoid. They are fast moving, dangerous, monstrous beasts just one step above hillbilly and zombie. They must be destroyed.

The post-9/11 vampire film *par excellence* is *30 Days of Night*. No angst-ridden teens, no slayer-dating noble souls, no aristocratic counts arrive in Alaska. Instead, a small group of inhuman but human looking evil monsters appear, not just to cause death but also pain and fear. They feed on the terror they generate in their victims. 'There is no escape. No hope. Only hunger and pain,' Marlow (Danny Huston), the leader of the vampires, tells one of his first victims, promoting despair before death. These vampires are clearly not American. They look 'foreign'. They speak English, but clearly as a second language. They have their own language (an invented one, to be sure, developed by a professor of linguistics), based on Eastern European models. They are outsiders, come to the United States to cause damage and fear. There is no seductive count, or vampire-with-a-soul threatening the souls of a few individuals. These vampires want to destroy an entire town. They arrive at a point when the sun will vanish for 30 days, since the town is so close to the North Pole. When they attack there is fire and smoke and destruction. There is not just damage to necks, but to property as well.

As in torture-porn, Sheriff Eben Oleson (Josh Hartnett) must become like them in order to defeat them. Just as Paxton in *Hostel*, Beth in *Hostel Part II* or Amanda in the *Saw* series become torturers after being tortured in order to defeat other torturers, Eben becomes a vampire in order to defeat vampires. In doing so, however, he himself must then die when the sun rises. As with the passengers on United 93, he must kill himself in order to prevent greater damage being done to the United States by these evil beings. This film presents the vampire as terrorist: they are not simply out to drink blood to survive. They are not sexy or aristocratic. They are out to destroy an entire American town.

It's their world now

Ghosts, zombies and vampires have also all appeared in films that imagine a world becoming dominated by these beings. The haunting of a remote hotel is terrifying enough in *The Shining*. A single vampire in London generates the fear of *Dracula*. After 9/11, though, fear is generated by a takeover of the world by the angry dead. Films such as *Zombieland*, *Land of the Dead*, *Dawn of the Dead* and *Last of the Living* posit a world in which the zombies significantly outnumber the living and yet still attempt to kill and devour the few remaining humans. *Stake Land* and *I Am Legend* imagine worlds in which the vampires now rule and in which small bands of survivors must work together to resist and, well, survive. *Pulse* shows a world in which angry ghosts bring more and more individuals into a kind of hellish afterlife, and a decreasing number of living humans band together. A small group of survivors also band together in *Vanishing on 7th Street*, which shows a world in which most of the people have become vicious, shadowy forms lurking in the darkness, hoping to convert the few remaining living human beings. These films manifest a fear of a changed world: one in which 'we' are no longer in control and in which 'they' dominate. This fear is a direct echo from 9/11, one of whose strongest clichés (including this book) is that it is a day that the world changed forever.

These films also manifest a fear of Islamic militants who wish to make the world theirs. Al Qaeda is not a national group, but a shadowy transnational organization, terrorists without borders, so to speak. Consider recent American concerns over Sharia law, in which several municipalities and states have either introduced or passed legislation outlawing the use of Sharia law. Oklahoma passed a constitutional amendment banning the use of Sharia in state courts, despite not a single instance of this happening, and a Muslim population of 15,000 out of 3.7 million people.[4] In fact, the only terrorism Oklahoma has suffered has been the bombing of the Alfred P. Murrah Federal Building by Timothy McVeigh, a right-wing, white supremacist Christian. There is also, as noted above, a fear of the different dead who appear to be sympathetic to 'us', but who turn on the living and attempt to kill them. The danger, these films assert, is that even those we believe to be friendly can turn at any moment and bring about horrible destruction and death.

Behind all films about the angry dead returning lies a fear of one's own death, and that after death one will not have any control. When one returns as a vampire, zombie or ghost, one no longer has a will of one's own but must obey supernatural instincts and appetites. There is, however, also something reassuring about the film featuring the dead that return, as it implies there is life after death and that our death is not the end. If such films, as noted above, help us cope with death and with those we mourn, we are reassured by the presence of the ghost, even an angry one, that the ones lost to us are not lost forever. Yet, as much comfort as we may take from that thought, the world in which the angry dead return (or worse yet, dominate) is one in which we are in constant danger and must remain vigilant. This attitude resonates with a post-9/11 world in which we never know when the next 9/11 is going to happen.

8

Manufacturing Fear

Fear-mongering

Horror cinema is rooted in the desire to feel fear. Indeed, Noël Carroll's two fundamental paradoxes of art horror are about its complex relationship to fear: 'how can anyone be frightened by what they know does not exist' and 'why would anyone even be interested in horror, since being horrified is so unpleasant' (1990: 8). After 9/11, the United States became dominated by fear in a manner unseen previously. That fear was, in many ways, out of proportion to the genuine threat. Furthermore, from the late nineties to the present, scholars from a variety of disciplines have argued that we live in a culture of fear, in which a variety of institutions (government, media, films, the scientific community, etc.) promote a constant state of alarm and worry, from Barry Glassner's *The Culture of Fear* (1999) to Frank Furedi's *The Culture of Fear* (2002), Marc Siegel's *False Alarm: The Truth about the Epidemic of Fear* (2005) and Peter Stearns' *American Fear* (2006). For Glassner, this fear is media-driven; for Stearns it is a combination of religious zeal, social isolation and parental anxiety; for all it is overblown in relationship to the genuine threats facing the American public (2006: 210–11). Our culture tells us to fear strangers, schools, transportation, planes, foreigners, terrorists, sharks, the home, family members, babysitters, teachers, clergy, vitamins, vaccinations, under-parenting, over-parenting, food and disease, to name but a few. We are instructed to be afraid, as all of these things *may* hurt or kill us.

Except, as Glassner, Furedi and Siegel all conclude, the evidence does not support the fear. We are actually, statistically speaking, much safer now than at any point previously in history. Crime statistics are at an all-time low, yet people fear crime waves. The nation was perhaps under much greater threat during the Cold War, with enough nuclear missiles pointed at us by the Soviet Union (and, conversely, at the Soviet Union by us) to destroy not just the nation but the planet many times over. The 'Doomsday Clock' approached midnight several times during this period. Yet, the ability of a single terrorist to attempt to blow up a plane with a home-made bomb seems to generate far greater fear both in the media and the public.

Peter N. Stearns argues for a 'distinctiveness of American fear', particularly after September 11 (2006: 25). Americans, despite the protection of two oceans and some of the most advanced technology, medicine, education and legal systems in the world, are also among the most fearful people in the world. That fear is, as often as not, irrational and not based in any genuine potential threat. Stearns cites a Carnegie Mellon study in the wake of September 11, which reported that, 'while most individuals claimed to feel that they were personally less vulnerable to terrorism than average; they still saw a high personal risk of harm or death by terrorism' (Furedi 2006: 25). In other words, even though most people knew that they themselves were not likely to be hurt or killed by terrorists, they still feared terrorist attacks and even believed that they might be killed by a terrorist, regardless of the likelihood.

Since 9/11, exactly 14 Americans have died in approximately three dozen Islamic-extremist terror plots targetted at the United States outside of war zones (Murphy 2011: A14). On the one hand, it can be argued that the attention and funds paid to the prevention of terror attacks is to be credited for keeping the number that low. Indeed, the odds of dying in a terror attack as of this writing are 1 in 3.5 million (Murphy 2011: A14). One is more likely to drown in one's bathtub than die at the hands of a terrorist. Yet the latter has generated much more fear than the former.

The constant barrage of fear makes it possible to perceive one's situation through paranoid eyes. In *Superpatriotism*, Michael Parents argues, 'Fed a lifelong diet of such offerings, many Americans have little difficulty accepting the picture painted by our leaders of a world full of vicious adversaries, lurking within and without our borders, just waiting to pounce upon us' (2004: 105). Our films begin to reflect that paranoia; that the world is full of killers out to get us. Horror films have actually in some sense become more plausible under this mindset, as the idea of killers and mass death have been confirmed for us by experience.

There is an awareness that the threat of terror has in some cases been overstated, but fear is a potent motivator and a potent tool. 'Since 9/11, dread and fear have regained prominence in the public sphere and become politically instrumental tools for a messianic Bush administration' (Thompson 2007: 17). In other words, there is cause enough for real fear, but the administration also appropriates such fears for its own political, military and social ends out of relation to the actual threat. Frank Furedi observes, 'The threat of terrorism has been appropriated to promote a bewildering variety of causes' (2007: 129). This assertion is proven by a recent study that reported the United States has spent 75 billion dollars each year since 9/11 in order to ensure the nation's safety (Murphy 2011: A1). Such spending has not only been on airport screening and training for law enforcement but also 'cattle nose leads, halters and electric prods – in case terrorists decided to mount biological warfare against cows'; lapel pins for officers in West Virginia; and an eight-foot-high fence around a veteran's hospital in North Carolina, not to mention the various military actions to which the government has committed (Murphy 2011: A1, A14). Kim Murphy is quick to point out that these expenditures, mostly in the form of Homeland Security Department grants to states, counties and municipalities have reaped many benefits over and above the prevention of or preparation for terror attacks. First responders have received much needed training, one consequence of which was that natural disasters have met with better responses, and communication has improved (2011: A15). 'I think it's important to understand the homeland security equipment wasn't bought to be tucked away for the day there would be some terrorism event', said one emergency management director in rural Nebraska (quoted in Murphy 2011, A15). This statement, however, merely proved Furedi's contention that the fear of terrorism is being used to promote other causes and meet other needs.

We have a politics of fear since the terror attacks. To cite but one example: during the 2004 election, Dick Cheney argued that voting for the Kerry/Edwards Democratic ticket would increase the likelihood of terrorist attacks on the United States. We have an economy of fear: billions of dollars have been spent on everything from duct tape and guns to panic rooms, space in survivor shelters, freeze dried food and emergency supplies. We have an entire media of books, talk shows, videos and other media to deal with various threats: inoculations and vaccinations, diet, health, medicine.

As a result, Hollywood has produced several films that present horrific situations that are then revealed to be completely manufactured. There is no real threat, or, more accurately, the threat is purely internal and manipulative. In other words, these films show a world in which the fear of the external is a tool of the internal. In films such as *The Village*, *Cry Wolf* and *Four Boxes* the plot twist at the climax is that there has never been an external threat to the community at all and the authority figures have generated the perceived threat, manufactured the fear, as it were, for their own purposes. Ironically, in these films, the manufacturing of the fear often becomes more dangerous than the ostensible threat itself.

In the wake of September 11, 'There is, if not a culture of fear, at least an American cultural vulnerability to fear' (2006: 202). The films mentioned above, which are analysed below, all demonstrate our culture's vulnerability to fear. We see shadows where there are shadows, but we also see shadows where there are none. And there are those within society who will exploit that fear. Ross Douthat argues that post-9/11 cinema is a 'return of the paranoid style', and certainly there is something of paranoia in films about manufactured fear (2008: 52). Pre-9/11 horror, thriller and action films frequently employed an inciting incident, what Hitchcock called a 'MacGuffin', a misleading entry at the start of the film that leads into a deeper conspiracy. In James Bond films, the initial investigation always leads to a greater and different threat than initially imagined. In *The Crazies*, what seems to be individuals going insane in a small town is revealed to be the accidental release of a government-manufactured virus. The threat in such films is external and usually and actually something other than what the threat is initially assumed to be. The threat is, however, real and the film's authority figure is behind the external threat, as in John Carpenter's *Vampires*, to give a single example. Cardinal Alba (Maximilian Schell) may be the organizer behind the plot, but the vampires are still real, as is the threat behind them. To give another example, The Colony and all who reside there may be werewolves, including the founder, Dr. George Waggner (Patrick Macnee), but the werewolves are still real in *The Howling*. It is a common trope in horror that a member or members of the community is or are actually part of the threat. In these films, the source of the threat may also be internal, but the threat is still genuine. In post-9/11 horror, the key difference is that the external threat may just be an artificial construct of those inside the community who manipulate and abuse it to their own ends. When that false fear generates real results, the manipulators further take advantage of the fear to confirm the reality of the ruse.

The Village: fear for our own good

M. Night Shyamalan's *The Village* (2004) is a film about a community built upon, run by and organized around fear on multiple levels. The fear is a manufactured one, but it is one designed to combat greater fears. The film also echoes the American obsession with quantifying fear ('how afraid should you be', is a common refrain in local news stories), most obviously in its use of colour to indicate when one should be afraid. The monsters that the villagers fear are also revealed to be the creation of those who lead the village, who then lose control of their creation. The entire film becomes an extended metaphor for the village of the United States after 9/11.

In the film's titular village, red is 'the bad color,' 'the color we fear' and 'the color that attracts Those We Don't Speak Of,' as Ivy (Bryce Dallas Howard) tells Noah (Adrien Brody). In the opening montage, when a girl sweeping spots a red flower, she immediately pulls the plant out of the ground and quickly buries it in the dirt away from the house. 'Those We Don't Speak of' dress in red robes. Late at night, upon witnessing a creature in a red robe pass under his watchtower, Finton (Michael) rings the bell. The entire village goes into a panic, as families gather together and rush to their frontier panic rooms, dirt cellars under trap doors under the house. Ivy waits for Lucius

(Joaquin Phoenix) as indistinct, red-hooded creatures grow closer. 'Don't let them in,' begs Kitty (Judy Greer). Lucius arrives in time to take Ivy into the cellar, but the creatures roam the house. Red represents a threat of invasion, of imminent attack, of the enemy already among us.

Those responsible for guarding the village wear yellow robes. Yellow banners mark the end of the village's territory and the beginning of the woods, where the creatures rule. Yellow is worn by those who patrol the woods and who throw sacrifices to the creatures. Yellow is a protective colour, it seems, but it, too is involved in the manufacture of fear. Yellow keeps us in fear, but is safer than red. Both colours are markers of the danger external to the village.

In March 2002, the Department of Homeland Security unveiled a colour-coded terrorism threat scale. Green represented 'Low', in which there was a 'low risk of terrorist attack'. Note that the chart assumes that there is always some risk; there is no colour or category for 'no risk of terrorist attack'. Blue represented 'Guarded', meaning there is a 'general risk of terrorist attack'. Yellow was termed 'Elevated' and meant a 'significant risk of terrorist attack'. Orange represented 'High' and red represented 'Severe', implying a terrorist attack was imminent if not already happening. Interestingly, in the nine years the scale was used, Green and Blue were never used; the nation never fell below 'Elevated' or Yellow. As in *The Village*, yellow is the constant state of fear; red is that which threatens the entire community. Red is 'the colour we fear' and yellow reminds us to stay alert and afraid, but is still safer than red. There is also a critique of the American approach to terrorism. If red is 'the colour that attracts Those We Do Not Speak Of', then terrorism is seen to be an effective means of achieving one's goals. To keep a society in a state of fear, in a state of terror, is to have achieved terrorism's goal. The effectiveness of red draws more red. The effectiveness of promoting terror promotes more terror. Later, Noah stabs Lucius, out of jealousy of his engagement to Ivy. His parents then see him with blood all over his hands, crying because they are covered in 'the bad colour'. Red thus has a secondary referent: the blood of the murder victims related to those who founded the village. The reminder is that red attracts red; blood generates more blood. One cannot escape crime and death.

The Village achieves its effect by pretending to be set a century ago. The opening shot of the film views a man (Brendan Gleeson) from a distance, over the heads of a crowd watching him. He sits by a grave, talking to the casket, clearly grieving a lost child. A shot of the tombstone shows the text: 'Here lies Daniel Nicholson Beloved Son of August Nicholson, June 17, 1890 – October 3, 1897'. Not only does this inscription confirm the death of a young child (seven at the time he passed from his illness), it also sets the relative date of the film: October 1897, since the child is dead and about to be buried. A voiceover from Edward Walker (William Hurt), Ivy's father and the village's de facto leader, transitions the film into the next scene in which the village as a whole sits down to dinner. 'Did we make the right decision to settle here?' he asks rhetorically, before confirming for the community that they did. A moaning is heard from the woods, establishing an unseen threat that has all the villagers nervous, if not in a state of fear. What follows is a montage of village life: planting, tending sheep, sweeping with homemade brooms, all of which, combined with the character's style of dress, tools and the buildings in which they live confirms that the setting is rural America at the end of the nineteenth century. Indeed, Walker's use of the word 'settle' directly implies American westward expansion in the post-civil war era. The overall impression of the film is the rural west (perhaps Colorado, Washington or Oregon) in the eighteen nineties.

The specific use of the word 'settle' also links the film to the history of the United States. Walker and the citizens of the village have chosen to live in a wooded valley. Yet, the moaning from the woods establishes that another group is present and, given the history of the nation, was probably there first. The villagers have displaced another group, echoing the European settlers' displacing of Native Americans. The film already suggests both the uncomfortable history of American settlers, praised for their pioneer spirit but indicted for their treatment of indigenous peoples, and also evokes tropes of that most American of film genres, the western. These are settlers threatened by an outside menace, determined quickly to be the 'creatures' that lived in this area before the settlers.

The twist of the film, of course, is that the film is actually set in the present. The great reveal about three quarters of the way through is that the villagers all live in a preserve outside Philadelphia in contemporary America. Over the course of the film various characters relate stories about the deaths of family members: Lucius' father went to a store in a town and never returned. Mrs. Clack's sister 'did not live past her twenty-third birthday', as some men in an alley killed her. August's brother was murdered. It is revealed at the end that the village elders all met in a support group for relatives of murdered people and decided to abandon the modern world for one of their own making. These are people who fled the reality of the United States of the present and chose to live in a nostalgic past. The threat of murder and death proved to be too much, and so they escaped into the past. But the past is never safe to live in, either. 'You may run from sorrow as we have; sorrow will find you,' says August. All of the elders of the village have sworn an oath never to return to the modern world but to live their lives in the village and raise subsequent generations in perpetuity to stay in their nostalgic simulacra of early modern life.

In a sense, this plot is a metaphor for the United States, which also sought to escape terror and fear by a return to the past. Susan Faludi sees the primary film referent after 9/11 as *The Searchers*, John Ford's film in which John Wayne goes in search of a virginal girl kidnapped by Indians: 'This was the Duke we were so desperate to "welcome back" in the aftermath of 9/11, a stone-cold killer and Indian-hater who would stand guard over our virginal girls' (2007: 7). In *The Village*, Walker is no John Wayne. He is a teacher (and former college professor) who responds to crises by reasoning about them. Faludi argues that American pop culture in this period was hungry for men of action; John Wayne types that punch, shoot and kill those who would hurt family members. *The Village* offers a John Wayne film scenario, but with a neo-con professor and his blind daughter as the heroes. Walker is a neo-con as he exploits his community's fears to reinforce the status quo. He neither wants nor needs Lucius to be heroic. In this John Wayne scenario, it is the blind girl, sent to 'rescue' the heroic man by bringing back the medicine he needs. *The Village* is a critique of the John Wayne approach to post-9/11 America.

The other great twist of the film is that the creatures of which the village lives in fear are not real. They are costumes worn by the village elders, who have also created an entire security system in which the entire village participates. Only a handful of elders know that here is no real threat. The younger generation has grown up with the threat of 'Those We Don't Speak of' and it is a normalized existence for them. They have always known the danger of the creatures. When Ivy tells the two young men she is with, that she has 'magic stones' and knows how to find their way around the creatures, the men abandon her, unable to conceive of a world in which the creatures are not a genuine threat to life and limb. They are terrified of the creatures and everything they do is rooted in their knowledge of the threat. The elders have done their job well: everyone but them believes the threat is real.

The Village is, in many ways, a film about secrets. 'There are secrets in every corner of this village,' Lucius tells his mother. Some of those secrets are about love; but there are also secrets about the true threats facing the community, the role that the leadership plays in maintaining those threats, and why the situation is what it is. Shyamalan might be famous for his twists, but this film is less about plot twists than secrets revealed, which utterly transform the reality of the film.

Read through the reality of the ending, the events of the film are understood significantly differently upon subsequent viewings. From the opening line 'Did we make the right decision to settle here?' (referring in this case to the decision to abandon the twentieth century and all of its technological and medicinal advances to live a pre-industrial revolution lifestyle), to the facts of the village's existence, every line carries an encoded double meaning. The elders willingly pretend at innocence, as if their world is pre-industrial, but they can never forget the past, nor erase the modern sensibilities they brought with them. Each line, in hindsight, carries additional meanings. The audience, like the younger generation of the village, remains ignorant of the secondary meanings until we learn the twin secrets of the village.

Just as the village has been created in the nostalgic past in order to escape the characters' real pasts, so too, do the creatures embody irony. They are referred to as 'Those We Don't Speak Of'. The irony is, of course, they speak about them a good deal, and think about them even more. Just as after 9/11, President Bush told the nation to be vigilant, but live our lives as if normal, to go shopping, and to engage in everyday activities, and yet all media were filled with stories of terrorism, tragedy and loss, so, too, the village, in creating their own monsters to escape the monsters of city life, now live in a constant state of peril. They have escaped a life of fear in the cities of contemporary America to give their children a life of constant fear on the frontier. Modern conveniences have been lost; fear remains.

The inciting incidents of the film are rooted in the younger generation finally rebelling against the state of fear in which the elders keep the village. Lucius wants to travel to the next village in order to get medicines to stop illness. He is 'not afraid' of the creatures as his intentions are pure, and he believes the creatures will sense this and allow him to pass, unmolested. The Elders clearly disapprove of his naïveté, which clearly reflects the dominant attitude towards terrorism in 2004. One cannot negotiate with the external threat, one cannot rely upon one's enemies knowing one's intentions are pure. The enemy can only be protected against or confronted and destroyed. Yet the greater concern is that if Lucius goes, he will learn the truth of the village.

In response to his request, the village is 'attacked' and some homes are painted with a red streak. The creatures are attacking, theorizes Walker, 'because they must feel threatened'. The elders use the narrative of external threat they have created in order to maintain the status quo. Real things begin happening, however. Various animals are found killed and skinned. The children believe the creatures in the woods are behind the animal mutilations, but the elders know it is not possible. Mr. Walker asks them, 'Children, Those We Don't Speak Of have not breached our borders for many years. We do not go into their woods, they do not come into our valley. It is a truce. We do not threaten them. Why would they do this?' It is a mystery to him as well, but the truth is eventually revealed. It is Noah, who is childlike, but also dangerously unstable, who is killing the animals. During Kitty's wedding, children see the creatures in the village again, leaving more marks. Walker knows this is impossible, as all the elders are at the wedding. Conspicuously absent is Noah, who has found the creature costumes and who now wears them upon occasion, leaving behind the animals he has killed and skinned, sparking additional panic.

When Noah stabs Lucius, it adds yet another level of fear and panic, this time genuine, to the leaders of the village. Walker tells this others, 'It is a crime what has happened to Lucius,' but he means this literally as well as metaphorically. A village founded to escape the evils of murder in contemporary American society finds itself with an attempted murder within. 'Our hope of something good and right', was the impetus to create the village, but they can neither escape human nature and its capacity for violence, nor can they escape fear.

Walker sends Ivy to the towns for medicine, to the consternation of the elders. Their new fear is that their established way of life will end. Ivy might expose their existence to the outside world. Walker argues that Ivy and Lucius represent the only hope for future generations. Once the elders begin to die, the ruse will have to be kept up by the next generation. A few must have knowledge of both the evil nature of modern society and the means of preserving the status quo in the village so that the other may maintain an unknowing happiness. 'That is what we have protected here: innocence,' Walker argues.

We might note that the manufacture of fear has now created genuine fears. By using fear to preserve a way of life and promote the status quo, the elders have created a situation in which that fear can be manipulated by others. Noah, who is simple, does not know to be afraid of the woods or the colour red. When he discovers the creature costumes, he wears them for fun. He then follows Ivy in the woods. Even though she knows the truth, she reacts out of fear when she encounters Noah dressed as one of the creatures. 'It's not real. It's not real,' she repeats to herself. She is genuinely afraid, even though she knows not to be.

The being in the woods with her, however, is real, even if it is just Noah in a costume. He attacks her, and she leads him on a chase which ends with his death, falling into a pit filled with sharp branches. Manufactured fears lead to a real death, which then confirms the reality of the false fear. When Ivy tells the elders that she has killed one of the creatures in the woods, they all realize the reality behind the statement. Walker tells Noah's parents, 'We will find him and give him a proper burial. We will tell everyone he was killed by the creatures. Your son has made our stories real. Noah has given us a chance to continue this place. If that is still something we wish for.' This is a pattern we will see repeated in *Cry Wolf* and *Four Boxes*:

what is intended as a prank or a deception has a real effect (often a death) that confirms the false fear.

Walker's intention to use Noah's death to further the village's narrative that enforces the status quo and ensures allegiance also calls to mind the official narratives of the death of Pat Tillman and the rescue of Jessica Lynch. In both cases, the 'official version' was later found not to conform to the actual events facts on the ground. Both events were portrayed as heroic Americans sacrificing themselves, but Tillman was killed by friendly fire and Lynch, who had been reported as fighting back against her capture in Iraq in March 2003, had never fired her weapon and later reports contested the official version of her rescue, noting that the Iraqi army may have fled the day before, which would make her rescue staged. Lynch herself also disputes the official report that she had been raped and tortured by Iraqis, later telling Diane Sawyer in an interview, 'They used me to symbolize all this stuff.' Instead, in *The Village*, as in Afghanistan and Iraq, the authority figures narrated events in a manner different from their actual occurrences in order to promote a story that supported the metanarrative of the authority figures.

When Walker revealed the first secret to Ivy, that the creatures are a 'farce' (but not the second, that the world is not what she thinks it is) he tells her the truth: the creatures are a narrative, a means of preventing anyone going 'to the towns', i.e. returning to modern society. Yet it is to the towns she must go in order to save Lucius. The very thing that will prevent an assault from becoming a murder is the very place from which the elders want to escape.

Ivy arrives outside the woods and it is revealed the village is located in 'Walker Nature Preserve', the film implying that Walker used his father's money and his own knowledge of American history to build a pre-industrial paradise in post-industrial Pennsylvania. Jay, the desk guard (M. Night Shyamalan), reveals that air traffic routes have been moved so that nothing flies over the preserve. Walker used all the modern resources he could to return the village to a pre-modern time. As Kevin the security guard (Charlie Hofheimer) gathers the medical supplies Ivy has asked him for, the audience can see the headlines of three articles in Jay's newspaper: 'Man sought in Multiple Slaying case', 'Body of 7 year old found after three days missing', and '11 die overseas in combat'. Simultaneously, the radio reports, 'There's an overturned tractor-trailer causing a one-hour delay in the Lincoln Tunnel. The body of seven-year-old Katrina Nelson was found today. She'd been missing for three days. Another 14 soldiers died in combat when a bomb exploded in their convoy', before Jay turns it off. The sole moment in the modern world is overwhelming with murder, war, death, kidnapping and the annoyances of everyday life in the New York area. Shyamalan, who places himself in his films, is never completely seen in this brief cameo. It is his point of view through which we hear the radio, read the paper and see Kevin surreptitiously grab first aid equipment. He cautions Kevin never to engage in conversation with anyone he meets while doing his job, as he does not want anyone asking questions about the preserve. It is almost as if Shyamalan is in agreement with the elders. The world is a terrible place. At best you are ignored and not engaged, at worst you are killed. Better to escape into the past, into a more civilized and polite society.

This view, however, is undermined by the very reason why Ivy had to leave in the first place. As with the biblical Cain and Abel, murder has been brought into paradise. The only saving grace is to be found in 'the towns', i.e. in modern civilization. This is perhaps the greatest fear to be found in *The Village*. We cannot safely escape into the past. We cannot live safely in the present. Horrible imaginings leave us in constant fear, which keeps us safe; but the secrets and lies that create those imaginings might lead to real dangers, real monsters and real deaths. Hiding in the red robe, with wooden claws and a pig mask might be an amoral simpleton with a taste for blood and death. The fear we were told was for our own good did not protect us from the real hazards, and instead has led us to fight monsters that do not exist and to ignore the ones that actually do: a powerful message as the United States entered its second year in Iraq with no end in sight.

Cry Wolf: fear to other ends

Cry Wolf employs the elements and tropes of the slasher film. Its marketing campaign focused on the image of its ostensible murderer, a serial killer dubbed 'The Wolf', who wears a camouflage jacket and orange neon ski mask while toting a serrated hunting knife. The opening of the film is a slasher cliché: a young woman runs through dark woods, screaming, pursued by an unseen hunter. The killer calls the young woman's cellphone, and the ring and light allow him to locate her hiding spot. She screams as the killer approaches and the film cuts to the opening credits. It is her murder that serves as one of the inciting incidents of the narrative.

The film then proceeds formulaically to introduce a circle of prep school students at the prestigious Westlake Preparatory Academy, who will serve as the victim pool for the film: Owen, the new student and protagonist, who also serves as 'final girl', in the first of one of many reversals in the film, Dodger, Tom, Randall, Regina, Graham, Lewis and Mercedes. Dodger is the ringleader of the circle of 'bored rich kids', playing 'shepherd' when they meet after curfew in the old chapel to play games. The favourite game is 'a lying game. The object: avoid suspicion, manipulate your friends, eliminate your enemies'. One student is 'the Wolf'; the others are the sheep. They question and accuse each other, voting in favour of or against each other as suspects until 'the Wolf' is revealed or the only one left.

Dodger's name is, of course, indicative of her true identity. She identifies her mother initially as a 'Dickens scholar' but then tells Owen she is actually a sixth grade teacher. Her name is a reference to 'The Artful Dodger' from *Oliver Twist*, the leader of a gang of child criminals, a thief, a pickpocket and a street urchin. While her name suggests education and literary knowledge, it also reflects her lower class origins. Among the 'bored rich kids', Dodger is 'the Wolf'. She is the child of a campus groundskeeper, which, combined with scholarships allows her to attend a school whose other students are the children of senators, wealthy business people and the elite. Because of school uniforms, she is able to pass among them as an equal and even their superior, but she is the child of working class parents and does not have the privilege and wealth of her friends. She must use her intelligence, her cunning and her ability to perform and manipulate (it helps to remember that 'artful' in Dodger's name is not necessarily a compliment, it implies falsehood and skill at criminality) to be their equal if not their superior. She creates 'the Wolf' in order to achieve her own ends.

The film's conclusion reveals that there is no killer. Only two people have died: the girl in the pre-credit sequence who was shot by

Dodger out of sexual jealousy as Mr Walker was having an affair with her as well, and Mr Walker, who was shot by Owen who thought he might be the Wolf. None of the students have been killed or injured. There was no real danger at any point. Despite this absence of genuine threat, however, Dodger and her friends succeed in creating a climate of menace in which even they become uncertain of what is true and what is prank, of what is fun and what is danger.

Dodger convinces Owen to start a new game: 'We'll play with the whole school. They're the sheep and we're the wolves'. They identify the key strategies of their original game: 'Lie your ass off. Defend your honor. Accuse your neighbor', and plot accordingly. What Owen believes is a prank on the school, however, is actually Dodger's plot for revenge. Dodger, who killed the girl, tells Owen, 'Nobody knows who killed that girl. So why don't we make an accusation? Let's convince them the murderer is on campus and he's just getting started'. They then literally create a serial killer based on the model of horror films, which Owen will then email to the entire school. They invent a name, 'the Wolf', characteristic clothing, especially a neon orange ski mask, which functions like Jason's hockey mask, Freddy's

Figure 8.1 *Cry Wolf* (2005): The email text forms the background of the conversation between Dodger (Lindy Booth) and Owen (Julian Morris).

fedora and sweater or the pig mask of Jigsaw, and a weapon: a serrated hunting knife. The irony, pointed out by Dodger herself, is that the first victim, the only victim really, was killed by a gun. 'A knife is scarier,' replies Owen. They invent a serial killer whose sole purpose is to be scary and to frighten their fellow students, or at least so Owen believes. Dodger, however, uses Owen in order to construct an environment of fear that will allow her to get away with the murder of the girl and to get revenge on Mr Walker.

As they write, the text of the email Owen is composing is superimposed on the screen, the words literally superimposing themselves over the student's reality (see figure 8.1). Certain words and phrases are highlighted. While Dodger and Owen speak, the word victims is in bold next to them, suggesting that they are both the creators of the Wolf, but they will also be his victims. The writing of the email is what makes the Wolf 'real' to the other students. They send the email, describing the Wolf as a killer who has killed at other schools and that the murder of the girl at the beginning of the film is similar to how the previous murders started. While we have seen this sort of thing before, most obviously in *Urban Legend*, in which a killer uses the motif of urban legends to kill a circle of friends at a college, *Cry Wolf* director Jeff Wadlow then features a montage that literalizes the metaphor. Two students receive the email and begin discussing it. The screen splits again and again, to show the spread of the email to other students, faculty and staff, like some sort of cinematic mitosis (figure 8.2). Finally, all the images form the back and head of 'the Wolf', his jacket and mask morphing out of the many conversations about him (figures 8.3, 8.4 and 8.5). The Wolf is literally created out of the images of people reading and talking about him. He does not exist in the film until this moment, but the reality of all of these individuals reading and believing the email demonstrates the potential for a climate of fear easily created through electronic media. The viral passing of the rumour and the email literally realizes the killer.

What is remarkable about the email, the story and the subsequent state of fear at the school is that none of the information in the email is correct. While the fiction of 'the Wolf' is obviously false, even the 'facts' are wrong. The email is entitled 'Murder on Campus', yet the murder took place off campus. The email describes a student being

Figures 8.2, 8.3, 8.4, 8.5 Literalization of a metaphor: The transformation of the transmission of the email about The Wolf into the physical body of The Wolf in *Cry Wolf*.

killed, except the girl who was killed was not a student. The email describes the killer using a knife, but the girl was shot. In other words, the receivers of this email already know a different story. The email is demonstrably false, yet the students begin to spread the rumour and believe the email instead of the facts. The text is more real than the reality.

Mr Walker is the journalism teacher at the school, and in his class an interesting discussion takes place near the beginning of the film. With the murder of the girl in the woods near the school, he asks the class what is the role of the media in serving the local community in relation to the local tragedy. Can simply reporting the story become exploitive, or is it necessarily informative, or does the media perpetuate fear based on rumour, hearsay and conjecture? The film never shows the local media reporting on the murder, but the students are able to exploit email and the internet to exploit the tragedy.

The second half of the film consists of a seemingly very straightforward slasher plot. All of the characters are suspects. Dodger and Owen are menaced in the library. The Wolf attacks Owen at his job as an after-hours janitor at the school cafeteria. Randall has gone missing, never showing up at his girlfriend's school for a weekend party and his bloody tongue stud left on Owen's desk. The Wolf trashes Tom's half of his and Owen's dorm room. Mercedes is attacked by the Wolf in the dormitory bathroom. Lewis is attacked when he goes to rescue Regina. Owen is attacked by the Wolf when he goes to check his roommate's car to see if there is any evidence that Randall took it.

It is at this moment that the plot begins to complicate. As Owen flees the Wolf, a campus policeman pulls his gun and threatens to shoot the Wolf. It is revealed that Owen's assailant is actually Mercedes playing a prank. When the group gathers in the chapel again that night, they each reveal that they all have been 'the Wolf' at one point or another to prank each other: Lewis trashed Tom's room, Tom was the attacker in the cafeteria, Regina was the stalker in the library, and Randall attacked Mercedes and Lewis. There was no serial killer. Except that Owen is now convinced that something is happening and he knows that Dodger is having an affair with Mr Walker. Owen finds himself in Walker's office and finds a gun and photos of the dead girl in her underwear. It appears to him that Walker may be the killer. He believes that Dodger has been killed by the real Wolf when he sees her tackled and stabbed by a man in the jacket and mask. He believes Randall has been killed by the Wolf and his body hidden in the chapel. He believes all of his remaining friends have fled the campus. All of these beliefs, however, are also the result of pranks.

When confronted by Mr Walker, who also is carrying a mask and jacket that he states he found (also probably true), Owen shoots him. Afterwards, the police reveal that the evidence indicates Walker killed the girl after having a sexual affair with her and that Owen acted in self-defence and will not be charged. Owen realizes that Dodger has set up the entire scenario and exploited it to its end. She ensured that he would believe Mr Walker might actually be a killer. She planted the gun in Walker's office and planted photos of her rival undressing. The police have found this evidence, and, combined with the dead Walker whom Owen found with knife, mask and jacket, conclude that Walker was the killer and Owen acted in self-defence. But there was no killer. Or, more accurately, Dodger was the killer. She has literally gotten away with murder twice, killing her rival and her lover. She is the Wolf. She manufactured fear. There was no killer. There was never any danger. None of the students were killed. In this sense, the film is a meta-slasher film different from the *Scream* series. While *Scream* is reflexive and self-aware, *Cry Wolf* is a straightforward presentation of someone using slasher tropes to manipulate her community into believing it is in danger, in order to pursue her own agenda of revenge.

Four Boxes: fear for its own sake

Four Boxes is also a film with an artificial threat, in this case three individuals creating a pseudo-documentary about a terrorist that inadvertently results in their actual deaths. Three friends, Trevor (Justin Kirk), Amber (Terryn Westbrook) and Rob (Sam Rosen) with a complex history (Amber used to date Trevor and is now engaged to Rob) operate an online auction business that disposes of the possessions of the recently deceased. They occupy a house formerly owned by Bill Zill that they are hired to clean out and discover a computer that has bookmarked a surveillance camera website called 'fourboxes.tv' that features four hidden cameras in the house of a hooded, bomb-making terrorist named Havoc and his assistant Ziploc. The apartment or house was wired by the previous tenants and Havoc does not know that he is being watched. He eventually discovers the cameras after the protagonists have witnessed him building bombs and disposing of bodies and comes looking for Trevor, Amber and Rob. Like a slasher, he begins stalking the three and the audience watches it unfold.

The film then reveals the entire scenario was a setup concocted by Amber, Trevor and Rob. They take turns playing Havoc and Ziploc on camera and have literally written a script that demonstrates how the whole thing will play out. They also plan to announce on fourboxes.tv that the whole thing has been an elaborate hoax and wait for the countdown on the website to go live. While they wait, Amber has inadvertently left the car running in the garage, the three are overcome by the fumes and die in the house before they can 'go live'. Their actual dead bodies are then displayed on the website and presumably discovered by the police. Their staged performance of three people discovering a terrorist on a website and the terrorist then stalking and killing them results in their deaths.

The film's tagline is 'Watching can be deadly', and it also marketed itself as '*Rear Window* on the internet', thus framing itself as a Hitchcockian thriller, as well as a slasher film with a terrorism angle. The idea is that if one watches dangerous people, who are then aware that they are being watched, the viewer is in danger. The reference to the internet, however is a reminder that going to websites is not a one-way street. Software now allows corporations, the government, and even any competent programmer, hacker or computer user to place 'cookies' in one's computer, track the websites one visits and send viruses or spyware that can cause genuine damage to one's computer and by extension, work and life. The idea that one is simply a passive user of the internet with no data flowing in the other direction is hopelessly naïve. To misquote Nietzsche, when we gaze into Amazon.com, Amazon gazes also into us.

There is also a literal meaning in this case. Trevor, Amber and Rob create a scenario in which they watch a website and then the person they are watching attacks them. That person, however, is a fictional construct. Havoc is also them. The entire world of the film is fictitious, created by the three so that they will be watched on the internet. It is their hope that viewers will watch them watching Havoc, and then believe Havoc has killed them. Everything in the film happens because Trevor, Amber and Rob want to be watched themselves. The scenario then posits that 'watching can be deadly', as they die while waiting to be watched. Watching something yourself is deadly, but so is someone watching you. The viewer is in danger, but so is the viewed.

The conclusion of *Four Boxes* is that ultimately, none of the things viewed on the internet or that happened in Bill Zill's house were real. The characters plotted to use the scenario in order to raise their own profiles on the internet, gaining many hits, so that they might be able to make films and other projects. Their fear of what they had discovered on the web was not real. They watched a terrorist make bombs, but it was not real. Their fear at watching the bomb maker was not real. They hoped to generate fear in their own web viewers until the big reveal that it was all a deception. Instead, they created a situation that resulted in their actual deaths, perhaps confirming for their viewers the reality of 'Havoc and Ziploc'. As with *Cry Wolf*, what began as an internet prank had real ramifications and resulted in death. The final, genuine horror comes from the realization of reality and the repercussions of the prank.

The difference with *Cry Wolf*, however, is that in that film, Dodger manipulated the other characters to create a fraudulent but believable killer in order to achieve a genuine revenge. In the case of *Four Boxes*, all three characters were in on the ruse, but the circumstances resulted in all of their accidental, unplanned deaths. There was no outside manipulator with a greater objective, who exploits the fear. In a sense, *Four Boxes* is an existential joke, a dark comedy in which individuals who planned on faking their own deaths and then revealing the joke to an internet audience inadvertently die unintentionally and cause their audience to believe in the reality of their manufactured fear, since they are not alive to reveal the ruse. It is not, however, a morality tale of the danger of manipulating fears. Indeed, their dead bodies become proof of the reality of the fear they sought to manufacture, a visual version of Kurt Vonnegut's warning in *Mother Night* (1966) to beware what one pretends to be, because in the end that is what one becomes.

Conclusion

The rational voices ('There are no such things as ghosts/vampires/zombies/Freddy/etc.') are always proven wrong in the horror film. The person who states, 'There is nothing out there,' is almost always demonstrably mistaken. Horror tells the viewer, 'You are right to be afraid, suspicious and even paranoid and, by extension, to be violent and aggressive. Only killing that which seeks to kill you will keep you safe. And it or they will not stop trying to kill you until you are forced to kill it or them.' Horror justifies fear.

Post-9/11, however, introduces complexity into this idea. What happens when there is actually nothing out there? Actions taken out of fear can have unintended consequences. As the cliché goes, just because you are paranoid does not mean there are not people out to get you. There are clear and real threats and dangers in the world for the United States and for Americans. But paranoia leads to overreaction or wrong reaction, which actually increases the danger. Sidney Hook reminds us:

> There is intelligent fear and unintelligent fear. Those who are completely fearless will not live long. Intelligent fear arms us against real danger and enables us, by modifying the environment or altering our behavior, to reduce the incidence of terror and pain. Intelligent fear must be proportionate to the dangers. It is the absence of any proportion between the danger and the fear which marks the panicky and hysterical response. (1974: 58)

The three films analysed in this chapter focus on a post-9/11 horror trope: the absence of proportion between danger and response. That fear in and of itself can be just as dangerous as the terror that generated the fear.

Conversely, these films also demonstrate that fear is also manufactured. When the elders of the village or Dodger or three young film-makers want to pursue their own objectives, they find fear is both the best means to achieve their goals and the best means to mask their true intentions. After 9/11 there was a good deal of genuine fear in the United States. By the time these three films had been made, however, the United States had invaded and occupied Iraq, a nation that had not attacked us, nor was involved in 9/11. It does not seem unreasonable to draw a line from the Iraq war, the USA PATRIOT Act and the media's and government's use of fear to the ideas in such films as *The Village*, *Cry Wolf* and *Four Boxes*. Sometimes there really is nothing out there. But the horror comes from the person who knows that, manipulating the fears of those who do not.

9

Horrific Nostalgia: Remaking the Slasher Film

Thousands of dangerous killers, schooled in the methods of murder, often supported by outlaw regimes, are now spreading throughout the world like ticking time bombs, set to go off without warning.

GEORGE W. BUSH
STATE OF THE UNION ADDRESS
29 JANUARY 2002

I watched him for fifteen years, sitting in a room, staring at a wall, not seeing the wall, looking past the wall – looking at this night, inhumanly patient, waiting for some secret, silent alarm to trigger him off. Death has come to your little town, Sheriff. Now you can either ignore it, or you can help me to stop it.

DR SAM LOOMIS (DONALD PLEASANCE)
HALLOWEEN

HORRIFIC NOSTALGIA: REMAKING THE SLASHER FILM 193

Susan Faludi argues that after 9/11 popular culture and social critics began to interpret events through the lens of a 'neofifties nuclear family, 'togetherness', redomesticated femininity, and reconstituted cold war manhood' (2007:3–4). She argues that 9/11 was used by neoconservatives to advance an Eisenhower-era, Cold War vision of the United States. Conversely, Ross Douthat sees the cinema of post-9/11 as echoing the seventies in an article entitled 'The Return of the Paranoid Style' (2008: 52). Douthat sees paranoia, distrust of government and corporations and a hermeneutics of scepticism towards all institutions as common tropes between the seventies and the first decade of the twenty-first century. I will not argue with either Faludi or Douthat, as their arguments are convincing, but I will add a third decade that is also evoked by horror after 9/11 and that is the eighties.

Post 9/11 horror is nostalgic for pre-9/11 horror, particularly that of the eighties. It is a reaction against the horror of the period immediately before September 11, primarily the nineties, and it seeks to reimagine the second Bush era as a second coming of Reagan. In this brief, final chapter, I propose to consider the remade slasher film as employing the slasher motif as emblematic of 9/11 and terrorists and that the remade slasher film is a form of nostalgia for the eighties. Nostalgia is a form of conservatism, which perceives the past through rose-coloured glasses and attempts to reimagine the present as the past. Although the current cycle of remakes began in the late nineties with remakes of such spectral early sixties fare as *House on Haunted Hill* (1959/1999), *The Haunting* (1963/1999), and *13 Ghosts* (1960/2001), the slasher film remake cycle began after 9/11 with the remake of *The Texas Chainsaw Massacre* (1974/2003), followed by *Black Christmas* (1974/2006), *When a Stranger Calls* (1979/2006), *Halloween* (1978/2007), *Prom Night* (1980/2008), *My Bloody Valentine* (1981/2009), *House on Sorority Row* (1983/remade as *Sorority Row*, 2009), *Friday the 13th* (1980/2009) and *A Nightmare on Elm Street* (1984/2010).[1] While the seventies began the slasher craze, it is most identified with the eighties, with the era of Reagan, and with a strong America.

The eighties slasher films represent a combination of human and inhuman killers. The killers of *The Burning*, *Prom Night*, *Happy Birthday to Me*, *Sleepaway Camp*, *Slumber Party Massacre* and

Terror Train, to name but a handful, are all too human, even if they are sexually confused or even transgendered. Even Michael Myers, despite his seemingly imperviousness to harm, is still a human being under the mask, although Dr Loomis continues to insist he is 'pure evil.' Jason and Freddy, on the other hand are no longer human. Freddy haunts and kills in dreams, Jason dies several times and is finally resurrected as an unstoppable inhuman killing machine.

The nineties, on the other hand featured predominantly human monsters in its slasher films. Beginning with *Silence of the Lambs* (1991), which gave us both Buffalo Bill (Ted Levine) and Hannibal 'The Cannibal' Lecter (Anthony Hopkins), and ending with *American Psycho* (2000), the serial killers of the decade were most decidedly human and not supernatural. The killers of the *Scream* series (1996, 1997, 2000 and 2011), *I Know What You Did Last Summer* (1997) and its sequel (1998), *Urban Legend* (1998) and the remake of *Psycho* (1998) are not supernatural at all, In fact, the films go out of the way to demonstrate they are simply disturbed humans. Unlike Jason, Freddy and Michael, when these killers are themselves killed, they stay dead

The eighties and nineties also displayed a penchant for likeable villains and wisecracking monsters. Hannibal Lecter, terrifying though he is, is also gregarious and quite droll. Chucky from the *Child's Play* series (1988, 1990, 1991, 1998 and 2004), Freddy Kruger, and even Ghostface from *Scream* are all witty and entertaining as they killed. Nineties horror is camp, in Susan Sontag's sense. Camp combats 'the threat of boredom. The relationship between boredom and Camp taste cannot be overestimated. Camp taste is by its nature possible only in affluent societies, in societies or circles capable of experiencing the psychopathology of affluence' (Sontag 1978: 290). No wonder most of the slasher films of the nineties concerned bored, affluent teens who knew the 'rules' of horror and still got killed.

Andrew Tudor sees the 'postmodern horror' of the nineties as exhibiting 'studied self-consciousness' and the 'use of pastiche' as well as the 'prominence of comedy' (2002: 107). The later films in the *Friday the 13th* and *Nightmare on Elm Street* series, as well as the more 'reflexive' horror of the *Scream* series and films such as *I Know What You Did Last Summer* offer fragmented horror and deconstructed deaths; they are not so much 'scary' as ironic.[2]

The terror attacks of 11 September 2001 presaged the return of the serious supernatural serial killer. The films of the eighties and early nineties began to be remade in the wake of 9/11. The sexual politics in the remakes are still regressive, as outlined by Creed, Clover and Twitchell. Twitchell is still right when it comes to slasher films: sexual anxieties are played out and sexuality is still subject to punishment. The influence of 9/11, as noted in the introduction, however, reshapes the gender politics and continues to empower women, even the sexually active ones, but allows gender to be ignored as a concern. As a result, there are fewer final girls and more final couples, as in *Hatchet* or the reboot of *Friday the 13th*. James Marriott posits, 'Gender confusion tends to be at the heart of the relationship between slasher and 'final girl', underlying both the killer's pathology … and the boyish and gender-free name of the final girl' (2007: 214). If there is no final girl, however, either because she is part of a couple or because she dies too (as in *Wolf Creek*, *The Devil's Rejects*, and *Martyrs*) indicates that gender confusion (and therefore gender issues) are of no importance in the post-9/11 horror film. This is not to suggest that gender is made irrelevant, only that gender confusion no longer drives the killer who, modelled after the terrorists, is often a personification of evil. Terrorists do not kill because their mothers forced them to dress as girls until young adulthood, in American popular myth (and in the government's rhetoric), they are simply 'evil', the same term Dr Sam Loomis uses to describe Michael in *Halloween*.

The Bush administration frequently evoked both a nostalgia for the eighties and a call to return to that period. President Reagan was invoked almost as much as Jesus in press conferences and the eighties was held up as an example of a paradigmatic period in which America was at a high point in its history. The Reagan era is remembered for its militarism in the name of protection and freedom from strife: 'Peace through strength' was one of Reagan's mottos. 'Morning in America' was his campaign slogan, evincing self-confidence, success in the world, a change for the better and a return to traditional values. Reagan himself promoted a nostalgia for the fifties, with 'traditional family values' as code for rolling back the sixties, the counterculture, the feminist and civil rights movements and the disappointments and defeats of Watergate, the Vietnam War and the Iran hostage crisis. Reagan projected strength, warmth and pride. The image nostalgia for his presidency inspires one to believe 9/11 could not have occurred on his watch.

The remade slasher film thus combines two elements: a nostalgia for a time in which America was strong (or at least perceived as strong on defence and the promotion of sexual morality), and the fear and nihilism of the post-9/11 horror film, resulting in an uneasy balance. The slasher film posits a sexual morality, in which those who engage in premarital intercourse or other 'sins' (drinking, doing drugs and disrespecting authority figures also target one for killing by a slasher, but the predominant cause of death is being sexually active) are killed, while resourceful young women, who remain 'pure' are able to triumph over the killer. This formula is a celebration of patriarchal values and the embodiment of the virtues promoted during the Reagan era. Problematizing the moral and sexual issues is the commitment of post-9/11 horror to seeing monsters as the embodiment of evil and being virtually unstoppable. These films also echo other concerns of the post-9/11 horror milieu.

The remade slasher films lose the camp humour and playfulness of the killers. By the second film of the *Nightmare on Elm Street* series, *Freddy's Revenge* (1985), Freddy (Robert Englund) was already being reduced to a wisecracking, punning villain, less scary than obnoxious. He was a child killer killed by parents. In the recent remake, Freddy (Jackie Earle Haley) has no sense of humour. He is a brutal, violent, sadistic killer again. His presence is fearful. His crimes are worse. Although the original Freddy was presented as a man who killed children but has been transformed by death into a vengeful comedian, Freddy is now a child molester who worked as a janitor at an elementary school and who violated children in a secret basement room. After their parents killed him, he returned from the grave to begin killing his victims. This Freddy is not a wisecracking comic monster, he is nothing short of a terrorist.

The remake of *Friday the 13th* is technically a remake of *Friday the 13th Part 2* (1981). Mrs Vorhees, avenging the death of her mentally challenged son who drowned when camp counsellors were having sex instead of watching him, was the killer in the first film. Jason did not begin killing until the second film, returning from the dead from the bottom of Crystal Lake. The remake offers the ending of the original as a pre-credit sequence. The film then takes up with a group of twenty-somethings who have come to the woods in order to find a stash of marijuana plants. Jason, now fully grown and never quite seen, kills three of the four and kidnaps Whitney (Amanda Rhigetti), holding her prisoner for months. The original Jason would have simple killed her, too, but this film implies she resembles his mother.

Whitney's brother Clay (Jared Padelecki) distributes fliers around Crystal Lake, searching for his sister. He runs into a group of wealthy, elite college students on their way to party at a private residence on Crystal Lake. These individuals will form Jason's next group of victims. Even the choice of victims reflects a different world. In the original film and its first sequels, the victims were camp counsellors attempting to reopen Camp Crystal Lake. These were individuals involved in rebuilding, preparing the camp for children and engaging in camp activities such as canoeing, archery and hiking. While they partied, drank and did drugs, all of that was secondary. The remake features victims, like those of *Hostel*, for whom the partying is primary. They do not seek to do anything beyond get drunk and have sex. There is no larger purpose: they are wasted youth (in all senses of the term). Jason slaughters them all. He does not distinguish between the sexually active and the 'pure'. While Whitney and her boyfriend do not have crazy, loud sex as their companions do, it is made clear that they, too, expect to have relations during the camping trip.

As I have written elsewhere: 'Unlike 9/11, which demonstrated that anyone, regardless of behavior or actions, could die simply by going to work or being in the wrong place at the wrong time, slasher films assert a morality and a meaningful cosmos' (2011: 92). The morality of the slasher film returns somewhat, both in the remakes of *Friday the 13th* and *Halloween* (2007), although random and anonymous death still dominates both films. The latter features an extended childhood sequence, showing the empty and ugly home life of Michael, his childhood killing incident in which he beats a school bully to death and then stabs his sister and her boyfriend to death render the horror somewhat less. Carpenter's original gave no reason or motivation for Michael's initial murder. A young boy dressed as a clown kills his sister in suburban America. Rob Zombie's remake shows a lower, working class family, the step-father is unable to work, the mother is a stripper and the whole family is dysfunctional and hostile, and solve problems through violence and self-medication. That Michael becomes a killer is unsurprising. He kills even those who have not violated the moral code of slasher films, however, and his desire to kill his baby sister (Scout Taylor-Compton) lies rooted not the sexual morality of the nineties but in the post-9/11 construction of monsters as terrorists. He, a primitive, hulking monster with a knife, invades suburbia and attempts to kill Laurie. She does not know who he is or why he hates her, he only seeks to kill her. He also kills everyone else he comes across. The original film shows suburbia is not safe from the evil within it. The remake shows that even those who rise out of poverty and live safe, comfortable lives of privilege are not safe from the evils they believe they escaped, the evils that exist outside of their perfect, sculpted, protected world.

Slasher films demonstrate the lessons of September 11. By remaking 'classic' ones, however, they also evoke nostalgia for a period when America was perceived as strong and a leader of the free world. The paradox of the remade slasher film is that it plays to our fears of terrorism: no one knows where the killer is, how and when he might strike next, and, in some cases, even who he is, while simultaneously comforting us with its familiarity and its message that the thing terrorizing us can be defeated. The remade slasher film allows us to contain and control our terror at the faceless killers who are out to get us.

In a sense, horror taught Americans how to understand 9/11 as well. Osama bin Laden is Jason, Freddy, Leatherface and especially Michael. Both Dick Cheney and Donald Rumsfeld, when speaking of the leaders of al Qaeda sound remarkably like Donald Pleasance in the original *Halloween*:

I met him fifteen years ago. I was told there was nothing left: no reason, no conscience, no understanding, even the most rudimentary sense of life or death, good or evil, right or wrong. I met this six year old child with this blank, pale, emotionless face with the blackest eyes, the devil's eyes. I spent eight years trying to reach him and then another seven trying to keep him locked up because I realized what was living behind that boy's eyes was purely and simply evil.

This passage could have been written by Rumsfeld about bin Laden. You do not negotiate with Michael Myers. You do not try to understand him. You can only kill him to prevent him from killing you and others, because he is 'simply evil'. Michael will never be put on trial, as even Hannibal Lecter was. Likewise, Osama bin Laden would never have faced a jury; the only American response to evil in that sense is to kill it outright.

Some of the elements of slasher films have shown up in other types of horror movies as well. *Hostel* has elements of slasher horror, although it violates traditional slasher morality. Paxton, who is a hard-drinking, sexually active hedonist lives, whereas Joshua, who is comparatively innocent and pure dies horribly. The only female victim we see, Hana, a Japanese girl who might be a 'final girl', is horribly disfigured and kills herself rather than allow herself to be rescued. The *Saw* series is obviously inspired by slasher films, not only in its gratuitous murder scenes but in the morality of its killer. In 2011 the slasher film has oddly become a kind of comfort horror: we know what to expect, we know how to react and we know that despite the deaths shown to the audience, at least one person can and will escape the killer (except when they do not).

There has not been a genuine 'final girl' since *Scream*. While *Scream* itself is meta-horror, horror that is aware it is an artificial construction, the sequels which followed extended the meta: *Scream* is a horror film about horror films. *Scream 2* is a sequel about sequels. *Scream 3* is a third film about trilogies. *Scream 4*, made over a decade after the previous one is a franchise reboot about franchise reboots and remakes. Kirby (Hayden Panettiere), answers a call from Ghostface, one of whose signatures is to ask questions about scary movies. Ghostface begins, 'What recent remake ... '. She does not even let him finish the question. She immediately rattles off about a dozen and a half of them: *Friday the 13th*, *Halloween*, *Prom Night*, *My Bloody Valentine*, *Sorority Row*, *House of Wax*, *The Fog*, etc. Not taking a chance, she names them all, demonstrating how the past decade and a half has been dominated by reboots and remakes, including *Scream 4*. The film calls attention to its own complicity in recycling the horrors of the past.

Ultimately, there is an element of the slasher film to the 9/11 attacks as well. Terrorists have historically planned their attacks to coincide with significant dates on the calendar. Many eighties slasher films were rooted in the idea of a return of a killer on a significant date or anniversary: *Halloween*, *Friday the 13th*, *Prom Night*, *Graduation Day*, etc.[3] The killers on 9/11 were low tech as well as high tech. They did slam airplanes into buildings, transforming them into people-filled missiles, killing thousands; but they took control of those planes armed with box cutters. They were slasher film killers, threatening and killing with knives in order to bring about a larger set of murders. Perhaps that is the final link between remade slasher films and the period in which they were made. After the irony of the nineties, we began to recognize once again that men with knives could indeed bring about a great deal of horror, and containing them to a single individual in the woods or in the suburbs would allow us to put that monster back in the box and feel control once more.

Conclusion

Ten Years of Post-9/11 Horror

I write these words a few weeks before the tenth anniversary of the terror attacks on September 11. *The 9/11 Commission Report* states that the failure of the United States government to anticipate and stop the terror attacks of September 11 was 'a failure of imagination' (National Commission on Terrorist Attacks upon the United States, 2004: 9). Horror cinema is a 're-imagining' of 9/11, and we have been re-imagining it for a decade since. If our imagination failed before that day, since that day our imagination has become a primary means of coping with and understanding the events of that day and events since. As I hope this volume has indicated, the cinema where horror is playing is where we interpret, understand and perhaps even reach a small catharsis about the terror attacks, or, conversely, reach no catharsis and descend into a bleak nihilism that reflects the reality of the past decade.

In the conclusion to her volume *The Dark Side*, subtitled *The Inside Story of How the War on Terror Turned into a War on American Ideals*, Jane Mayer writes, '[I]t is clear that what began on September 11, 2001 as a battle for America's security became, and continues to be, a battle for the country's soul' (2008: 327). Horror movies remind us that sometimes we are the monster. In *Saw*, in *Hostel Part 2*, in *The Mist*, and in *30 Days of Night* we are reminded that we make poor decisions, that torture is being done in our names, that we become the monsters we fight and therefore are as scary if not scarier than them. In the battle for the country's soul, as *The Exorcism of Emily Rose* and *The Last Exorcism* teach us, sometime the exorcist dies, sometimes the one he is trying to save does not survive. Post-9/11 horror reminds us that evil is real, but sometimes it can be contained.

In this conclusion I wish to return to two films one last time: *Cloverfield* and *The Strangers*, for a brief comparison of how they replicate 9/11 on the screen. *Cloverfield* is post-9/11 horror writ large. Conversely, *The Strangers* is post-9/11 horror writ small, but with the same effect to the same intent as the larger film. The key difference is in *Cloverfield* we recapitulate the experience of watching 9/11 happen on the screen from a distance, afterwards, whereas *The Strangers* recapitulates the experience of those on the planes, watching as it unfolds. *Cloverfield* is mediated horror; *The Strangers* is unmediated. The killers in *The Strangers* are a small group of unknown individuals. They employ knives to kill (reminiscent of the box cutters employed by the terrorists). As noted in Chapter 3, what is particularly chilling is the idea of random selection of victims, that one dies because of location ('Why are you doing this to us?' 'Because you were home'). In *The Strangers*, unlike in *Cloverfield*, the psychological effect is important, if not more so than physical. *Cloverfield* depicts an event – a random, destructive attack on New York City in which individuals are not important (in fact, according to the film's creators in the DVD behind-the-scenes feature, the monster is actually a baby, more frightened of us than we are of it! Thus, the situation is also fraught with misunderstanding and overreactions on both parts). *The Strangers* depicts the killing and terrorizing of individuals. The latter is a film about psychological terror, knowing that individuals have randomly targetted you, but are now out to kill you no matter what. As in the previous film, the victims all die, none survive, and the 'bad guys' get away with it. This film is 9/11 writ on the personal level, 9/11 understood as one's own random, purposeless death.

In *The Strangers* random people (terrorists?) use everyday items to frighten and then kill random people. What is that if not a reflection of our own fears? No experience, no hope could save you from being ploughed into a building if you were on American Airlines Flight 88. The best you could hope for, if you were on United 93, was to plough the plane into the ground so only you died and not a building full of people, too. That is our fear: that the best we can hope for is to die without too many others dying with us. The deaths seem senseless. The killers themselves escape justice, at least recognizable justice. The world is not fair. We live in inexplicable fear and the worst fear is that we do not know what is going to happen next or why, only that it is going to be real bad. While an honest assessment of 9/11 would say we understand who did it, why they did it, what their motivations were and what they hoped to achieve, on a child-like level, we still do not get it. We can call them evil, but it still seems like meaningless, motiveless malevolence.

Now, one might prefer one's horror to end in hope, or that experience will allow the triumph of good, or that the threat can be defeated, even if only in the last few minutes. And if one does, *The Strangers* is an ugly movie. I (for now at least) am a fan of horror that does not merely play at horror, horror that does not compromise at the end, horror that embraces the nihilism of its time and shows us what we fear the most. The only way to conquer fear is to go to the worst possible place you can and look at it with eyes wide open. Otherwise, you should just watch *Ghostbusters* or even *The Exorcist* –because these are films that promise a meaningful, logical universe in which action by a few brave individuals can save us. But, as we all know in the wake of 9/11, the universe is not so kind. David L. Scruton offers the cautionary understanding that, 'Fear is our society speaking to us through our own voice, insistently reminding us of what it means to live in the world' (1986: 42). We watch horror films because we lived through 9/11.

We should recognize as well that 9/11 and subsequent events are not only reproduced through horror films, they are also interpreted through horror cinema. Nick Muntean and Matthew Thomas Payne state, 'The September 11 attacks, then, functioned according to a logic quite similar to that of the zombie films, albeit with terrifyingly real consequences' (2009: 243). We 'understood' 9/11 in the moment, since it resembled a movie. The terror attacks of September 11 taught us about horror, but horror also teaches us about the world after 9/11. In doing so, even without catharsis, these films offer us an opportunity to understand the world and to contain and overcome the horror of terror.

Notes

Notes on Introduction

1. This assertion is actually not entirely true. The proliferation in the past decade of the superhero fantasy genre is also a direct response to 9/11, everything from the *Spiderman* and *Batman* series to *Thor* and *Superman Returns* to *V for Vendetta* and *Watchmen* can be seen as a form of wish-fulfilment fantasy for heroes (no matter how flawed) who might save us from 'bad guys'. Often in these films, however, the focus is on the hero as dysfunctional and on the frequent inadequacy of the hero to sufficiently respond to various crises in a manner that reintegrates society. Just as frequently the battles between hero and his or her nemesis causes a great deal of collateral damage. Villains such as the Joker serve as a stand-in for terrorists, causing terror to American urban landscapes. In the case of *Iron Man*, villain Obadiah Stane (Jeff Bridges) is literally in league with terrorists in Afghanistan. Yet these films also represent a form of wish fulfilment, in which a flawed individual with superior powers is able to defeat, capture and perhaps even kill those who would harm innocent citizens.
2. Despite these pronouncements, it is important to note that not all horror films after September 11 are so bleak, nihilistic and hopeless, nor are all films before that day hopeful, or at least contain the possibility of redemption. I speak here in terms of broad trends and dominant motifs.
3. See Wetmore 2009 for an argument that the similarity between these two cultural crises is what allowed J-horror to succeed so well in the American marketplace, in addition to the novelty factor.
4. This 'official' number comes from *The 9/11 Commission Report* (2004: 311).
5. Although more commonly known and cited as 'the Patriot Act', the title is actually an acronym which stands for United and Strengthening America by Providing Appropriate Tools to Intercept and Obstruct Terrorism Act of 2001, the official title of the bill and

subsequent law. Ironically, it did not actually unite America as many of its provisions proved quite controversial.

6 Information on the attacks is primarily from David Willman's *The Mirage Man: Bruce Ivins, the Anthrax Attacks and America's Rush to War* (New York: Bantam, 2011), the most complete and up-to-date history of the anthrax attacks as of this writing.

7 Noël Carroll links 'the psychology of horror' back to Aristotle (1990: 168–78). For Carroll, the great questions of horror cinema are its two fundamental paradoxes: 'how can anyone be frightened by what they know does not exist' and 'why would anyone even be interested in horror, since being horrified is so unpleasant' (1990: 8). He then distinguishes between 'art horror' (i.e. horror films) and 'natural horror' (i.e. the experience of 9/11) (1990: 12). For Carroll, art horror is fundamentally rooted in catharsis. The answers to his two questions are that we allow ourselves to be frightened by the non-existent to gain psychological control over those 'unpleasant' emotions, a very Aristotelian conclusion.

8 For an excellent recent volume on suffering, death and representations of catastrophe in Greek tragedy, the reader is directed to Edith Hall's *Greek Tragedy: Suffering under the Sun* (Oxford: Oxford University Press, 2010). Justina Gregory's edited volume *Companion to Greek Tragedy* (Malden, MA: Blackwell, 2005) also gives an excellent background to Greek tragedy, catharsis and Phrynicus. For those interested in Aristotle, many good translations of the *Poetics* can be found, but Kenneth Telford's 1961 translation and analysis is one of the best and offers a unique and accurate understanding of Aristotle's concepts (Chicago: Henry Regnery, 1961).

9 These terms for subgenres and hybrid genres were coined by the following: 'torture porn' (Edelstein 2006), 'post millennial horror road movie' (Ballard 2008), 'military horror film' (Hantke 2010) and 'post-torture porn retro-slasher' (The Gore-Met 2010).

Notes on Chapter 1

1 To a certain extent, this aspect is still true, as borne out by such films as *2012*, which concerns the destruction of the entire world, but the first scenes are set in, and the most prolonged and gleeful destruction is of, Los Angeles, and such films as *Battle: Los Angeles*, which, like *Skyline*, sees Los Angeles as 'ground zero' for an alien invasion. So while New York has primacy of destruction, Los

Angeles still sees its fair share of attacks and mayhem. As a fellow Los Angelino once asked me about *Battle: Los Angeles* when the posters began appearing around town: 'How do we all die now?', demonstrating the flippancy of natives to the almost ludicrous number of depictions of our hometown being destroyed. Perhaps nature and aliens are not cinema fans. Also, the destruction of New York is always played as tragedy, but the destruction of Los Angeles is played as farce (see, for example, *Independence Day*).

2 C. James, 'Live images make viewers witnesses to horror' New York Times (12 September 2001): A25. Quoted in Zelizer and Allan, 2002: 5.

3 This image is also used to great effect in the television series *Battlestar Galactica*.

Notes on Chapter 3

1 The term 'megadeath' originated in Herman Kahn's *On Thermonuclear War*, although he first coined the neologism in 1953. It was a means of reducing mass deaths during a global nuclear war to comprehensible numbers.

2 Stated in an interview on the *National Geographic: Inside 9/11* DVD.

3 For those interested in a nuanced and complex understanding of the reasons behind al Qaeda and its particular approach to terrorism, see Lawrence Wright's Pulitzer Prize-winning study *The Looming Tower: Al Qaeda and the Road to 9/11* (2006).

4 Although I fully concede I use it here in a slightly different meaning than Coleridge does.

5 Stated in an interview in 'The Elements of Terror', a behind-the-scenes documentary on *The Strangers* DVD.

6 Quotes are taken from the interview with Haneke on the DVD of *Funny Games*.

7 The film is *Benny's Video* (1992), about a young man who likes to watch violent movies.

8 Haneke himself makes the observation in the DVD interview that by 2005 (when the interview was taking place), the original film had lost much of its punch. He was also concerned that audiences did not understand his point and were simply watching the film for its unmitigated brutality.

Notes on Chapter 4

1 Quoted in *The 9/11 Commission Report* (2004: 47).
2 Quoted in Danner, 2004: 29.
3 Quoted in Priest and Gellman, 2002: A1.

Notes on Chapter 6

1 Frum 2003: 140.
2 Schlesinger 2004: 116.

Notes on Chapter 7

1 I would argue that, in fact, not a single film of M. Night Shyamalan's has been as well received as *The Sixth Sense* because he has maintained a pre-9/11 sensibility in many of his films. Shyamalan's films are ultimately about people with special abilities transcending crises and fixing the world. From *Unbreakable* to *Signs* (which was in production when 9/11 happened) to *The Village* to *The Lady in the Water* to *The Happening*, some of which, as this volume has argued, have post-9/11 characteristics and images, Shyamalan's films function in the heroic mode and his characters are ordinary people who discover they are actually extraordinary. This aspect, more than the supposed twists he is known for, dominates his cinema and feels false in contemporary America. Audiences will embrace the improbable and the storytelling mode, but in a horror film, the heroic fails to generate much horror.

2 As I have noted elsewhere, 'heading for an island' is a theme in many of Romero's zombie films. Islands represent places of escape, safety and freedom from the factors that made the zombie apocalypse happen. Characters head to islands in *Dawn of the Dead*, *Day of the Dead*, and *Survival of the Dead*, although in the last Romero reveals that islands are just as unsafe and problematic. Also, it bears pointing out that there are no habitable islands in the Great Lake in which Steve's boat is located, so the remake of *Dawn* is also geographically incorrect.

3 I argue in *Back from the Dead* that the fact that Ken's closest relationship is with someone he has never met in a gun shop a

quarter mile away is emblematic of one of the major themes of the *Dawn* remake: that we are incapable of building and maintaining real relationships. We instead surround ourselves with (distanced) acquaintances so as to avoid any real emotional connection. More and more, relationships are lived 'virtually' in every sense of the word. The film makes this fact obvious.

4 Information on the law and state demographics from 'Sharia law banned', 2010.

Notes on Chapter 9

1 The first decade of the twenty-first century also saw numerous non-slasher horror films being remade: *The Wolfman* (1941/2010), *Willard* (1971/2003), *The Wicker Man* (1973/2006), *The Crazies* (1973/2010), *The Omen* (1976/2006), *Dawn of the Dead* (1978/2004), *The Toolbox Murders* (1978/2004), *The Amityville Horror* (1979/2005), *The Fog* (1980/2005), *The Hitcher* (1986/2007), *The Stepfather* (1987/2009) and *Night of the Demons* (1988/2010). Clearly a much larger trend is manifesting in this period, partly having to do with Hollywood relying upon known properties and established stories to ensure an audience and more box office. We might also note that films other than horror get remade and that other periods, including the late seventies and early eighties were periods of more remakes as well. All of these remakes also contain post-9/11 horror elements as well.

2 The fragmented nature of the narratives of the late eighties/early nineties horror is clearly demonstrated by the 'jump to a death' feature on most DVDs of horror films from the period. Plot is less important that the variety and creativity of the murders within *Jason Takes Manhattan*, *Jason X* or *Nightmare on Elm Street 5*. The victims are interchangeable. What distinguishes them is not personality or identity but how they are killed.

3 As I write this, the news media reports concerns of a 'serious, credible but unconfirmed threat' of a terror attack planned for the anniversary of the attacks. Just like cinematic serial killers, real world terrorists value anniversaries.

Filmography

9/11. Dir. James Hanlon, Rob Klug, Jules Naudet and Gedeon Naudet. Screenplay by Tom Forman and Greg Kandra. CBS. 2002.
28 Days Later. Dir. Danny Boyle. Screenplay by Alex Garland. DNA Films. 2002.
28 Weeks Later. Dir. Juan Carlos Fresnadillo. Screenplay by Rowan Joffe, Juan Carlos Fresnadillo and Enrique López Lavigne. Fox Atomic. 2007.
30 Days of Night. Dir. David Slade. Screenplay by Steve Niles, Stuart Beattie and Brian Nelson. Ghost House Pictures. 2007.
1408. Dir. Mikael Håfström. Screenplay by Matt Greenberg, Scott Alexander and Larry Karaszewski. Dimension Films. 2007.
Apollo 18. Dir. Gonzalo López-Gallego. Screenplay by Brian Miller. Apollo 18 Productions. 2011.
Battle: Los Angeles. Dir. Jonathan Leibsman. Screenplay by Christopher Bertolini. Columbia Pictures. 2011.
Behind the Mask: The Rise of Leslie Vernon. Dir. Scott Glosserman. Screenplay by Scott Glosserman and David J. Stieve. Glenn Echo Entertainment. 2006.
Black Christmas. Dir. Bob Clark. Screenplay by Roy Moore. Warner Brothers. 1974.
Black Christmas. Dir. Glen Morgan. Screenplay by Glen Morgan. Dimension Films. 2006.
Black Death. Dir. Christopher Smith. Screenplay by Dario Poloni. Egoli Tosselli Film. 2010.
The Blair Witch Project. Dir. Daniel Myrick and Eduardo Sánchez. Screenplay by Daniel Myrick and Eduardo Sánchez. Haxan Films. 1999.
Buried. Dir. Rodrigo Cortés. Screenplay by Chris Sparling. Versus Entertainment. 2010.
Cabin Fever. Dir. Eli Roth. Screenplay by Eli Roth and Randy Pearlstein. Black Sky Entertainment. 2002.
The Candy Snatchers. Dir. Guerdon Trueblood. Screenplay by Bryan Gindoff. Marmot Productions. 1973.
Cannibal Holocaust. Dir. Ruggero Deodato. Screenplay by Gianfranco Clerici. F.D. Cinematografica. 1980.
Carrie. Dir. Brian DePalma. Screenplay by Lawrence D. Cohen. Redbank Films. 1976.

Chain Letter. Dir. Deon Taylor. Screenplay by Michael J. Pagan, Deon Taylor and Diana Erwin. Tiger Tail Entertainment. 2010.
Cloverfield. Dir. Matt Reeves. Screenplay by Drew Goddard. Bad Robot. 2008.
The Collector. Dir. Marcus Dunstan. Screenplay by Marcus Dunstan and Patrick Melton. Liddell Entertainment. 2009.
Constantine. Dir. Francis Lawrence. Screenplay by Kevin Brodbin and Frank Cappello. Warner Brothers. 2005.
The Crazies. Dir. George A. Romero. Screenplay by George A. Romero and Paul McCullough. Pittsburgh Films. 1973.
The Crazies. Dir. Breck Eisner. Screenplay by Scott Kosar and Ray Wright. Overture Films. 2010.
Cry Wolf. Dir. Jeff Wadlow. Screenplay by Beau Bauman and Jeff Wadlow. Hypnotic. 2005.
Dawn of the Dead. Dir. George A. Romero. Screenplay by George A. Romero. Laurel Group. 1978.
Dawn of the Dead. Dir. Zach Snyder. Screenplay by James Gunn. Strike Entertainment. 2004.
The Descent. Dir. Neil Marshall. Screenplay by Neil Marshall. Celador Films. 2005.
Devil. Dir. John Erick Dowdle. Screenplay by Brian Nelson. Story by M. Night Shyamalan. Media Rights. 2010.
The Devil's Rejects. Dir. Rob Zombie. Screenplay by Rob Zombie. Lionsgate. 2005.
Diary of the Dead. Dir. George A. Romero. Screenplay by George A. Romero. Artfire Films. 2007.
Dominion: Prequel to the Exorcist. Dir. Paul Schrader. Screenplay by William Wisher. Jr. and Caleb Carr. Morgan Creek. 2005.
Drag Me to Hell. Dir. Sam Raimi. Screenplay by Sam Raimi and Ivan Raimi. Universal Pictures. 2009.
Dread. Dir. Anthony DiBlasi. Screenplay by Anthony DiBlasi. Matador Pictures. 2009.
End of the Line. Dir. Maurice Devereaux. Screenplay by Maurice Devereaux. Maurice Devereaux Productions. 2007.
The Exorcism of Emily Rose. Dir. Scott Derrickson. Screenplay by Paul Harris Boardman and Scott Derrickson. Screen Gems. 2005.
The Exorcist. Dir. William Friedkin. Screenplay by William Peter Blatty. Warner Brothers. 1973.
Exorcist: The Beginning. Dir. Renny Harlin. Screenplay by William Wisher, Jr., Caleb Carr and Alexi Hawley. Morgan Creek. 2004.
Fahrenheit 9/11. Dir. Michael Moore. Screenplay by Michael Moore. Miramax Films. 2004.
Feast. Dir. John Gulager. Screenplay by Marcus Dunstan and Patrick Melton. Dimension Films. 2005.

FILMOGRAPHY

The Final. Dir. Joey Stewart. Screenplay by Jason Kabolati. Agora Entertainment. 2010.

Final Destination. Dir. James Wong. Screenplay by Glen Morgan, James Wong and Jeffrey Riddick. New Line Cinema. 2000.

Final Destination 2. Dir. David R. Ellis. Screenplay by J. Mackye Gruber and Eric Bress. New Line Cinema. 2003.

Final Destination 3. Dir. James Wong. Screenplay by Glen Morgan and James Wong. New Line Cinema. 2006.

The Final Destination. Dir. David R. Ellis. Screenplay by Eric Bress. New Line Cinema. 2009.

Final Destination 5. Dir. Steven Quale. Screenplay by Eric Heisserer. New Line Cinema. 2011.

Four Boxes. Dir. Wyatt McDill. Screenplay by Wyatt McDill. Lake Street Productions. 2009.

Freddy vs. Jason. Dir. Ronnie Yu. Screenplay by Damien Shannon. New Line Cinema. 2003.

Friday the 13th. Dir. Sean S. Cunningham. Screenplay by Victor Miller. Paramount. 1980.

Friday the 13th. Dir. Marcus Nispel. Screenplay by Damien Shannon and Mark Swift. New Line. 2009.

Friday the 13th V: A New Beginning. Dir. Danny Steinmann. Screenplay by Martin Kitrosser, David Cohen and Danny Steinmann. Paramount Pictures. 1985.

Frozen. Dir. Adam Green. Screenplay by Adam Green. A Bigger Boat Pictures. 2010.

Funny Games. Dir. Michael Haneke. Screenplay by Michael Haneke. Austrian Film Institute. 1997.

Funny Games. Dir. Michael Haneke. Screenplay by Michael Haneke. Celluloid Dreams. 2007.

Ghost. Dir. Jerry Zucker. Screenplay by Bruce Joel Rubin. Paramount. 1990.

Ghosts of Abu Ghraib. Dir. Rory Kennedy. Screenplay by Jack Youngelson and Mark Bailey. Moxie Firecracker Films. 2007.

Ginipiggu: Akuma no Jikken (Guinea Pig: Devil's Experiment). Dir. Ogura Satoru. Sai Enterprise. 1988

Grindhouse. Directed by Robert Rodriguez and Quentin Tarentino. Screenplay by Robert Rodriguez and Quentin Tarentino. Dimension Films. 2007.

The Happening. Dir. M. Night Shyamalan. Screenplay by M. Night Shyamalan. Twentieth Century Fox. 2008.

Hard Candy. Dir. David Slade. Screenplay by Brian Nelson. Vulcan Productions. 2006.

Halloween. Dir. John Carpenter. Screenplay by John Carpenter and Debra Hill. Compass Entertainment. 1978.

Halloween. Dir. Rob Zombie. Screenplay by Rob Zombie. Dimension Films. 2007.
Halloween III: Season of the Witch. Dir. Tommy Lee Wallace. Screenplay by Tommy Lee Wallace. Dino Di Laurentiis Company. 1982.
Hatchet. Dir. Adam Green. Screenplay by Adam Green. Ariescope. 2006.
High Tension. (*Haute Tension*). Dir. Alexandre Aja. Screenplay by Alexandre Aja and Gregory Levasseur. Alexandre Films. 2003.
The Hills Have Eyes. Dir. Wes Craven. Screenplay by Wes Craven. Blood Relations. 1977.
The Hills Have Eyes. Dir. Alexandre Aja. Screenplay by Alexandre Aja and Gregory Levasseur. Fox Atomic. 2006.
The Hills Have Eyes II. Dir. Martin Weisz. Screenplay by Wes Craven and Jonathan Craven. Fox Atomic. 2007.
Hostel. Dir. Eli Roth. Screenplay by Eli Roth. Hostel LLC. 2005.
Hostel Part 2. Dir. Eli Roth. Screenplay by Eli Roth. Lionsgate. 2007.
House of 1000 Corpses. Dir. Rob Zombie. Screenplay by Rob Zombie. Spectacle Entertainment. 2003.
House of the Devil. Dir. Ti West. Screenplay by Ti West. MPI Media Group. 2009.
The House on Sorority Row. Dir. Mark Rosman. Screenplay by Mark Rosman and Bobby Fine. VAE. 1983.
The Howling. Dir. Joe Dante. Screenplay by John Sayles. AVCO Embassy. 1981.
I Am Legend. Dir. Francis Lawrence. Screenplay by Akiva Goldman and Mark Protosevich. Warner Brothers. 2007.
I Spit on Your Grave. Dir. Meir Zarchi. Screenplay by Meir Zarchi. Cinemagic Pictures. 1978.
I Spit on Your Grave. Dir. Steven R. Monroe. Screenplay by Stuart Morse. Family of the Year Productions. 2010.
Independence Day. Dir. Roland Emmerich. Screenplay by Roland Emmerich and Dean Devlin. Twentieth Century Fox. 2006.
Insidious. Dir. James Wan. Screenplay by Leigh Whannell. Alliance Films. 2010.
Jennifer's Body. Dir. Karyn Kusama. Screenplay by Diablo Cody. Fox Atomic. 2009.
Kill Theory. Dir. Chris Moore. Screenplay by Kelly C. Palmer. Benderspink. 2009.
Knowing. Dir. Alex Proyas. Screenplay by Ryne Douglas Pearson, Juliet Snowden, and Stiles White. Summit Entertainment. 2009.
Lake Mungo. Dir. Joel Anderson. Screenplay by Joel Anderson. Mungo Productions. 2008.
Land of the Dead. Dir. George A. Romero. Screenplay by George A. Romero. Universal. 2005.

The Last Broadcast. Dir. Stefan Avalos and Lance Weiler. Screenplay by Stefan Avalos and Lance Weiler. FFM Productions. 1998.
The Last Exorcism. Dir. Daniel Stamm. Screenplay by Huck Botko and Andrew Gurland. Strike Entertainment. 2010.
Last of the Living. Dir. Logan McMillan. Screenplay by Logan McMillan. Gorilla Pictures. 2009.
Loose Change 9/11: An American Coup. Dir. Dylan Avery. Screenplay by Dylan Avery. Collective Minds Media. 2009.
Man Bites Dog. (C'est arrivé près de chez vous) Dir. Rémy Belvaux, André Bonzel and Benoît Poelvoorde. Screenplay by Rémy Belvaux, André Bonzel, Benoît Poelvoorde and Vincent Tavier. Les Artistes Anonymes. 1992.
Martyrs. Dir. Pascal Laugier. Screenplay by Pascal Laugier. Canal Horizons. 2008.
The Mist. Dir. Frank Darabont. Screenplay by Frank Darabont. Dimension Pictures. 2007.
Monsters. Dir. Gareth Edwards. Screenplay by Gareth Edwards. Vertigo Films. 2010.
Mulberry Street. Dir. Jim Mickle. Screenplay by Jim Mickle and Nick Damici. Belladonna Productions. 2006.
My Bloody Valentine. Dir. George Mihalka. Screenplay by Stephen A. Miller and John Beaird. Canadian Film Development Corp. 1981.
My Bloody Valentine. Dir. Patrick Lussier. Screenplay by Todd Farmer and Zane Smith. Lionsgate. 2009.
My Soul to Take. Dir. Wes Craven. Screenplay by Wes Craven. Rogue. 2010.
National Geographic: Inside 9/11. Written by Michael Eldridge and Lance Hori. Tower Productions. 2005.
National Geographic: Ultimate Explorer: Witness 9/11. National Geographic. Original Airdate: 7 September 2003.
New Nightmare. Dir. Wes Craven. Screenplay by Wes Craven. New Line. 1994.
Night of the Living Dead. Dir. George A. Romero. Screenplay by John Russo and George A. Romero. Image Ten. 1968.
A Nightmare on Elm Street. Dir. Wes Craven. Screenplay by Wes Craven. New Line. 1984.
A Nightmare on Elm Street. Dir. Samuel Bayer. Screenplay by Wesley Strick and Eric Heisserer. New Line. 2010.
A Nightmare on Elm Street 4: The Dream Master. Dir. Renny Harlin. Screenplay by Brian Helgeland and Scott Pierce. New Line Cinema. 1988.
The Omen. Dir. Richard Donner. Screenplay by David Seltzer. Twentieth Century Fox. 1976.
Open House. Dir. Andrew Paquin. Screenplay by Andrew Paquin. Lionsgate. 2010.

Open Water. Dir. Chris Keritis. Screenplay by Chris Keritis. Plunge Pictures. 2003.
Paranormal Activity. Dir. Oren Peli. Screenplay by Oren Peli. Blumhouse Productions. 2007.
Paranormal Activity 2. Dir. Tod Williams. Screenplay by Michael R. Perry, Christopher Landon and Tom Pabst. Paramount Pictures. 2010.
Paranormal Activity 3. Dir. Henry Joost and Ariel Shulman. Screenplay by Michael R. Perry. Paramount Pictures. 2011.
Priest. Dir. Scott Charles Stewart. Screenplay by Cory Goodman. Screen Gems. 2011.
Prince of Darkness. Dir. John Carpenter. Screenplay by John Carpenter. Alive Films. 1987.
Prom Night. Dir. Paul Lynch. Screenplay by William Gray and Robert Guza, Jr. Quadrant. 1980.
Prom Night. Dir. Nelson McCormick. Screenplay by J. S. Cardone. Alliance Pictures. 2008.
Psycho. Dir. Alfred Hitchcock. Screenplay by Joseph Stefano. Shamley Productions. 1960.
Pulse. Dir. Jim Sonzero. Screenplay by Wes Craven and Ray Wright. The Weinstein Company. 2006.
Quarantine. Dir. John Erick Dowdle. Screenplay by John Erick Dowdle and Drew Dowdle. Andale Pictures. 2008.
The Reaping. Dir. Stephen Hopkins. Screenplay by Carey Hayes, Chad Hayes and Brian Rousso. Warner Brothers. 2007.
[REC]. Dir. Jaume Balagueró and Paco Plaza. Screenplay by Jaume Balagueró and Luis Berdejo. Filmax. 2007.
Red Sands. Dir. Alex Turner. Screenplay by Simon Barrett. Tricky Pictures. 2009.
The Reeds. Dir. Nick Cohen. Screenplay by Chris Baker and Mark Anthony Galluzzo. Delacheroy Films. 2009.
Resident Evil. Dir. Paul W. S. Anderson. Screenplay by Paul W. S. Anderson. Constantin Film Produktion. 2002.
Resident Evil: Afterlife. Dir. Paul W. S. Anderson. Screenplay by Paul W. S. Anderson. Constantin Film Produktion. 2010.
Resident Evil: Apocalypse. Dir. Alexander Witt. Screenplay by Paul W. S. Anderson. Constantin Film Produktion. 2004.
Resident Evil: Extinction. Dir. Russell Mulcahy. Screenplay by Paul W. S. Anderson. Resident Evil Productions. 2007.
The Ring. Dir. Gore Verbinski. Screenplay by Ehren Kruger. Dreamworks SKG. 2002.
The Rite. Dir. Mikael Håfström. Screenplay by Michael Petroni. Contrafilm. 2011.
The Ruins. Dir. Carter Smith. Screenplay by Scott B. Smith. Dreamworks SKG. 2008.

Saving Private Ryan. Dir. Steven Spielberg. Screenplay by Robert Rodat. Amblin Entertainment. 1998.
Saw. Dir. James Wan. Screenplay by Leigh Whannell and James Wan. Evolution. 2004.
Saw II. Dir. Darren Lynn Bousman. Screenplay by Leigh Whannell and Darren Lynn Bousman. Twisted Pictures. 2005.
Saw III. Dir. Darren Lynn Bousman. Screenplay by Leigh Whannell and James Wan. Twisted Pictures. 2006.
Saw 3D. Dir. Kevin Greutert. Screenplay by Marcus Dunstan and Patrick Melton. Twisted Pictures. 2010.
Saw IV. Dir. Darren Lynn Bousman. Screenplay by Marcus Dunstan and Patrick Melton. Twisted Pictures. 2007.
Saw V. Dir. David Hackl. Screenplay by Marcus Dunstan and Patrick Melton. Twisted Pictures. 2008.
Saw VI. Dir. Kevin Greutert. Screenplay by Marcus Dunstan and Patrick Melton. Twisted Pictures. 2009.
Scary Movie. Dir. Keenen Ivory Wayans. Screenplay by Marlan Wayans, Shawn Wayans. and Buddy Johnson. Dimension Pictures. 2000.
Scream. Dir. Wes Craven. Screenplay by Kevin Williamson. Dimension Films. 1996.
Scream 2. Dir. Wes Craven. Screenplay by Kevin Williamson. Dimension Films. 1997.
Scream 3. Dir. Wes Craven. Screenplay by Kevin Williamson and Ehren Kruger. Dimension Films. 2000.
Scream 4. Dir. Wes Craven. Screenplay by Kevin Williamson. Dimension Films. 2011.
The Searchers. Dir. John Ford. Screenplay by Frank S. Nugent. Warner Brothers. 1956.
Season of the Witch. Dir. Dominic Sena. Screenplay by Bragi F. Schut. Atlas Entertainment & Relativity Media. 2011.
Seconds Apart. Dir. Antonio Negret. Screenplay by George Richards. After Dark Films. 2011.
The Sixth Sense. Dir. M. Night Shyamalan. Screenplay by M. Night Shyamalan. Barry Mendel Productions. 1999.
Skyline. Dir. Colin Straus and Greg Straus. Screenplay by Joshua Cordes and Liam O'Donnell. Black Monday. 2010.
Sorority Row. Dir. Stewart Hendler. Screenplay by Josh Stolberg and Pete Goldfinger. Karz Entertainment. 2009.
Stag Night. Dir. Peter A. Dowling. Screenplay by Peter A. Dowling. Film Tiger. 2008.
Stake Land. Dir. Jim Mickle. Screenplay by Nick Damici and Jim Mickle. Glass Eye Pix. 2010.
Standard Operating Procedure. Dir. Errol Morris. Participant Productions. 2008.

The Strangers. Dir. Bryan Bertino. Screenplay by Bryan Bertino. Rogue Pictures. 2008.
Survival of the Dead. Dir. George A. Romero. Screenplay by George A. Romero. Blank of the Dead Productions. 2009.
Targets. Dir. Peter Bogdanovich. Screenplay by Peter Bogdanovich and Polly Platt. Saticoy Productions. 1968.
The Texas Chainsaw Massacre. Dir. Tobe Hooper. Screenplay by Tobe Hooper and Kim Henkel. Vortex. 1974.
The Texas Chainsaw Massacre. Dir. Marcus Nispel. Screenplay by Scott Kosar. New Line. 2003.
The Thing. Dir. John Carpenter. Screenplay by Bill Lancaster. Universal. 1982.
Tooth and Nail. Dir. Mark Young. Screenplay by Mark Young. Morningstar Films. 2007.
Trick 'r Treat. Dir. Michael Dougherty. Screenplay by Michael Dougherty. Bad Hat Harry Productions. 2008.
Trolljegeren (*Trollhunter*). Dir. André Øvredal. Screenplay by André Øvredal. Filmkameratene A/S. 2010.
Turistas. Dir. John Stockwell. Screenplay by Michael Ross. Stone Village Pictures. 2006.
The Unborn. Dir. David S. Goyer. Screenplay by David S. Goyer. Rogue Pictures. 2009.
United 93. Dir. Paul Greenglass. Screenplay by Paul Greenglass. Universal Pictures. 2006.
The Untouchables. Dir. Brian DePalma. Screenplay by David Mamet. Paramount Pictures. 1987.
Vampires. Dir. John Carpenter. Screenplay by Don Jakoby. Largo Entertainment. 1998.
Vanishing on 7th Street. Dir. Brad Anderson. Screenplay by Anthony Jaswinski. Herrick Entertainment. 2010.
The Village. Dir. M. Night Shyamalan. Screenplay by M. Night Shyamalan. Buena Vista. 2004.
Wait Until Dark. Dir. Terence Young. Screenplay by Robert Carrington and Jane-Howard Carrington. Warner Brothers. 1967.
The War Game. Dir. Peter Watkins. Screenplay by Peter Watkins. BBC. 1965.
War of the Worlds. Dir. Byron Haskin. Screenplay by Barre Lyndon. Paramount Pictures. 1953.
War of the Worlds. Dir. Stephen Spielberg. Screenplay by David Koepp and Josh Friedman. Paramount Pictures. 2005.
What Dreams May Come. Dir. Vincent Ward. Screenplay by Ronald Bass. Polygram. 1998.
When a Stranger Calls. Dir. Fred Walton. Screenplay by Steve Feke and Fred Walton. Columbia Pictures. 1979.

When a Stranger Calls. Dir. Simon West. Screenplay by Jake Wade Wall. Screen Gems. 2006.
Wolf Creek. Dir. Greg Mclean. Screenplay by Greg Mclean. Australian Film Finance Corporation. 2005.
World Trade Center. Dir. Oliver Stone. Screenplay by Andrea Berloff. Paramount Pictures. 2006.
Wrong Turn. Dir. Rob Schmidt. Screenplay by Alan B. McElroy. Summit Entertainment. 2003.
ZMD: Zombies of Mass Destruction. Dir. Kevin Hamedani. Screenplay by Kevin Hamedani and Ramon Isao. Typecast Pictures. 2009.
Zombie Strippers. Dir. Jay Lee. Screenplay by Jay Lee. Stage Six Films. 2008.
Zombieland. Dir. Ruben Fleischer. Screenplay by Rhett Reese and Paul Wernick. Columbia Pictures. 2009.

Bibliography

Anonymous (2007), 'Torture in Abu Ghraib'. *The Phenomenon of Torture: Readings and Commentary*. William F. Schultz ed. Philadelphia: University of Pennsylvania Press.

Aristotle (1961), *Poetics: Translation and Analysis*. Trans. Kenneth A. Telford. Chicago: Henry Regnery.

Arkin, William M. (2003), 'The Pentagon Unleashes a Holy Warrior'. *Los Angeles Times* (16 October 2003): A1.

Baglio, Matt (2010), *The Rite: The Making of a Modern Exorcist*. New York: Image.

Baigent, Michael (2009), *Racing Toward Armageddon*. New York: HarperOne.

Ballard, Finn (2008), 'No Trespassing: The Post-Millennial Road-Horror Movie'. *The Irish Journal of Gothic and Horror Studies*. 4 (2008): <http://irishgothichorrorjournal.homestead.com/roadhorror.html>. Accessed 10 October 2010.

Beer, Gillian (July 1978), 'Ghosts'. *Essays in Criticism* 28): 259–64.

Berman, A. S. (2009), *The New Horror Handbook*. Duncan, OK: BearManor.

Bernstein, Richard J. (2005), *The Abuse of Evil: The Corruption of Politics and Religion Since 9/11*. Cambridge: Polity.

Blake, Linnie (2008), *The Wounds of Nations: Horror cinema, historical trauma and national identity*. Manchester: Manchester University Press.

Broderick, Mick (2010), 'Better the Devil You Know: Film Antichrists at the Millennium'. *Horror Zone: The Cultural Experience of Contemporary Horror Cinema*. Ian Conrich ed. London: I. B. Tauris. 227–44.

Bryant, John (2002), *The Fluid Text: A Theory of Revision and Editing for Book and Screen*. Ann Arbor: University of Michigan Press.

Canetti, Elias (1962), *Crowds and Power*. Carol Stewart (trans.). New York: Viking.

Carroll, Noël (1990), *The Philosophy of Horror*. New York: Routledge.

Clover, Carol J. (1992), *Men, Women and Chainsaws: Gender in the Modern Horror Film*. Princeton: Princeton University Press.

Coleridge, Samuel Taylor (1987), *Lectures 1808–1819: On Literature*. R. A. Foakes ed. Volume 2. Princeton, New Jersey: Princeton University Press.

BIBLIOGRAPHY

Collins, Jo and John Jervis (eds) (2008), *Uncanny Modernity: Cultural Theories, Modern Anxieties*. New York: Palgrave Macmillan.
Conrich, Ian ed. (2010), *Horror Zone: The Cultural Experience of Contemporary Horror Cinema*. London: I. B. Tauris.
Cooper, Richard T. (2003), 'General Casts War in Religious Terms'. *Los Angeles Times* (16 October 2003): A1.
Cowan, Douglas E. (2008), *Sacred Terror: Religion and Horror on the Silver Screen*. Waco, TX: Baylor University Press.
Creed, Barbara (1993), *The Monstrous-Feminine: Film, Feminism, and Psychoanalysis*. London: Routledge.
Daniels, Les (1975), *Living in Fear: A History of Horror in the Mass Media*. New York: Scribner.
Danner, Mark (2004), *Torture and Truth: America, Abu Ghraib, and the War on Terror*. New York: New York Review of Books.
Davis, Mike (1999), *Ecology of Fear: Los Angeles and the Imagination of Disaster*. New York: Vintage Books.
Dixon, Wheeler Winston ed. (2004), *Film and Television after 9/11*. Carbondale: Southern Illinois University Press.
Douthat, Ross (2008), 'The Return of the Paranoid Style'. *Atlantic Monthly* 301.3 (April 2008): 52–9.
Dwyer, Jim and Kevin Flynn (2004), *102 Minutes: The Untold Story of the Fight to Survive inside the Twin Towers*. New York: Times Books.
Edelstein, David (2006), 'Now Playing at Your Local Multiplex: Torture Porn'. *New York Magazine* (28 January 2006) <http://nymag.com/movies/features/15622>. Accessed 2 May 2011.
Edwards, Les (2005), '*The War of the Worlds* by H. G. Wells'. *Horror: Another 100 Best Books*. Stephen Jones and Kim Newman (eds). New York: Carroll and Graf
Engelhardt, Tom (2006), '9/11 in a Movie-Made World'. *The Nation* 283.9 (25 September 2006): 15–21.
Fahy, Thomas ed. (2010). 'Introduction'. *The Philosophy of Horror*. Lexington: The University of Kentucky Press, 1–13.
Faludi, Susan (2007), *The Terror Dream: Fear and Fantasy in Post-9/11 America*. New York: Henry Holt and Company.
Flynn, Kevin and Jim Dwyer (2004), 'Falling Bodies: A 9/11 Image Edited in Pain'. *New York Times* (10 September 2004): A1, B8.
Fowkes, Katherine A. (2004), 'Melodramatic Specters: Cinema and *The Sixth Sense*'. *Spectral America: Phantoms and the National Imagination*. Jeffrey Andrew Weinstock ed. Madison: University of Wisconsin Press. 185–206.
Freeland, Cynthia A. (2000), *The Naked and the Undead: Evil and the Appeal of Horror*. Boulder, CO: Westview.
Frum, David (2003), *The Right Man*. New York: Random House.
Furedi, Frank (2006), *Culture of Fear*. 4th edn. London: Continuum.

—(2007), *Invitation to Terror: The Expanding Empire of the Unknown*. New York: Continuum.
Gelder, Ken ed. (2003), *The Horror Reader*. London: Routledge.
Glassner, Barry (1999), *The Culture of Fear: Why Americans Are Afraid of the Wrong Things*. New York: Basic Books.
Goodman, Felicitas D. (1981), *The Exorcism of Anneliese Michel*. Eugene: Resource Publications.
Gordon, Andrew M. (2008), *Empire of Dreams: The Science Fiction and Fantasy Films of Steven Spielberg*. Lanham, MD: Rowan and Littlefield,
Gordon, Devin (2006), 'Horror Show'. *Newsweek* 147.14 (3 April 2006): 60–2.
The Gore-Met (2010), 'Das Blood 'N' Guts Is Gut, Ja?' *Rue Morgue* 103 (August 2010): 60.
Grant, Barry Keith ed. (1996), *The Dread of Difference: Gender and the Horror Film*. Austin: University of Texas Press.
Gregory, Justina ed. (2005), *A Companion to Greek Tragedy*. Malden, MA: Blackwell.
Hall, Edith (2010), *Greek Tragedy: Suffering under the Sun*. Oxford: Oxford University Press.
Hantke, Steffen (2010), 'The Military Horror Film: Speculations on a Hybrid Genre'. *The Journal of Popular Culture* 43.4: 701–19.
Harries, Martin (2007), *Forgetting Lot's Wife: On Destructive Spectatorship*. New York: Fordham University Press.
Hawkins, Joan (2000), *Cutting Edge: Art-Horror and the Horrific Avant-Garde*. Minneapolis: University of Minnesota Press.
Heller, Dana ed. (2005), *The Selling of 9/11: How a National Tragedy Became a Commodity*. New York: Palgrave.
Herman, Edward S. and Gerry O'Sullivan (1989), *The Terrorism Industry*. New York: Pantheon.
Hook, Sidney (1974), *Pragmatism and the Tragic Sense of Life*. New York: Basic Books.
Ignatieff, Michael (2004), 'The Terrorist as Auteur'. *New York Times Magazine* (14 November 2004): 50–8.
Jacoby, Susan (2008), *The Age of American Unreason*. New York: Pantheon.
Jancovich, Mark (1992), *Horror*. London: B. T. Batsford.
—(2002), *Horror: The Film Reader*. New York: Routledge.
Jenkins, Brian Michael (1975), *International Terrorism: A New Mode of Conflict*. Los Angeles: Crescent.
Johnson, Reed (2011), 'How attacks changed our psyches'. *Los Angeles Times* (4 September 2011): E7.
Junod, Tom (2003), 'The Falling Man'. *Esquire* 140.3 (September 2003): 177–85.

Kahn, Herman (1960), *On Thermonuclear War*. Princeton: Princeton University Press.
Kenny, Glenn (2008), '"Cloverfield" has nothing to lose'. *Los Angeles Times* (6 February 2008): E3.
King, Stephen (1982), *Danse Macabre*. New York: Berkeley.
—(1985), *Skeleton Crew*. New York. G. P. Putnam's Sons.
King, Susan (2011), 'Devil, meet your match'. *Los Angeles Times* (27 January 2011): D3.
Kristeva, Julia (1982), *Powers of Horror*. Trans. Leon S. Roudiez. New York: Columbia University Press.
Kuebler, Monica S. (2011), 'Piety and Pestilence'. *Rue Morgue* 108 (Jan/Feb 2011): 16–18, 20, 22.
Lawrynowicz, Lea (2009), 'Divinity in Darkness: The Rise of Christian Horror'. *Rue Morgue Magazine* No. 87 (March 2009): 24–8.
Lee, Chris (2005), 'Horror returns to make a killing'. *Los Angeles Times* (30 January 2005): E1; E8.
Lewis, Sinclair (1970), *Elmer Gantry*. New York: Signet Classics.
Lifton, Robert Jay (1999), *Destroying the World to Save It: Aum Shinrikyō, Apocalyptic Violence and the New Global Terrorism*. New York: Metropolitan.
—(2003), *Superpower Syndrome: America's Apocalyptic Confrontation with the World*. New York: Thunder's Mouth Press.
Lowenstein, Adam (2005), *Shocking Representations: Historical Trauma, National Cinema and the Modern Horror Film*. New York: Columbia University Press.
Marriott, James (2007), *Horror Films*. London: Virgin.
Mather, Cotton (1970), *Wonders of the Invisible World*. [1693] Amherst, WI: Amherst Press.
Mayer, Jane (2008), *The Dark Side: The Inside Story of How the War on Terror Turned into a War on American Ideals*. New York: Doubleday.
McIntyre, Gina (2010), '"Piranha" director goes for the gory'. *Brand X* (25 August 2010): 10.
Melnick, Jeffrey Paul (2009), *9/11 Culture: America Under Construction*. Malden, MA: Wiley-Blackwell.
Milgram, Stanley (1974), *Obedience to Authority*. New York: Harper and Row.
Mitchell, W. J. T. (2011), *Cloning Terror: The War of Images, 9/11 to the Present*. Chicago: University of Chicago Press.
Morgan, Matthew J. (2009), 'Introduction'. *The Impact of 9/11 on the Media, Arts and Entertainment: The Day that Changed Everything?* Matthew J. Morgan ed. New York: Palgrave MacMillan. 1–5.
Morris, Jeremy (2010), 'The Justification of Torture Horror'. *The Philosophy of Horror*. Thomas Fahy ed. Lexington: University of Kentucky Press. 42–56.

Muller, Christine (2009), 'Witnessing the Fall: September 11 and the Crisis of the Permeable Self'. *The War on Terror and American Popular Culture*. Andrew Schopp and Matthew B. Hill (eds) Madison: Fairleigh Dickinson University Press. 45–64.

Muntean, Nick and Matthew Thomas Payne (2009), 'Attack of the Livid Dead: Recalibrating Terror in the Post-September 11 Zombie Film'. *The War on Terror and American Popular Culture*. Andrew Schopp and Matthew B. Hill (eds) Madison: Fairleigh Dickinson University Press. 239–58.

Murphy, Kim (2011), 'Has All the Spending Paid Off?' *Los Angeles Times* (28 August 2011): A1, A14–A15.

National Commission on Terrorist Attacks upon the United States (2004), *The 9/11 Commission Report*. New York: W. W. Norton.

Natoli, Joseph (2007), *This Is a Picture and Not the World: Movies and a Post-9/11 America*. Albany: State University of New York Press.

Navasky, Victor (2002), 'Foreword', *Journalism after September 11*. Barbie Zelizer and Stuart Allen (eds). London: Routledge. xiii–xviii.

Newman, Kim (1988), *Nightmare Movies: A Critical Guide to Contemporary Horror Films*. New York: Harmony.

Noah, Timothy (2005), '9/11 Was No Summer Movie'. *Slate* (19 July 2005) <www.slate.com/id/2123008>. Accessed 21 March 2011.

O'Hara, Jessica (2010), 'Making their Presence Known: TV's Ghost Hunter Phenomenon in a "Post" World', in *The Philosophy of Horror*. Thomas Fahy ed. Lexington: University of Kentucky Press. 72–85.

Olsen, Mark (2011), 'It takes light years for the creeps to build up'. *Los Angeles Times* (3 September 2011): D8.

Orr, John and Dragan Klaić (1990), *Terrorism and modern drama*. Edinburgh: Edinburgh University Press.

Pahl, John (2010), *Empire of Sacrifice: The Religious Origins of American Violence*. New York: New York University Press.

Parents, Michael (2004), *Superpatriotism*. San Francisco: City Lights.

Pinedo, Isabel Christina (1997), *Recreational Terror: Women and the Pleasures of Horror Film Viewing*. Albany: State University of New York Press.

Priest, Dana and Barton Gellman (2002), 'U.S. decries abuse but defends interrogations'. *Washington Post* (26 December 2002): A1.

Prince, Stephen ed. (2004), *The Horror Film*. New Brunswick: Rutgers University Press.

—(2009), *Firestorm: American Film in the Age of Terrorism*. New York: Columbia University Press.

Prior, Lindsay (1997), 'Actuarial Visions of Death: Life, Death and Chance in the Modern World'. *The Changing Face of Death: Historical Accounts of Death and Disposal*. Peter C. Jupp and Glennys Howarth (eds). Hampshire: Macmillan Press. 177–91.

Roche, David (2011), '"That's Real! That's What You Want!": Producing Fear in George A. Romero's Dawn of the Dead (1978) vs Zack Snyder's Remake (2004)'. *Horror Studies* 2.1): 75–87.
Schlesinger, Jr., Arthur M. (2004), *War and the American Presidency*. New York: W. W. Norton.
Schopp, Andrew (2009), 'Interrogating the Manipulation of Fear: *V for Vendetta*, *Batman Begins*, *Good Night and Good Luck*, and America's "War on Terror"'. *The War on Terror and American Popular Culture*. Andrew Schopp and Matthew B. Hill (eds). Madison, NJ: Fairleigh Dickinson University Press. 259–86.
Schopp, Andrew and Matthew B. Hill (2009), 'Introduction: The Curious Knot'. *The War on Terror and American Popular Culture*. Andrew Schopp and Matthew B. Hill (eds). Madison, NJ: Fairleigh Dickinson University Press. 11–42.
Schneider, Steven Jay and Daniel Shaw (eds) (2003), *Dark Thoughts: Philosophical Reflections on Cinematic Horror*. Lanham, MD: Scarecrow.
Scruton, David L. (1986), 'The Anthropology of an Emotion'. *Sociophobics: The Anthropology of Fear*. David L. Scruton ed. Boulder, CO: Westview Press. 7–49.
'Sharia Law Banned: Oklahoma to become the first U.S. state to veto use of Islamic code' (2011), the *Daily Mail Online* (2 November 2010) < http://www.dailymail.co.uk/news/article-1325986/Sharia-law-banned-Oklahoma-US-state-veto-Islamic-code.html>. Accessed 10 July 2011.
Siegel, Marc (2005), *False Alarm: The Truth about the Epidemic of Fear*. New York: John Wiley and Sons, Inc.
Singer, Peter (2004), *The President of Good and Evil: The Ethics of George W. Bush*. New York: Dutton.
Skal, David J. (1993), *The Monster Show: A Cultural History of Horror*. New York: W. W. Norton.
Sontag, Susan (1978), *Against Interpretation and Other Essays*. New York: Octagon.
—(2004) 'The photographs are us'. *New York Times Magazine* (23 May 2004): 24–9, 42.
Spigel, Lynn (2004), 'Entertainment Wars: Television Culture after 9/11' *American Quarterly* 56.2 (June 2004): 235–70.
Stearns, Peter N. (2006), *American Fear: The Causes and Consequences of High Anxiety*. London: Routledge.
Strozier, Charles (1994), *Apocalypse: On the Psychology of Fundamentalism in America*. Boston: Beacon.
—(2005), 'From Ground Zero: Thoughts on Apocalyptic Violence and the New Terrorism'. *War in Heaven, Heaven on Earth: Theories of the Apocalyptic*. Stephen O'Leary and Glen S. McGhee (eds). London: Equinox.

Thompson, Kristen Moana (2007), *Apocalyptic Dread: American Film at the Turn of the Millennium*. Albany: State University of New York Press.
'The Torture Trail' (2010), *Los Angeles Times* (21 July 2010): A16.
Tudor, Andrew (1989), *Monsters and Mad Scientists: A Cultural History of the Horror Movie*. Oxford: Basil Blackwell.
—(2002), 'From Paranoia to Postmodernism: The Horror Movie in Late Modern Society'. *Genre and Contemporary Hollywood*. Steve Neale ed. London: BFI Publishing.
Twitchell, James (1985), *Dreadful Pleasures: An Anatomy of Modern Horror*. Oxford: Oxford University Press.
Valenti, Jack (2001), 'Hollywood, and our nation, will meet this test'. *Variety* (27 September 2001): 1. Also available at <http://www.variety.com/article/VR1117853266?refcatid=9>. Accessed 15 June 2010.
Versluys, Kristiaan (2009), *Out of the Blue: September 11 and the Novel*. New York: Columbia University Press.
Vonnegut, Kurt (1966), *Mother Night*. New York: Delacort Press.
Weimann, Gabriel (1988), 'Mass Mediated Theatre of Terror – Must the Show Go On?' *The News Media and Terrorism*. Peter A. Bruck ed. Ottowa: Carleton: Carleton University Center for Communication, Culture and Society.
Weinstock, Jeffrey Andrew (2004), 'Introduction: The Spectral Turn'. *Spectral America: Phantoms and the National Imagination*. Jeffrey Andrew Weinstock ed. Madison: University of Wisconsin Press.
Welch, Michael (2006), *Scapegoats of September 11th*. New Brunswick: Rutgers University Press,
Wells, Paul (2000), *The Horror Genre: From Beelzebub to Blair Witch*. London: Wallflower.
Wetmore, Jr., Kevin J. (2009), 'Technoghosts and Culture Shocks: Sociocultural Shifts in American Remakes of J-Horror'. *PostScript* 28.2): 72–81.
—(2011), *Back from the Dead: Remakes of the Romero Zombie Films as Markers of Their Times*. Jefferson, NC: McFarland & Company.
Williams, Tony (1996), *Hearths of Darkness: The Family in the American Horror Film*. Madison, NJ: Fairleigh Dickenson University Press.
Willman, David (2011), *The Mirage Man: Bruce Ivins, The Anthrax Attacks and America's Rush to War*. New York: Bantam.
Wood, Robin (2003), *Hollywood from Vietnam to Reagan ... and Beyond*. Revised edn. New York: Columbia University Press.
Wright, Lawrence (2006), *The Looming Tower: Al-Qaeda and the Road to 9/11*. New York: Knopf,
Zacharek, Stephanie (2005) '*War of the Worlds*'. *Salon.com*. (29 June

2005) <www.salon.com/entertainment/movie/review/2005/06/29/war/index.html>. Accessed 21 March 2011.

—(2008), '*Cloverfield*: Do we really need the horror of 9/11 to be repackaged and presented to us as an amusement-park ride?' *Salon.com*. (17 January 2008). http://www.salon.com/ent/movies/review/2008/01/18/cloverfield/>. Accessed 21 March 2011.

Zelizer, Barbie and Stuart Allan (2002), 'Introduction: When Trauma Shapes the News'. *Journalism after September 11*. Barbie Zelizer and Stuart Allan (eds) New York: Routledge, 1–24.

Zimbardo, Philip (2007), *The Lucifer Effect: Understanding How Good People Turn Evil*. New York: Random House.

Žižek, Slavoj (2002), *Welcome to the Desert of the Real*. London: Verso.

Index

9/11 (film) 61, 62, 63, 70, 71
28 Days Later 9, 34, 105, 159
28 Weeks Later 34, 159, 164
30 Days of Night 4, 13, 60, 98, 165–6, 201
1408 38, 143, 157–8

Abu Ghraib 96, 97, 101, 113
Afghanistan 1, 19, 55, 84, 97, 138, 140, 163, 179, 204
After Dark Horrorfest 13, 55
al Qaeda 7–8, 11, 104, 126, 151, 166, 198
Alien 4, 46, 78
Aliens 127
America's Next Top Model 78
Anthrax attacks (2001) 8–9
Apollo 18 19, 60, 72–3, 80
Aristotle 17, 205
  Poetics, The 17, 205

Battle: Los Angeles 43, 46, 205–6
Behind Enemy Lines 46
Behind the Mask 60, 61–2
Berg, Nicholas 59
Black Christmas 21
Black Death 9, 141, 149–50
Blade 165
Blair Witch Project, The 12, 59–60, 61, 64–5, 80
Bless the Child 140
Blood Monkey 22
Boykin, Lt. General William G. "Jerry" 138
Buffy the Vampire Slayer 3, 135, 164
Buried 5, 85, 99, 117, 133–4

Burning, The 193
Burnt Offerings 12
Bush, George W. 21, 43, 81, 137, 138, 142, 176, 192

Cabin Fever 9, 108, 109
Cannibal Holocaust 12, 59, 61
Carrie 140
Children Shouldn't Play with Dead Things 12, 116
Child's Play 194
C.H.U.D. 12
Cloverfield 2, 3, 13, 19, 23, 29, 30, 31, 32, 34, 38, 43, 51–5, 56, 57, 60, 61, 62, 63, 65–8, 69, 70, 74, 202
Constantine 141
Crazies, The (2010) 9, 171, 208
Cronenberg, David 12
Cry Wolf 21, 171, 178, 180–7, 189, 191

Darabont, Frank 120, 123, 127, 128
Dawn of the Dead (1978) 159, 161, 162
Dawn of the Dead (2004) 7, 159, 160–3, 166, 207–8
Day of the Dead 159, 207
Descent, The 38
Devil 42, 135, 141
Devil's Rejects, the 13, 15, 96, 195
Diary of the Dead 19, 32, 34, 60, 61–2, 63, 64–5, 70–1
Don't Look Now 100
Dracula 100, 164, 166

Drag Me to Hell 20, 117, 132, 135, 140, 141

Elmer Gantry 139
End of Days 140
End of the Line, The 20, 145
Evil Dead 14
Exorcism of Emily Rose, The 60, 132, 140, 141, 143, 144, 202
Exorcist, The 2, 4, 22, 63, 131, 135, 139, 140, 144, 203

Falling Man 37, 38–42
Fahrenheit 9/11 1, 73–4
Final, The 98, 113–14
Final Destination 20, 92–3, 94
Final Destination sequels 92–3, 94
Fog, The 199, 208
Four Boxes 21, 171, 178, 187–90, 191
Fox, Megan 61
Freddy's Dead: The Final Nightmare 22
Friday the 13th (1980) 13, 63, 194
Friday the 13th (2009) 13, 15, 21, 195–6, 197, 199, 200
Friday the 13th (sequels) 85, 87, 208
Frozen 41–2
Funny Games (1997) 6, 20, 65, 76, 81, 89–91, 93, 119, 206
Funny Games (2007) 6, 20, 65, 85, 88, 89–91, 94

Ghost 156
Ghostbusters 203
ghosts 21, 154, 155–9, 166, 167
Ghosts of Abu Ghraib, The 105
Ginipiggu: Akuma no Jikken 59
Godzilla 29
Guantánomo (U.S. Detention Camp) 97, 113

Halloween (1978) 63, 78, 87, 135, 192, 193, 195, 197, 199, 200
Halloween (2007) 21, 193, 197–8
Halloween III: Season of the Witch 116–17
Happening, The 26, 29, 38–9, 40, 42, 43, 77
Happy Birthday to Me 193
Hatchet 15, 60, 127, 195
Hell's Kitchen 78
Henry: Portrait of a Serial Killer 76
Hills Have Eyes, The 45, 46
Hills Have Eyes II, The 45
Hopkins, Anthony 61, 194
Hostel 96, 97, 98, 99, 101, 104–7, 103–9, 166, 197, 199
Hostel Part 2 97, 98, 99, 100, 105, 107–9, 166, 201
House of the Devil 20, 141, 143, 147
House of Wax 199
Howling, The 172
Hurricane Katrina 8, 19, 163
Hurt Locker, The 1

I Am Legend (novel) 25
I Am Legend (2007) 25, 34, 166
I Know What You Did Last Summer 194
I Spit on Your Grave 98, 100, 112–13
Independence Day 29, 42–3, 47
Inside 9/11 30, 31, 34, 83–4
Insidious 117, 132–3, 135, 141, 158–9
Invasion of the Body Snatchers 12, 48
Iraq 1, 19, 21, 55, 84, 85, 96, 97, 123, 133–4, 138, 140, 163, 179, 180

'J-horror' 6, 14, 19, 157, 204
Jason X 13
Jennifer's Body 61, 134–5

INDEX

Kairo 27
Karloff, Boris 82
King, Stephen 3, 13, 119
King Kong 12
Knowing 27
Kruger, Freddy 4, 85, 87, 194, 196, 198

Land of the Dead 7, 166
Last Broadcast, The 59, 61
Last Exorcism, The 20, 60, 61, 62, 63, 71–2, 74, 117, 132, 140, 141, 144, 147, 148–9, 152, 202
Last House on the Left 81, 91
Last of the Living 34, 166
Last Resort, The 98, 99–100, 109, 111
Leprechaun in the Hood 22
Loose Change 9/11: An American Coup 73
Los Angeles 24, 42, 84, 205–6
Lost Souls 140
Lynch, Jessica 179

Martyrs 15, 99, 195
Masters of Horror (Showtime series) 13
    Homecoming 159
Mist, The (film) 3, 13, 20, 117, 119, 120–30, 146–7, 201
Mist, The (novella) 119–20, 127
Monsters 46
Mulberry Street 23, 43, 44, 55–6
My Bloody Valentine 21, 193, 199

Natural Born Killers 81
Near Dark 164, 165
New York City 23, 24–6, 34, 36, 38, 39, 46, 54–6, 62, 67, 157
Night of the Living Dead (1968) 12, 22, 82, 116, 127, 159

Night of the Living Dead (1990) 159
Nightmare on Elm Street (1984) 13, 135, 193, 194, 196
Nightmare on Elm Street (2010) 13, 21, 196
Nightmare on Elm Street (sequels) 4, 13, 85, 196, 208

Omega Man, The 25
Omen, The 139, 208
Open Water 60, 73

Paranormal Activity 3, 7, 19, 20, 60, 61, 62, 63, 65, 68–9, 70, 74, 80, 117, 131, 133, 135
Paranormal Activity 2 3, 60, 63, 72, 74, 131–2, 135
Paranormal Activity 3 60
Passion of the Christ, The 96
Pearl, Daniel 59
Priest 141, 151, 165
Prince of Darkness 3
Prom Night 21, 193, 199, 200
Pulse 27, 34, 36–7, 38

Q 12
Quarantine 6, 19, 38, 43, 60, 62, 63, 68, 69–70

Raimi, Sam 14
Reaping, The 20, 141, 144, 147–8
[Rec] 6, 19, 60, 61, 62, 63, 65, 68, 69–70
Red Sands 140
Rendition 97
Resident Evil 9, 60
Rice, Anne 164
Ring, The 6, 38, 157
Ringu 6, 22
Rite, The 61, 132, 140, 143
Rosemary's Baby 12, 135, 141, 147

Roth, Eli 96
Ruins, The 60, 97, 98, 99, 109–11

Saving Private Ryan 47, 49
Saw 5, 20, 74–6, 96, 101–3, 104, 105, 130–1, 135, 201
Saw II 13, 76, 99, 103–4
Saw III 99, 102, 103
Saw 3D 102
Saw VI 85
Saw sequels 97, 98, 100, 117, 131, 166, 199
Scarlet Letter, The 139
Scream 62, 76, 87, 88, 187, 194, 199
Scream 2 199
Scream 3 199
Scream 4 93, 199
Searchers, The 175
Season of the Witch 9, 141, 149, 150–1
Seconds Apart 77
Se7en 116
Shaun of the Dead 13
Signs 143–4, 207
Silence of the Lambs 194
Silent Night Deadly Night 85
Sixth Sense, The 156, 157, 207
Skyline 4, 25, 33, 34, 40–1, 43, 46, 205
Sleepaway Camp 193
Slumber Party Massacre 193
sociophobics 17–18, 163
Sorority Row 21, 193, 199
Stag Night 26, 46
Stake Land 166
Standard Operating Procedure 105
Stigmata 140
Strangers, The 3, 13, 20, 79–80, 81, 83, 85, 86–9, 93, 94, 119, 202–3, 206
Straw Dogs 91
Syriana 97

Taliban 8
Tarantino, Quentin 6
Targets 81–2
Terror Train 194
terrorism 7–11, 12
Texas Chainsaw Massacre (1974) 45, 81, 82, 193
Thing, The 4, 12, 116
"torture porn" 20, 96–8, 205
Transformers 61
Transportation Safety Administration (TSA) 4
trauma studies 16–17
Trollhunter 60
True Blood 165
Turistas 98, 99, 109, 111
Twilight Saga 4, 5, 154, 164–5
Twin Towers *see* World Trade Center

Unborn, The 140
United 93 1, 118
Untouchables, The 11
Urban Legend 183, 194
USA PATRIOT Act 4, 8, 191, 204–5

vampires 21, 154, 164–7
Vanishing on 7th Street 26, 27, 33, 34, 35, 43, 166
Village, The 21, 171, 172–80, 191, 207

War Game, The 59
War of the Worlds (novel) 25, 47, 48
War of the Worlds (1953) 25, 29, 48
War of the Worlds (2005) 2, 23, 25, 27–9, 30, 34, 35, 36, 36, 42, 43, 46, 47–51, 54, 56, 78–9, 121
What Dreams May Come 156
When a Stranger Calls 193

Whitman, Charles 82
Wishmaster 140
Witness 9/11 57–8
Wolf Creek 15, 96, 195
World Trade Center 7, 23, 32, 34, 37–8, 56, 84, 118
   North Tower 37, 39, 117
World Trade Center 1, 2, 118

Wrong Turn 108

ZMD: Zombies of Mass Destruction 159
Zombie Strippers 13, 159
Zombieland 159, 166
zombies 21, 153–4, 159–64, 166, 167

www.ingramcontent.com/pod-product-compliance
Lightning Source LLC
Chambersburg PA
CBHW062141300426
44115CB00012BA/2000